Text and Corpus Analysis

OWL

Language in Society

GENERAL EDITOR
Peter Trudgill, Professor in the Department of Language and Linguistics, University of Lausanne

ADVISORY EDITORS
Ralph Fasold, Professor of Linguistics, Georgetown University
William Labov, Professor of Linguistics, University of Pennsylvania

Text and Corpus Analysis

Computer-assisted Studies of Language and Culture

Michael Stubbs

First published 1996

2 4 6 8 10 9 7 5 3 1

Blackwell Publishers Ltd
108 Cowley Road
Oxford OX4 1JF
UK

Blackwell Publishers Inc.
238 Main Street
Cambridge, Massachusetts 02142
USA

British Library Cataloguing in Publication Data

A CIP catalogue record for this book is available from the British Library.

Library of Congress Cataloging-in-Publication Data
Stubbs, Michael, 1947–
Text and corpus analysis: computer-assisted studies of language and culture / Michael Stubbs.
p.   cm. — (Language in society; 23)
Includes bibliographical references and indexes.
ISBN 0-631-19511-4. — ISBN 0-631-19512-2 (pbk.)
1. Discourse analysis.   2. Discourse analysis — Data processing.
3. Language and culture.   4. English language — Modality.   I. Title.   II. Series: Language in society (Oxford, England); 23.
P302.S773   1996
401'.41 — dc20   95-31070
CIP

1 0 0 3 3 2 5 6 7 8

Typeset in 10½ on 12 pt Ehrhardt
by Best-set Typesetter Ltd., Hong Kong

Printed and bound in Great Britain by Marston Lindsay Ross International Ltd, Oxfordshire

Contents

Figures, Concordances and Tables

Figure

Concordances

Tables

Series Editor's Preface

It is one of the traditions of this series that its volumes have a strong orientation towards linguistic data. Our contention is that the best sorts of work in linguistics are those which, as our title 'Language in Society' suggests, are based on research employing as data instances of language as actually used by real people in their everyday lives. We would not deny that research based on linguists' intuitions about their own native varieties has been responsible for very considerable theoretical progress. But, in the final analysis, if linguistics is not about language as it is actually spoken and written by human beings, then it is about nothing at all. Michael Stubbs's volume demonstrates this point with perhaps greater clarity than any previous volume in the series. Here is a work that is based not just on real language data rather than on intuitions, but on vast amounts of real language data. This computer-aided research, based on the immense linguistic corpora which are now available, gives Stubbs's findings a degree of reliability that is unusual in linguistics, and reveals patterns of usage of which we previously had only a vague notion, or even no knowledge whatsoever.

Stubbs has also taken pains to situate his work in the British, Firthian tradition, which goes back many decades but has tended to be lost from view in recent years. It is probably not too much to claim that this book, relying as it does on the approach of British linguists such as Halliday and Sinclair, represents something of a renaissance of this tradition. It is clear, however, that it will appeal to all linguistics and sociolinguistics scholars, whatever their intellectual background, who would like to see the findings of linguistic science grounded in real language. Some will find this work controversial, but all will find it stimulating. Stubbs covers a wide scale of topics, ranging from the relationship between syntax and pragmatics to the issue of sexism in language, but all his analyses are presented with the confidence that only corpora-based studies can provide. In keeping with the Firthian tradition, as well as the aims of this series, Stubbs also discusses the problem of transmitting without distortion linguists' expert knowledge about language to those non-linguists who can benefit from it, in such a way that they can comprehend it. Stubbs has elsewhere shown himself to be very competent in this respect, and this book can only add to his stature in the field.

Peter Trudgill
University of Lausanne

Acknowledgements

I am grateful to many friends and colleagues who provided helpful criticism on earlier versions of this book. Philip Carpenter, Florian Coulmas and Norman Fairclough encouraged the project at an early stage. Judy Delin, Gabi Keck, Greg Myers and Joan Swann made detailed comments on a complete draft. Dwight Atkinson, Wolfram Bublitz, Joanna Channell, Jenny Cheshire, Gill Francis, Andrea Gerbig, Bob Hodge, Susan Hunston, Anthony Johnson, John Sinclair and Dick Watts made helpful comments on various chapters. The book is much better for their good advice. Andrea Gerbig also helped with some of the data analyses and provided text E (for chapter 6). And Anthony Johnson insisted, several times, that I should read Giddens's work.

Work in corpus linguistics is always based on previous work by many people. Jeremy Clear and Tim Lane helped me to extract data from corpora at Cobuild. My student research assistants in Trier, Anja Helfrich and Susanne Jarczok, helped with text and corpus preparation; and Brigitte Grote, Oliver Jakobs and Oliver Hardt wrote programs for analysing lexical density, producing concordances and analysing collocations.

The texts of Baden-Powell's last messages to the Girl Guides and the Boy Scouts were obtained from archivists of the Girl Guides Association and the Scout Association. I am most grateful to them for permission to reproduce the texts (in chapter 4), and also for details of their composition and publication. For permission to use the transcript of courtroom data (in chapter 5), I am grateful to the defendant in the case: for obvious reasons, I will not name him here. Simon & Schuster Education, Hemel Hempstead, UK, gave permission to store text G (in chapter 6) in computer readable form and to cite extracts; the text is *The British Isles*, copyright N. Punnett and P. Webber, Blackwell, 1984. Text E (in chapter 6) is *The Ozone Message* by D. Kinnear, P. Preuss and J. Rogers, Australian Conservation Foundation, 1989. For permission to use corpus materials, I am most grateful to: the Norwegian Computing Centre for the Humanities; Longmans Group UK

Ltd; and colleagues at the University of Birmingham and at Cobuild, especially Gwynneth Fox, John Sinclair and Malcolm Coulthard, for arranging access to the Cobuild corpus, the Bank of English.

I am grateful to publishers for permission to use material from published articles: in all cases the material has been extensively revised. Chapter 2 is considerably revised from an article in M. Baker et al., eds (1993) *Text and Technology*, published by John Benjamins. Chapter 3 uses material from an article in M. Pütz, ed. (1992) *Thirty Years of Linguistic Evolution*, published by John Benjamins, but several sections are new. Chapter 5 is considerably revised from an article in C. Uhlig and R. Zimmermann, eds (1991) *Anglistentag 1990 Marburg: Proceedings*, published by Max Niemeyer; the chapter also contains much new material. Chapter 6 is revised from an article in *Applied Linguistics*, 15, 2 (1994); the chapter also contains much new material. Chapter 7 uses some material from an article in *Language and Education*, 3, 4 (1989), published by Multilingual Matters, but the main part is previously unpublished. Chapter 8 uses material from an article in *Applied Linguistics*, 7, 1 (1986), published by Oxford University Press; the chapter also contains much new material. Other chapters are previously unpublished.

The publishers apologize for any errors or omissions in the above list and would be grateful to be notified of any corrections that should be incorporated in the next edition or reprint of this book.

Data Conventions and Terminology

1   An important feature of the book is that all data which are analysed in detail are attested in naturally occurring language use. The status of examples is indicated as follows.

[A]   *attested, actual, authentic* data: data which have occurred naturally in a real social context without the intervention of the analyst.

[M]   *modified* data: examples which are based on attested data, but which have been modified (e.g. abbreviated) to exclude features deemed irrelevant to the current analysis.

[I]   *intuitive, introspective, invented* data: data invented purely to *illustrate* a point in a linguistic argument.

Chapter 2 discusses the importance of such distinctions. Individual examples are not always marked in this way if their status is clear from the surrounding discussion.

2   Other conventions used are more standard.

2.1   Double quotation marks " " for meanings of linguistic expressions.

2.2   *Italics* for short forms cited within the text, e.g. The German sentence *Sie soll sehr klug sein* means "She is said to be very clever".

2.3   CAPITAL LETTERS for lemmas. Alternative terms for lemma include dictionary head-word and lexeme. A lemma is abstracted from a set of morphological variants. Conventionally the base form of verbs and the singular of nouns are used to represent lemmas. For example, *do* and *does* are forms of the lemma DO.

2.4   Asterisk (*) for ill-formed sequences, e.g. ungrammatical or semantically anomalous sentences. For example, *He must can come. *He is a vegetarian and eats meat.

2.5   A question mark (?) before a form denotes a string of doubtful or marginal acceptability, e.g. *?he mayn't come.* By definition, such asterisked and questioned items cannot be attested, and such intuitive judgements on ill-formedness should be treated with care. Corpus data often reveal forms which are thought intuitively not to occur, but which occur frequently and are used systematically. See especially chapter 8.

Notes on Corpus Data and Software

The first generation of computer-readable corpora (up to around one million words) was set up in the 1960s and 1970s. The Brown Corpus is so named because it was prepared at Brown University in the USA by W. Nelson Francis. This consists of one million words of written American English, published in 1961, and sampled as text fragments of 2,000 words each. Such corpora now seem very small, and can easily be handled on desktop PCs. One of the most important points about such corpus work is that linguistic data become public and accessible to other scholars, who can therefore check the interpretations and analyses proposed (see sections 2.9, 9.1).

The following are the computer-readable corpora of spoken and written English which I have used in various ways in this book.

1   London–Lund corpus: 435,000 words of spoken British English. I have used a version of this corpus, which consists of 435,000 running words, comprising 87 texts of 5,000-word samples of adult educated usage, including face-to-face and telephone conversations, lectures, discussions and radio commentaries. The speakers are university academics, students, civil servants, doctors, secretaries, broadcasters and other professional people. Speakers are on variously intimate and distant personal and social terms with each other. (The corpus contains much coded prosodic information, such as tone unit boundaries, pitch, stress and pause phenomena. I have omitted such codings in citing examples.) The sections comprising face-to-face conversation are published in Svartvik and Quirk (1980) which gives a detailed description of the corpus. Other details of the corpus and of work based on it are given in Svartvik et al. (1982) and in Biber (1988). This corpus was one part of the data gathered by the Survey of English Usage at the University of London, in the preparation of Quirk et al.'s (1972) *A Grammar of Contemporary English*, and other associated grammars (e.g. Quirk et al., 1985). (See section 2.5.)

2   LOB (Lancaster–Oslo–Bergen) corpus: one million words of written

British English. The LOB corpus was designed as the British equivalent of the Brown corpus: one million words of written British English, also published in 1961, and also sampled as text fragments of 2,000 words each. These samples are from informative texts, such as newspaper texts, learned and scientific writing and imaginative fiction. For a detailed list of the textual categories represented, see *ICAME News*, 5, 1981, p. 4 (*International Computer Archive of Modern English*, Bergen). This corpus aims to provide a range of samples of different varieties of English, but could never be representative of the whole English language. There are, for example, many genres which are not represented in LOB. Since it contains samples only of published language, it contains no samples of business correspondence: a huge genre in the modern world.

3 Longman–Lancaster corpus: 30 million words of written English (only small selections are used here). The Longman–Lancaster corpus consists of about 30 million words of written (published) English. For some comparative purposes in this book, I have taken 2,000 word samples from each file, in order to construct a sub-corpus which can be compared with LOB. The corpus contains both fiction and non-fiction, some well known literary works but also published works randomly sampled from books in print. The non-fiction texts are sampled from broad topic fields, including the natural and social sciences, world affairs, commerce and finance, the arts and leisure. Summers (1993) provides details of the design of the corpus.

4 Cobuild corpus of written and spoken English (The Bank of English). This corpus is held at Cobuild in Birmingham, where it is used in the construction of major dictionaries and grammars (including Sinclair, 1987a, 1990, 1995), published by HarperCollins. For description of the early corpus development, see Renouf (1987) and Sinclair (1991a, pp. 13–26). For several articles based on the corpus, see Baker *et al.* (1993). In 1995, the corpus totalled some 200 million words. For the analyses in this book (e.g. chapter 7), about 120 million words of spoken and written British English were used. This comprises books on many different topics, both fiction and non-fiction, daily newspapers and samples of spoken English, face-to-face interaction, telephone calls and many types of radio programmes.

Several chapters present concordances. These were produced by running computer-readable texts through a computer program, which searches for words in the text, and prints them out in the centre of the page, with a half line of context (usually up to ten words) on each side. This provides a convenient layout for studying how a speaker or writer uses certain words and phrases, and whether there are particular patterns in his or her use of language. I have used commercially available software: the Longman Mini-

Concordancer, written for MS-DOS machines by Brian Chandler and available from Longman. This is an interactive program, extremely easy to use, with powerful pattern matching, which can handle texts of up to 50,000 words (given 640 kb available RAM). I would highly recommended it for anyone who wants to start work in this area. I have also used other batch software, written by my students in Trier. See the acknowledgements above.

Part I
Concepts and History

1

Texts and Text Types

Attested language text duly recorded is in the focus of attention for the linguist. (Firth, 1957b, p. 29)

The main question discussed in this book is as follows:

> How can an analysis of the patterns of words and grammar in a text
> contribute to an understanding of the meaning of the text?

I discuss traditions of text analysis in (mainly) British linguistics, and computer-assisted methods of text and corpus analysis. And I provide analyses of several shorter and longer texts, and also of patterns of language across millions of words of text corpora. The main emphasis is on the analysis of attested, naturally occurring textual data. An exclusive concentration on the text alone is, however, not an adequate basis for text interpretation, and this introductory chapter discusses the appropriate balance for text analysis, between the text itself and its production and reception.

Such analyses of attested texts are important for both practical and theoretical reasons, and the main reasons can be easily and briefly stated. First, there are many areas of the everyday world in which the systematic and critical interpretation of texts is an important social skill. One striking example occurs in courtrooms, where very important decisions, by juries as well as lawyers, can depend on such interpretations. Second, much of theoretical linguistics over the past fifty years has been based on the study of isolated sentences. This approach has some severe limitations and it is important to show what can be learned by studying patterns of language across texts and corpora.

1.1   The Data

By text, I mean an instance of language in use, either spoken or written: a piece of language behaviour which has occurred naturally, without the intervention of the linguist. This excludes examples of language which have been invented by a linguist merely to illustrate a point in a linguistic theory. Examples of real instances of language in use might include: a conversation, a lecture, a sermon, an advert, a recipe, a newspaper article, a scientific research paper, a novel, a school textbook and so on. The list is open-ended, and probably endless. In chapter 2, I discuss in more detail the advantages of basing linguistic description and theory on attested instances of language use.

One brief point of terminology. There is considerable variation in how terms such as *text* and *discourse* are used in linguistics. Sometimes this terminological variation signals important conceptual distinctions, but often it does not, and terminological debates are usually of little interest. These distinctions in terminology and concept will only occasionally be relevant for my argument, and when they are, I will draw attention to them (e.g. in section 7.2).

It is an important feature of the book that all the data which are analysed in any detail are attested in this sense. Where this is not absolutely clear from the context, I will use the following conventions (see also pp. xv–xvi on data conventions and terminology) to mark the source of examples:

[A]   actual, authentic, attested data;
[M]   modified data;
[I]   invented, intuitive, introspective data.

Almost all examples in the book are [A]. Occasionally, it is convenient to modify (for example, to abbreviate) or to invent an example, and I will always warn the reader when I have done this.

Possibly the most central problem in contemporary linguistics is: what counts as data? This question has major implications for descriptive and theoretical linguistics. What precisely is the evidence on which theories of syntax and semantics are based? But questions of what counts as evidence, corroboration or proof are also important in applied linguistics, and I will discuss in detail texts from the mass media, education and courtrooms. In such cases, linguists have a responsibility to say how confident they are that their analyses are correct 'beyond reasonable doubt'.

1.2 The Organization of the Book

Chapters 1 to 3 discuss the concepts of text, text type and genre, with particular reference to the British neo-Firthian tradition of linguistics, as it has been developed by Halliday and Sinclair. This tradition has led to major grammars and dictionaries of English, and to significant advances in methods of computer-assisted text and corpus analysis.

Chapters 4 to 8 provide analyses of texts and text corpora. One descriptive focus of these chapters is texts and text types which are public and/or authoritative: two widely circulated speeches (chapter 4), the summing-up by a judge in a criminal trial (chapter 5), two school textbooks (chapter 6), statements by public figures (chapter 7) and various corpus data (chapters 7 and 8). These chapters progress from little things to big things:

- from short texts (of a few hundred words) to long texts (whole books of tens of thousands of words);
- from a comparison of one text with another, to a comparison of patterns in texts with patterns in corpora;
- from single texts to text corpora: that is, collections of texts of millions of words in length.

This progression is important for two reasons. First, it should facilitate the use of the book in teaching. These chapters introduce various methods of computer-assisted text and corpus analysis: in particular, the use of concordances for studying patterns of language use. Later chapters also introduce other methods for studying the most frequent and characteristic syntactic constructions and lexical collocations in which words occur.

Second, it facilitates a discussion of criteria for text analysis. These include: the need to analyse not only short text fragments, but also whole long texts; and the need for the stylistic analysis of individual texts to be based on comparisons with other texts and with corpus data which represent (however imperfectly) the language. The main descriptive and theoretical arguments in the book concern findings about language which could not conceivably result from intuitive data in the form of invented sentences, but which require large quantities of corpus data. (See especially chapters 2, 7 and 8.)

1.3   A Simple Model: Texts, Production and Reception

This opening chapter makes some introductory points about the relations between texts, text types and social institutions, and gives some examples of different studies.

A problem which crops up in various forms is: where is the meaning of a text located? Is the meaning inside the text itself? Or inside the mind of the person who makes sense of it? Or is it in the speech community somewhere – perhaps in the form of a consensus interpretation on which we could all agree?

Suppose I receive a legal document, which I read, but do not fully understand. I might ring up a friend who is a lawyer and read a problematic sentence over the phone. My friend might then explain to me what this sentence means. I will have read it, but the lawyer will have interpreted it. So was the meaning in the text? Possibly, although it seems to require the knowledge of the lawyer to get the meaning out. And note the ambiguity of the word *read*. It sometimes refers merely to the words on the page: I have read a sentence aloud over the telephone. And it sometimes means "read and understand", as when I say that I have read a good book on holiday.

Here is a very simple model of the relation between text and context. In common sense terms, it seems clear that the meaning of a text depends on at least three things: the language of the text itself, who produced it and who is responding to it. By the language itself I mean the words actually spoken or written, and their patterns of lexical collocations and of syntactic and rhetorical structures. Some meanings are created by the words themselves and their observable interrelationships, and several chapters below are concerned with analysing such patterns. But some meanings depend on our knowledge of the point of view of the author. We may interpret things quite differently, depending on when and where and by whom the language was produced – for example, depending on the status or authority of the speaker or writer: a person in the street, an expert, a government minister, a government committee, an author of a school textbook, a judge summing up in court and so on. And some meanings are brought to the text by readers or listeners: according to their specialist knowledge, their cultural assumptions or their familiarity with other related texts. Readers and listeners also have different points of view, and respond to texts in different ways.

The text-production-reception model emphasizes immediately that meanings and interpretations are mediated by social institutions. It is difficult to discuss examples of language, say from a textbook or a judicial summing-up, without referring to the status of speakers and listeners in institutions such as education and the law.

This simple view of different factors in the meaning of texts is reflected in the history of literary criticism over the past hundred years or so (Eagleton (1983) provides a good discussion of this history). There was a period when the main focus was on the author: his or her biography and social background were felt to be crucial to an understanding of a text. This tradition is still represented in the essays of literary reference books. An essay on Wordsworth, for example, might combine comments on the themes of his poetry with a brief account of his life and references to contemporary historical events, such as the French Revolution.

In the 1920s, various approaches shifted the focus to the text itself, the words on the page. Critics emphasized the formal aspects of texts, and saw literature as a particular organization of language, sometimes even downgrading content in favour of form. Close critical reading of the text, sometimes in deliberately maintained ignorance of the author (since this might influence interpretations), was recommended by I. A. Richards (1929) in his approach to practical criticism. As part of the view which treated literary works as objects, independent of their historical and social contexts of production, the intentional fallacy refers to the argument that we do not (or cannot or need not) know the intention of an author in order to interpret his or her text. The text is autonomous; the author is irrelevant to its interpretation.

But the practical criticism position already implies that readers' interpretations can be influenced by what they know: that is, by things outside the text. And more recently, the focus has been on the reader. Reader response theory emphasizes that meanings are constructed by active readers: they are not derivable from texts in a passive way. This position is represented in influential work by Iser (1974) and Fish (1980).

Views are still shifting on the relation between text, author and reader. After more extreme views on the 'death of the author', literary critics have begun more recently to argue again that an author's biography may, after all, shed light on the text, and many well publicized literary biographies have recently appeared. In addition, the concept of authorship, and dependent concepts such as copyright and plagiarism, are themselves historically variable. In fact, the concept of an individual creative author is a relatively recent historical invention: largely a product of Romanticism. We do not know the authors of some famous Middle English literary texts (such as *Sir Gawain and the Green Knight*, written some time before 1400): they seem not to have been important enough to record. And most texts in the modern world, such as government reports, advertisements and even many newspaper articles, have no identifiable author. They are anonymous, or have multiple authors or ghost authors.

These shifts in the fashion and theory of literary criticism, along with historical shifts in how authors are regarded, show the constantly changing relation between authorship and authority. And they all seem to indicate that the meaning of a text is not in any single place. An exclusive reliance on any one of these sources of meaning is not adequate, since all three contribute to our interpretations of texts. This simple model, which relates the text itself, speakers or writers, and listeners or readers, draws attention to relations which are essential in text analysis. A balanced approach must take into account both product and process: not only the text itself, but also its production and reception.

Usually, given a text, it is possible to infer quite a lot about who produced it for whom; and given information about author and audience, it is often possible to predict quite a lot about what kind of thing the author is likely to say in what way. We can do this because even creative literary authors are not entirely free to express things as they wish. An author's freedom is always constrained by how other speakers use the language and by accepted ways of speaking and writing. The concepts of prediction and probability are central to the view of language which I develop below.

Most chapters in this book discuss texts with reference both to their linguistic patterning and to their contexts of production and reception. But it is not possible to study everything at once, and some chapters focus largely on the text itself, whereas others emphasize relations between a text and its social and political background..

I will also discuss patterns which are in the language. Literary and linguistic theory have also emphasized that it is not only texts which can be anonymous. The language itself is anonymous. It is never the property of individual speakers. Individuals have to take over ways of speaking from previous generations of the speech community (see section 3.4). Along with individual words and grammatical rules, speakers acquire routine expressions, common ways of formulating things and collocations, which encode commonly accepted ideas (see chapters 4 and 7).

1.4   Content, Author and Audience

This simple three-part model for thinking about language and interpretation provides a route into several aspects of text analysis. The model draws attention both to the expression of content and to the expression of relations between author and audience. For example, in analyses of a school textbook, it is natural for the focus to be on the content of the text. This is likely to be what the author was concentrating on: a school textbook is about some subject, such as mathematics or geography. But it may be important to pay attention also to interpersonal meaning: does the author admit to being a fallible human being, or claim unassailable authority for the truth of what is written? (A detailed example is given in section 6.10.)

The model also emphasizes that texts do not have absolute and unchanging interpretations, but are interpreted differently in different historical periods, and in different cultural contexts. Indeed, a major source of misinterpretation is when texts are read outside a specialist context. (Section 7.3 gives examples of what can happen to linguistic arguments when they are recontextualized in educational and political debates.)

Each genre of text, such as Bible translations, novels, reading primers, textbooks and newspapers, has served social and cultural functions. The authority of textbooks is related to the view that the meaning is in the text. But very different views of knowledge are implied by different relations between text and audience: texts can be dictated, learned by rote, read silently in private or aloud in public, discussed in groups and so on. The most basic distinction is perhaps between an unmediated reading and an expert interpretation.

It is worth remembering that the Reformation turned on debates about who could interpret what. When Luther posted his theses on the door of a church in Wittenberg in 1517, he was challenging the Papal authority to interpret the scriptures, arguing that everyone should read the Bible for themselves. The translation of the Bible from Latin into German was a challenge to the mediation of the text by the organized Church. Luther's view was that people should study the text itself, not rely on the claimed authority of other people's interpretations: 'The meaning of the Scripture depends, not upon the doctrine of the Church, but on a deeper reading of the text.' He was thereby aiming to change the relations between text, social institution and authoritative interpretation. Such questions of text, audience and interpretation are not, as they say, merely of academic interest (not merely of interest to literary theory, for example). Changed views about their relations have been at the root of religious and social revolutions (and different religions have taken very different views about text and translation).

A model which emphasizes the relations among text, production and reception points the way to a critical model of text interpretation, in which listeners and readers do not simply accept received opinion, but can identify and discuss cases where evidence is given for views versus cases of personal opinion, unsupported assertion, innuendo or bias, and can better understand the differences between what the words mean, what the writer/speaker means and what the reader/listener understands.

In Shakespeare's play *Julius Caesar* (III, 2), after Caesar's murder by Brutus and others, Antonius gives his famous speech which starts *Friends, Romans, Countrymen, lend me your ears.* He repeats several times Brutus' claim that Caesar was ambitious, and says, also several times, that *Brutus is an honourable man.* The words mean one thing, the speaker means something else and the listener's understanding of the words changes as Antonius repeats them throughout his speech. The words have a micro-history in the text (see section 4.5). Nowadays this Shakespearean line is so well known that it can itself be quoted to draw attention to such ambiguous and shifting meanings. I recently overheard a conversation in which a speaker was criticizing a colleague, but concluded, *But he is an honourable man,* to which the response was: *Brutus was an honourable man.* Words and fixed phrases also have a history in the language (see chapter 7).

A method of teaching students, including school pupils, to interpret the points of view from which texts are written has many educational implications. This will not be a central focus in this book, although I will draw attention to educational implications of the argument when this is particularly striking. (See section 4.9 and chapter 6.)

1.5   Texts and Text Types

In chapters 4 to 6, I will analyse examples of different texts which represent different configurations of text type, author and audience.

- Two speeches: produced by a public figure, and interpreted by a wide range of readers, including children.
- A summing-up in a criminal trial: produced by the judge, and interpreted by lawyers, the defendant and members of the jury.
- Two school textbooks: produced by authors, and interpreted by pupils and teachers.

I will also give briefer examples (section 7.3) of what can happen when ideas about language and education are discussed in the mass media by public figures. Other corpus data which I analyse comprise samples from many other text types. These various analyses will show how messages are conveyed: not only explicitly, by words themselves, but also implicitly, by lexical and syntactic patterning.

Again terms are variable. Some authors distinguish between text type and genre: I will not. Text types or genres are events which define the culture. They are conventional ways of expressing meanings: purposeful, goal-directed language activities, socially recognized text types, which form patterns of meaning in the social world (Kress, 1989). An essential concept is purpose for audience. Text types also imply different ways of producing, distributing and consuming texts (Fairclough, 1992, p. 71). They may be produced individually (a personal letter) or collectively (a committee report); the author may be named (a novel) or anonymous (a television ad); they may be published, xeroxed, faxed; they may be read once and thrown away, or read repeatedly (a work of literature), or learned by heart by successive generations (famous poems, or many religious texts); they may be private or public.

Genre, as a traditional category in literary studies, includes short story, novel, play, autobiography, diary, sonnet, epic and fable. It therefore fits naturally into a study of the aesthetic functions of language. However, the concept is also relevant to broader forms of cultural analysis. Popular culture provides examples such as science fiction, detective fiction, romance, comic strip and western. Some genres have developed for use in television and radio: documentary, soap opera, phone-in, panel discussion, news broadcast, travel programme, light entertainment and quiz show. These examples emphasize that genres change and evolve. Relatively recent genres include the blues, the presidential press conference, the television game show, the music video (Swales, 1990, pp. 33–5). And the concept applies equally to everyday uses of spoken and written language, such as joke, story, chat, gossip, song, sermon, argument, debate, committee meeting, instructions and signs. When one is using various corpora of contemporary English (such as LOB and the Longman–Lancaster corpus), it is important to bear in mind that many such genres are not represented: diaries, personal letters, business correspondence (a huge genre), company reports, writing for teenagers and so on.

A genre which has become prominent in modern life consists of guides and manuals: books and articles offering practical, easy-to-read, concise, comprehensive advice on various subjects. Any bookshop contains many such books and magazines, which provide advice on self-help, self-management, self-realization, self-knowledge, lifestyle and efficiency. Common topics include: the body (health, fitness, diet, etc.); personal relations (in marriage and divorce, in child-care, at work, etc.); the home (buying and selling houses, moving house, do-it-yourself, gardening, cooking, etc.). One can buy a book of advice on almost anything: how to cure migraine, how to set up a business, how to avoid paying too much tax, how to cross the

Australian outback in a four-wheel drive vehicle. Whole magazines are devoted to topics such as health and diet, personal relations, work and travel. Giddens (1991) has pointed to this vast literature as a feature of modernity. There is no clear dividing line between the technical or expert and the popular, between social science and guides to life, and some writers produce both (for example, Deborah Tannen writes both on discourse analysis and on communication problems in marriage). Giddens sees this ambiguity as an important part of the reflexivity of modernity.

Genres can also go out of fashion or become less useful. The essay form no longer has the prestige it had in the eighteenth century when Addison and Steele were writing for the *Tatler* and the *Spectator*, though a few periodicals still publish essays on general political and social issues. The pastoral and the epic poem are today dead as literary genres. And the role of genres in society changes: think of political satire, proverbs, traditional tales, sermons and funeral orations.

The concept of text type is clear enough in general, but although many categorizations have been proposed, none is comprehensive or generally accepted. There is no implication that such genres are categories with neatly defined boundaries; although the focal members of genres are usually easy to identify. Genres can, for example, be combined. The important point is not knowing in some mechanical way which genre an example fits into, but knowing how the category can make a difference to the way in which it is interpreted. The emphasis in all such study is on the conventions which govern the uses and meanings of language. The ability to identify and compare different genres contributes to our ability to understand them. Misunderstandings, and even dislike, of texts of different kinds can often be due to a lack of understanding of the different conventions involved.

1.6 Text Types and Institutions

Social institutions and text types are mutually defining. An example is provided by the public media – radio, television, newspapers – where new text types have developed with the media, and now help to define them. Some valuable historical studies are available.

Püschel (1991a,b) discusses the development of new types of newspaper article which arose in Germany in the nineteenth century. He discusses the shift from merely reporting that events had taken place to more detailed commentary on events and to the formation of public opinion through rational public political debate. This involved the differentiation of genres such as short news items and longer reports, on-the-spot and eye-witness reports, background coverage, commentary and leading editorial articles. It also involved page layout, which helped readers to distinguish between different types of item, such as readers' letters. The letter to the editor was itself a genre which had to be invented and developed.

Scannell (1986) discusses the development of documentary programmes on BBC radio from the 1920s to the 1940s. The BBC had an explicit policy of finding new forms of communication to transmit socially contentious issues to a new mass audience. They broke with established literary modes, and attempted to record 'what actually happened' and to allow people and events to 'speak for themselves'. They saw the audience as being within family groups in the home, for which intimate, informal styles were appropriate. They deliberately contrasted the points of view of officialdom and of working-class people. This all represented attempts to reconstruct the relations between the institution of the BBC, the subject matter of programmes, the people who had access to the microphone and the audience. There were also sharp differences between national broadcasting from the south of England (in London) and regional programmes produced in the north (in Manchester). A new concept of a general public was developed, with a more local working-class public for regional programmes. And new genres were developed: documentaries, features, social reportage, eye-witness reports, dramatized reconstructions, studio discussions, dialect plays. The sound of a live audience for the first time in a radio programme was heard as a major innovation. Interviewing was a new technique and had to be invented. News programmes only existed from 1934. News interviews were not used until after the Second World War.

Scannell (1986) documents the changing relations between institution, genre, subject matter, speakers and audience, and the ways in which a new institution and new genres were developed in tandem. (He does not provide any textual or corpus analysis to ground his analysis, though, to be fair, much broadcasting of the period was live, and there are no surviving recordings to analyse!)

Another set of links between genres and institutions can be seen if we look at professions which specialize in discourse (Bernstein, 1990, pp. 135ff), such as priests, scientists, lawyers, teachers and administrators. Priests, for example, are specialists in particular types of discourse, such as prayers, sermons, confessionals, baptisms, excommunications and exorcisms! And they are experts in the interpretation of particular types of written texts: scriptures and related genres. Some professions write and sell texts: advertisers and journalists. Some professions reproduce and mediate texts: teachers, priests, actors. A public relations agency is paid to transform one text into another, to create new texts from different sources, in order to try to change people's beliefs, persuade them of a point of view or alter the actions of politicians.

Such transformations can lead to long intertextual sequences. For example, scientists write research reports and articles on the destruction of the ozone layer. These technical texts are interpreted by experts in other fields (for example, those drafting industrial legislation, or environmental organizations) and by journalists. They are also rewritten by public relations agencies who prepare position papers and speeches for industrial clients opposed to the legislation. A detailed case study of the mediation of knowledge in this area by different interest groups is provided by Gerbig (1993).

In addition, there are several relatively new professions which not only specialize in discourse, but whose discourse is designed to regulate psychological and social relations. These are the professions to do with counselling and guidance: child guidance and marriage guidance, personnel officer, social worker, psychoanalyst, psychotherapist, public relations agency. The growth of such professions since the eighteenth century, and the kinds of power they have, based on the new kinds of knowledge developed within the social and behavioural sciences, is one of Foucault's (1980) main themes. The colonization of new areas of life by the discourse of counselling is discussed by Fairclough (1992). (See section 7.10 for the importance of cultural key words such as *expert* and *professional*.)

A German magazine reported recently on a new profession which is competing with the clergy in providing funeral speeches for atheists: its members comprise mainly retired or out-of-work teachers and actors. Of several currently used terms, practitioners seem less happy with *Grabredner* ("graveside orator"), and to prefer *freigeistlicher Redner* ("freethinking orator") or simply *Consultant*.

1.7   Three Studies

When we look at published studies of texts and text types, we find all conceivable combinations of focus on text, production and reception. Studies focus variously on: the text itself, patterns of words or grammar; the relations between one text and another, patterns that we recognize from other texts we have heard or read; text corpora, patterns across large collections of texts; and the context, relations between text, author and audience, or the broader social and political context of the text.

The literature on text and genre is vast. Rather than attempt a bland overview, I will discuss three studies in very different styles. They are all based on corpora of texts which represent important public uses of language: advertising, newspapers and scientific articles. All three studies have valuable features, and they all raise different problems concerning the relation between text, corpus and meaning.

1.7.1 *Advertising*

There have been many studies of the language of advertising: two worth consulting are Leech (1966) and Myers (1994).

Cook (1992) provides a highly readable, and often witty, study of advertisements in British magazines and television. He discusses the genre in general, different types of ads (for products, charities, health campaigns and so on) and changes in advertising fashion from the 1950s to the 1990s. His analytic method is line-by-line commentary on the short texts and their visual and musical components, and his observations on individual ads are invariably perceptive. However, ultimately, the method is simply that of confident personal literary judgement. Thus a poem in one ad is condemned (p. 123) as 'outstandingly banal and clumsy . . . a bad ad as well as a bad poem'.

Cook mentions several methodological issues, but does not draw the consequences in his own analyses. He emphasizes (p. 199) that people have 'vast and daily experience' of advertisements and that 'each new ad is encountered through knowledge of thousands of earlier ads'. But the book is not based on a defined corpus of data, and he can only appeal to our intuitions that a particular television ad is 'fairly ordinary' (p. 38) or that other examples are 'prototypical' (p. 8). He admits (p. 11) that he ignores the numerically largest sub-type in the genre, small ads in newspapers.

He proposes sampling a wide range of data: it is 'most instructive to look at ads which occupy extreme points' in the genre (p. 11). But he looks in detail at only one such point, the allusion and verbal play in soft-sell ads. Here he picks his own favourites (which is what all literary critics do), concentrating on memorable or famous examples, but does not analyse the majority(?) which merely provide useful information and/or are just banal. His examples are mainly of the type where buying a brand of chewing gum, four-wheel drive car, jeans or instant coffee makes you intelligent, good-looking, loved by your family or desired by the opposite sex (in that order?). He mentions many other types (for example, for political parties, famine relief, anti-drink/drive campaigns), but does not analyse examples. And he does not discuss other extreme points, such as the marketing of the American President, or radio travel programmes which are extended advertising for package holidays.

Cook's study contains precise and interesting commentary on individual short texts, and his analyses draw attention to features I would certainly not have noticed. However, given its basis in personal commentary, and the failure to specify the corpus, it is difficult to see how the study could be replicated. He emphasizes that people are not cultural dopes who believe everything in soap operas or ads. But his only audience research refers (pp. 106, 112) to 'an informal survey of forty young adults' (some of his students?).

Cook mentions all the following themes, but has no explicit theory to explain:

- how an individual text can have meaning only as a sample of an enormously large body of texts;
- how typical or representative texts can be identified;
- how the relation between text and audience could be studied.

1.7.2   Newspapers

There are also many analyses of newspaper language: Bell (1984, 1991) and Fowler (1991b) are particularly useful studies.

In a study which is very different from Cook's in style and method, Jucker (1992) provides a detailed analysis of a sample of British newspapers, based on a well defined sub-set of English grammar, the structure and complexity of noun phrases (NPs), and on a well defined corpus. The corpus comprises samples, from a few days in 1987–8, of all eleven British national daily newspapers, up-, middle- and down-market. Based on circulation figures, he provides empirical evidence of their audiences. He then makes detailed comparisons across the newspapers, and also across different sections (genres?) within them (UK and foreign news, business, arts and sports). The 371 articles studied provide 43,000 NPs. He describes the syntax of the NPs, with statistics on their distribution in different newspaper types and sections, to give a careful grammar of NPs, with probabilities attached, on the basis of a precisely defined, though narrow, sample of real written data.

However, what is missing is a semantic analysis. This is not an oversight, of course, but a deliberate part of the methodology. Yet without a discussion of meaning, it is difficult to know what to make of the detailed descriptive statistics. As Jucker himself admits, it is 'a complex step to reach any conclusions about the stylistic aims of specific newspapers and newspaper sections' (p. 148). Three (out of many) clear findings are as follows. The average number of modifiers per 1,000 NPs distinguishes the newspaper types: up-markets have more (p. 108). NP-appositions stratify the three newspaper types more distinctly than any other structural property of NPs (p. 107). And the down-market papers always omit the determiner (*a*, *the*) in NP-appositions (p. 230), e.g. *Royal relative Katie Baring, left-wing firebrand Derek Hatton*. But Jucker provides little explanation of what these differences might mean.

An interpretation might proceed as follows. A language always provides different ways of describing a common world, and Jucker shows that different newspapers have different ways of referring to the same people, things and events. NPs provide ways of referring to people (*Tory health fanatic Edwina Currie, a splendidly gloomy Vladimir*), things (*Perth jail, a 130 mph silver X-registered BMW coupe*), and events (*a devastating onslaught, the tragic news*). (These are attested examples from the book.) But what is missing is a discussion of what these nomenclatures imply about how the world is encoded. For example, there are many illustrations of the elaborate taxonomies used for professions, titles and personal descriptions (*father, husband, billionaire, minister, gun fanatic, student nurse, crackpot, curvacious cutie*, etc., etc.), but no analysis of how such taxonomies condense and classify experience. (See chapter 7 on cultural keywords, and section 8.8.1 on words such as *cutie*.)

Two types of information, which would permit such an interpretation, are missing. First, Jucker provides no semantic information on the NPs. Most examples refer to people (presumably in line with the well known tendency of the press to personalize stories), but he gives no statistics on what the 43,000 NPs most often refer to. Events? Things? People? Women? Men? Presumably women and men are categorized with different modifiers. Name? Profession? Appearance? With such semantic information we could better interpret the kind of world which is being constructed. Second, the corpus is not in fact a sample of texts, but the list of NPs, extracted and studied independently of their co-text. Jucker studies the NPs in the context of type of publication (up- and down-market) and text type (e.g. sports versus arts section), but he ignores the data needed to interpret the isolated grammatical constructions. Since he ignores the intervening layers of sentence and text, he cannot explain how such NPs are used to construct arguments.

Jucker's careful quantitative study of the frequency of syntactic constructions across text types provides normative data which will be very helpful in future comparative studies of the meaning of syntactic patterns. But Jucker's study stops short of several questions:

- there is analysis of the distribution of grammatical structures across texts, but no analysis of their meanings;

- there is no interpretation of syntactic features in their co-text;
- there are statistics of features of the corpus, without any study of the constituent, individual texts.

1.7.3   Scientific research articles

There are also many analyses of scientific English. The study by Halliday and Martin (1993) is particularly relevant to chapter 6 below.

Swales (1990) provides a study of scientific research articles, which is an important contribution to understanding academic discourse and also to genre theory. It discusses major approaches to genre in folklore studies, literary studies, linguistics and rhetoric. A genre is seen as a class of communicative events, with shared communicative purposes. Discourse communities share agreed public goals and mechanisms of communication, and possess one or more genres. Competence in the genre(s) is required for membership of the community.

Swales sees science as comprising various international discourse communities, whose central communicative mechanism is the research article, plus associated genres such as abstract, research presentation, grant proposal and thesis. He points out (p. 95) that the research article is a huge genre: there are perhaps 100,000 research journals in the world, in science, technology and other subjects, publishing perhaps five million articles per year. Some journals are slim and intermittent, but others are huge: *Physical Review* published 30 million words in 1980.

He provides an account of the historical development of scientific English out of personal letters among scientists from the mid–1600s onwards. The genre was consciously developed by scientists who required ways of expressing generally accepted knowledge about experimental matters of fact. He then summarizes a great deal of work on the syntax and discourse structures preferred in research articles, including: tenses, modals, nominals, actives and passives, commitment and hedging, topic sentences, text structures (e.g. problem–solution, introduction–methods–results–discussion), authorial comments, citation patterns and information density. He refuses any simplistic clichés, such as that scientific language uses an impersonal nominalized style.

Swales emphasizes the role of language in science, the 'sheer importance of the writing' (p. 127), and talks of the documentary world (p. 122) of science, in which articles are products and in which the discussion of written formulations is a major activity. Swales sees reality as linguistically constructed. He discusses the 'construction of research articles', the 'long process of rhetorical construction' (p. 121) from experimental work via laboratory reports (a very different genre) to publication, and the 'creation of facts' (p. 112) through this 'complexly distanced' (p. 175) rhetorical construction, where the aim of the rhetoric is to convince the reader that there is no rhetoric. He seems unhappy about the subjectivist implications of this constructionist view (p. 122), although he has a concrete and institutional view of process and product. Knowledge is produced by scientists working in institutions. The main product of this knowledge-manufacturing industry is research articles (pp. 95, 125), which are distributed along communicative networks: they may be selected for inclusion in journals, further selected by abstracting services, requested as reprints by other scientists, mediated by science journalists in popularized accounts and required by universities for promotion. Swales's discussion of these gate-keeping policies provides much empirical evidence for a theory of the relations between texts, knowledge and communicative networks.

One unclear point is his use of the term translation to refer to journalists mediating original research articles and turning them into popularizations. It is possible to translate between languages, dialects or styles, where it is meaningful, if approximate, to talk of the same content being conveyed in different forms. But when the shift is between genres (technical and popular), then it is not the same content in different words, but different content. Scientists produce the original texts. These are then both modified and simplified, and also recontextualized by being put into contact with different texts: no longer other research texts, but, say, news items about politics. (On the recontextualization of knowledge, see chapter 6 on school textbooks, and section 7.3 on public figures making statements about education.)

An omission in the argument is as follows. Swales points to the great variation in the scale and level of linguistic analysis in work on research articles. Some studies are based on a single, sometimes atypical, article; other studies give no indication of what data they are based on! But Swales himself makes no attempt to compare this special genre with academic English in general, or with written and spoken English more widely. Any study of genres must be located in a description of variation in the language overall. Swales reviews many linguistic features which have been found in scientific research articles, but does not relate this to a theory of variation in English. As Biber (1988, p. 178) has shown, there is a wide range of variation within academic prose, and therefore no individual text represents this genre adequately. Furthermore, the range of texts within natural science is even more striking, depending on the sub-discipline: say, engineering versus biology (Biber, 1988, p. 193).

Swales could also have developed his argument with reference to Popper (1972, 1994), who argues the importance of formulating things in written language for a critical view of knowledge. For Popper (e.g. 1972, p. 73), 'objective knowledge' includes theories which are published in journals and books, the logical content of books, libraries, computer memories and so on. Swales provides substantial textual and ethnographic evidence for the phenomena which Popper discusses (see section 9.1).

Concepts which seem underdeveloped in Swales' study are:

*   the mediation of knowledge by language;
*   the comparative analysis of a text type against the background of variation in the language as a whole.

These three studies are very different in style, and have different strengths and weaknesses. Other important case studies are discussed elsewhere: see chapter 5, appendix, for a discussion of Berk-Seligson's (1990) analysis of a corpus of courtroom data.

1.8   Summary

As a group, these three studies raise a range of questions which have to be tackled by a theory of text interpretation:

*   the relations of text to corpus, and of instance to system;
*   the concepts of sample, representativeness and typicality;
*   the probabilistic nature of many textual patterns;
*   the meaning of patterns of frequency and distribution;
*   the function of syntactic units in texts;
*   the mediation of knowledge in language;
*   the dissemination of texts from authors to audience.

I will discuss all of these questions below, and propose techniques for making some progress with them.

So, this book is about the computer-assisted analysis of text semantics. It represents part of a research programme on the relations between texts, text types, text corpora and social institutions. The linguistic focus is on lexical and grammatical patterns in texts, particularly those patterns which express the point of view of the speaker or writer. The descriptive focus is on texts which are public and/or authoritative, such as newspaper articles, school textbooks, government reports and legal judgements. This leads to a sociological focus on the relation between the micro structure of texts and the macro structure of social institutions, such as schools and courtrooms. Texts, spoken and written, comprise much of the empirical foundation of society: they help to construct social reality. And textual analysis is a perspective from which to observe society: it makes ideological structures tangible.

Much of this deep patterning is beyond human observation and memory. It is observable only indirectly in the probabilities associated with lexical and grammatical choices across long texts and corpora. This therefore leads in turn to a methodological focus on computer-assisted and quantitative methods, particularly in cases where native speaker intuitions are very limited, and where description can proceed only on the basis of attested corpus data.

The major intellectual puzzle in the social sciences is the relation between micro and macro. How is it that routine everyday behaviour, from moment to moment, can create and maintain social institutions over long periods of time? (See sections 3.4, 3.5.) Institutions are networks of commitments: they are based on contracts, promises, requests, authorizations and other speech acts. And the many things created by texts and by ways of talking include the mass media, education, government and the law. Text and corpus analysis provide methods for studying the empirical basis of society in these micro—macro relations.

The rest of the book now presents some history and principles of text and corpus analysis (chapters 2 and 3) and some computer-assisted analyses of texts and corpora (chapters 4 to 8).

2

British Traditions in Text Analysis: Firth, Halliday and Sinclair

The use of machines in linguistic analysis is now established. (Firth, 1957b, p. 31)

It is my belief that a new understanding of the nature and structure of language will shortly be available as a result of the examination by computer of large collections of texts. (Sinclair, 1991b, p. 489)

This chapter discusses a cluster of ideas which have been developed in British linguistics from the 1930s to the 1990s, and which form an enduring and distinctive vision of language study. The basic philosophy has been very stable, but it has left great scope for individual initiatives, and it has recently been given a substantial new impetus by computer-assisted corpus linguistics. The tradition is visible mainly in the work of Firth, Halliday and Sinclair, and it is Sinclair's work in corpus linguistics which is particularly relevant here.

I will refer briefly to some of the historical origins of these ideas, especially in work by J. R. Firth (e.g. 1935, 1957a, b), and I will point out how Firth's 'contextual theory of meaning' has led to significant progress in grammatical and lexical theory and to significant grammars and dictionaries of English (e.g. Halliday, 1985a, 1992; Sinclair, 1987a, 1990, 1995).

However, the chapter is not a chronology of people and influences. Rather, it concentrates on the principles underlying the work. These principles demand studying the use of real language in written and spoken discourse, both across corpora of data and also with reference to the functions of language in social institutions. The major ideas have therefore clustered around the textual analysis of naturally occurring language – as it is used without the intervention of the analyst – and also around the practical importance of language study in the real world.

In the appendix to this chapter I provide some notes on the intellectual background. And beyond the Firth–Halliday–Sinclair line of development, there is also a broader British tradition of corpus linguistics, in work by Quirk, Leech and others (e.g. Quirk et al., 1972, 1985; Garside et al., 1987), and links to work elsewhere in Europe. In important ways, however, this work differs from Sinclair's and I comment further on this below.

2.1 Principles: from Firth via Halliday to Sinclair

At the risk of over-simplifying the work of different linguists, I will try to formulate as simply as possible some principles which have been central to much British linguistics, and which have been developed in detailed and concrete ways. These principles concern the following.

- The nature of linguistics: that it is essentially a social science and an applied science, with practical implications, especially in education (see section 4.9 and chapter 6).
- The nature of data for linguistics: that language should be studied in attested, authentic instances of use (not as intuitive, invented sentences); that language should be studied as whole texts (not as isolated sentences or text fragments); and that texts must be studied comparatively across text corpora.
- The essential subject of linguistics: that linguistics should study meaning; that form and meaning are inseparable; and that lexis and grammar are interdependent (see this chapter for many examples).
- The nature of linguistic behaviour: that language in use involves both routine and creation; and that language in use transmits culture (see chapter 7 for a detailed argument).
- The conceptual structure of the discipline: that Saussurian dualisms (especially *langue–parole* and syntagmatic–paradigmatic) require radical revision.

2.2 Alternative Traditions

Work by Halliday and Sinclair has covered the thirty years from the 1960s to the 1990s. This is precisely the period of the rise and heyday of Chomskyan linguistics. Firth (1957b) published one of his most famous papers, 'A synopsis of linguistic theory, 1930–1955', in the same year that Chomsky (1957) published *Syntactic Structures*. And it is a Chomskyan approach which has formed the basic training and legitimated a way of study for a whole generation of linguists, and which must be used as one point of reference because it is still the source of so many assumptions in linguistics.

However, a comparison of Chomskyan principles with the neo-Firthian principles summarized above shows how deep and systematic are the differences. Chomsky argues that linguistics is a branch of cognitive psychology (and ultimately of biology), that it can be based on intuitive data and isolated sentences, that corpus data are unrevealing, that the study of language in use is essentially uninteresting and that linguistics can be based on a variant of the Saussurian *langue–parole* dualism. As an initial example, contrast these sharply opposed positions on the appropriate data for linguistics:

1a   'The critical problem for grammatical theory today is not a paucity of evidence but rather the inadequacy of present theories of language to account for masses of evidence that are hardly open to serious question' (Chomsky, 1965, pp. 19–20).
1b   'Starved of adequate data, linguistics languished – indeed it became almost totally introverted' (Sinclair, 1991a, p. 1).
2a   'Like most facts of interest and importance . . . information about the speaker-hearer's competence . . . is neither presented for direct observation nor extractable from data by inductive procedures of any known sort' (Chomsky, 1965, p. 18).
2b   'The ability to examine large text corpora in a systematic manner allows access to a quality of evidence that has not been available before' (Sinclair, 1991a, p. 4).

The Chomskyan view on these matters has not significantly changed in over twenty-five years. There have certainly been changes of direction within Chomskyan linguistics. Major events include the rise (and collapse) of generative semantics and the development of work in universal grammar. But in the underlying approach to language, very little has changed. (See, for example, the introduction to a major textbook on government and binding theory (Haegeman, 1991), where the assumptions about the data and the explanatory tasks for linguistics have not changed at all from Chomsky (1965). See also Chomsky (1992), first published in 1987, for an essentially unchanged position.)

2.3   Linguistics as an Applied Social Science

So, this chapter is about work which provides a substantial and well documented alternative to the use of intuitive data, and shows how computer-assisted analysis of texts and corpora can provide new understanding of form–meaning relations. Here, then, are the principles and a discussion of their development.

> Principle 1. Linguistics is essentially a social science and an applied science.

Strictly speaking, this formulation collapses two points into one: social scientific study need not have practical applications. However, it is easy to see why the two things have often gone together in language study.

Over the past fifty years much British linguistics has been deeply empirical, involved in practical problems of language and society, such as teaching English as a foreign language or mother tongue, speech pathology, teacher training and dictionary making. And British linguists have often been deeply involved in public debates and language planning around Standard English and the English curriculum in schools (see section 7.3). This is certainly true of the tradition developed by Firth, Halliday and Sinclair. They have made major descriptive and theoretical contributions to linguistics, and have insisted on the integrity of linguistic methods. But they have never espoused the autonomous linguistics of much recent American and other British work, in the sense of work divorced from all social relevance. Firth describes his work as essentially sociological. And Halliday regards his work as ultimately applied and as being in particular a contribution to educational linguistics.

Both Sinclair and Halliday have done major work in educational linguistics: with reference to teaching English as both mother tongue and second language, and to teacher training. In a series of battles with the English mother tongue teaching establishment, Sinclair (1982) is uncompromising about the 'sadly watered down and trivialized' material about language which is often served to English teachers, and about the rejection of precise technical knowledge about language in their training. For example, he draws ironic analogies between the professional training of English teachers and of doctors:

> Subjects like anatomy, physiology and all that are much too technical. Everyone knows medical students are not from the top of the academic pile, and they'll soon get confused by all those long Latin names and cutting people up. . . . In reality, anyone knows when a chap's ill – you don't have to be a doctor to take his temperature – and if a few of us get together for a chat we'll surely work out what's wrong with him. (Sinclair, 1982, pp. 21–2)

Sinclair is here pointing ironically to the different attitudes to systematic knowledge in the training of two groups of professionals, doctors and teachers. No one would argue in this way with respect to medical students. But views of professionalism in teacher training are often very differently conceived. Sinclair argues here that it is patronizing to think that teachers are incapable of an academically based training which is as demanding as that given to doctors. And he has always emphasized that principled knowledge about language should underlie the teaching of language.[1]

Much British work on linguistic description – of lexis, syntax and discourse – is inseparable from applied issues, such as teacher education, the preparation of teaching materials and the writing of dictionaries. For example, Sinclair (1991a, p. xvii) expresses the aim of 'exploit[ing] the relevance to teaching of an increased emphasis on the description of naturally occurring stretches of language.'

Several other areas of applied linguistics could be mentioned. One is the design of Seaspeak (Strevens and Weeks, 1985). This is the regularized subset of English designed for use over VHF radio in ship-to-ship and ship-to-shore maritime communications (analogous to the language of international air traffic control). Because of its contexts of use (the vital importance of correctly understood messages, the frequently poor radio reception, its use by non-native speakers), the system demands use of a controlled vocabulary, syntax and discourse rules, and increased redundancy. Seaspeak is an important example of the planning of a restricted language: a central concept of Firth's.[2]

2.4   Grammar and Discourse: Data and Models

One well known development of Firthian work is in discourse analysis. And the most widely known work is on classroom discourse (Sinclair and Coulthard, 1975; Sinclair and Brazil, 1982), but work on naturally occurring texts and discourse is much wider than this. Substantial work on lexis (Sinclair, 1966b) and on the computer-assisted analysis of a corpus of spoken language (Sinclair et al., 1970) and other stylistic work (e.g. Halliday, 1971; Sinclair, 1965, 1966a, 1968) came first, and computational work came to the fore again in work on lexis and grammar in the 1980s and 1990s (Halliday, 1991, 1992; Sinclair, 1991a).

Sinclair's first grammar of English (Sinclair, 1972) is based on Hallidayan scale-and-category theory, and analyses purely invented, intuitive, illustrative examples. It was significant at the time, as it represented a distinct shift away from the then dominant deep structural grammars, towards surface grammar, and therefore towards lexico-grammar. The discourse model of exchange and transaction structure (Sinclair and Coulthard, 1975) was constructed as the upward projection of this same Hallidayan rank–scale model, which had been designed for lower syntactic units. This was 'a reasonable tactic for getting started' in a new area (Sinclair, 1992a). But the model does not always fit the classroom data. (The appendix to the book codes exchanges in ways ruled out by the descriptive system.) And in a review of related work by Sinclair and Brazil (1982), I argued that the authors are unclear on the nature of the data: whether it is attested, or modified, or purely intuitive (Stubbs, 1984).

In the classroom discourse studies, there is a clear commitment to authentic data in the form of transcriptions of audio–recordings made in real classrooms. But this early work suffers from severe problems with the descriptive system: problems in grounding a pre–existing descriptive model in the recalcitrant data. This well known work on classroom data shows that spoken discourse is amenable to structural description, just as syntax is. The essential proposal is that exchanges in classroom discourse have a three–part structure of initiation–response–feedback. This IRF structure can be seen intuitively in examples (Sinclair and Coulthard, 1975, p. 48) such as [A]:

Teacher:	Do you know what we mean by accent?
Pupil:	It's the way you talk.
Teacher:	The way you talk. This is a very broad comment.

It is evident from our experience of classrooms and also from much ethnographic educational research that teachers often ask such pseudo–questions, to which they already know the answer, and that they evaluate pupils' responses in line with their own expectations. Sinclair and Coulthard (1975) provide a detailed examination of such discourse.

One interpretative problem with this work was that it had two audiences, educational and linguistic, and was therefore read within very different intellectual contexts. Within education, it was naturally interpreted as a contribution to classroom ethnography, and often criticized as being based on a narrow corpus, which represents only a narrow range of formal chalk–and–talk teaching. The description of classroom discourse was further often interpreted by educationalists as a prescription of how teachers should or should not (depending on one's ideological position) talk to pupils. And all of this in the post–1968 debates over teacher control and pupil autonomy!

From the beginning, however, this work was presented by its authors as contributing to central linguistic problems as 'one stage in a continuing investigation of language functions and the organization of linguistic units above the rank of the clause', and as an investigation of 'the extent of linguistic patterning in long texts' (Sinclair and Coulthard, 1975, pp. 1, 19).

A comparison of this 1970s work with Sinclair's more recent text analysis shows several developments, as the relations between data, existing linguistic models and new models are radically rethought. Rather than attempting to develop a pre-existing rank-scale model of linguistic description by projecting it 'upwards' to larger discourse units, Sinclair proposes highly general and elegant models of prospective and retrospective organization. From a beginning with relatively restricted data on classroom discourse, elegant hypotheses about spoken interaction in general are proposed. These more recent models relate observations about linguistic organization at the levels of lexis, syntax and discourse. And rather than imposing such a model on the data, Sinclair looks for ways of deriving the theory from the data: the concept of data-driven description becomes central. One of the most frequent words in recent titles and articles by Sinclair is 'evidence'. These points are developed below.

2.5   Methodology: Attested Data and Text Corpora

At the centre of work by Firth, Halliday and Sinclair are proposals about the nature of such evidence and about the empirical foundations of the discipline.

Principle 2. Language should be studied in actual, attested, authentic instances of use, not as intuitive, invented, isolated sentences.

This principle contrasts the American Chomskyan tradition with the British neo-Firthian tradition and also with earlier American structuralist work which was corpus-based. In the 1950s and 1960s, American scholars such as C. C. Fries, H. Kucera and W. N. Francis made major contributions to corpus study.

From its beginnings, Chomskyan linguistics had a very abstract and indirect concept of data: not observed instances of attested language behaviour, but sentences elicited from informants (often the linguist her or himself) in order to illustrate some grammatical point. Often the data were more indirect still: not even invented sentences themselves, but native speaker intuitions (usually the linguist's own) about the well-formedness of such invented sentences. This view of data had the merit of revealing the depth of abstractness and complexity of native speakers' knowledge of their language. But two points deserve special emphasis. First, only narrow aspects of human linguistic competence can be revealed by such methods. They can reveal nothing of the many aspects of language about which speakers have only inaccurate intuitions or simply no useful intuitions at all. Second, this is a very strange notion of data. Normally one expects a scientist to develop theories to describe and explain some phenomena which already exist, independently of the scientist. One does not expect a scientist to make up the data at the same time as the theory, or even to make up the data afterwards, in order to illustrate the theory.

Mey and Talbot (1988), in their highly critical review of Chomskyan-influenced pragmatics (Sperber and Wilson, 1986), make the same point as Sinclair (1987a, p. 15) that in relevance theory, 'examples are not . . . chosen to vouchsafe for the outside reality . . . but to make a point of theory'. And even within approaches very much influenced by Chomsky, the concept of intuitive data has been strongly criticized. Major criticisms have been: the uncertainty or inconsistency of native speaker judgements in cases central to the theory; the frequent discrepancies between linguists' intuitive judgements and observed linguistic behaviour, even their own; and the circularity of linguists using their own intuitions as data in analyses where they know what they would like to prove. Labov (1975) sharply attacks exclusive reliance on introspective data, with reference to these points.

As Pullum (1991a, p. 85), a committed Chomskyan, puts it (admittedly in an aggressively critical and ironic mood, and not in a mainstream academic article):

> The median number of speakers on whom the entire corpus of examples in an English syntax paper is checked before publication, including its author, is zero. The median number of informants used for study of a foreign language is one. The median number of children used in an acquisition study is one.

(I guess Pullum means *mode*, not *median*, but let's not quibble.)

There are actually two points in Principle 2. Much linguistics is based on invented sentences. In addition, often only a very small number of invented sentences are discussed. It is easy to forget or ignore how few data (either invented sentences or real texts) are actually analysed in the most influential literature in twentieth-century linguistics. Saussure (1916) in his *Cours de Linguistique Générale* analyses no textual data and few examples of any kind. Bloomfield in his influential textbook *Language* (1933, p. 22) rejects mentalism, and proposes turning to the 'observation of normal speech'. But the famous account of Jack, Jill and the apple, which immediately follows this proposal, and which is a key move in his argument about the analysis of meaning, is an entirely hypothetical, and rather implausible, story – anecdote as data. Chomsky (1957, 1965) analyses, respectively, only 28 and 24 invented sentences, some of them several times (De Beaugrande, 1991, p. 176, has counted!). Other example sentences are quoted as either grammatical or deviant, but without analysis. Lyons (1977) in his massive two volume *Semantics* does not analyse a single authentic text or text fragment.

One of the ironies of speech act theory (influential for Sinclair and Coulthard, 1975) is that it is based on 'seeing what we can screw out of ordinary language' (Austin, 1962, p. 122), yet, again, in the work by Austin and Searle which defines the field, all the data are invented. In Searle's (1969, pp. 50ff) proposals for an institutional theory of language, there are no actual instances of language use in institutions (see chapter 3 and section 8.3). The tradition continues in work by Grice (1967) and in further developments in relevance theory by Sperber and Wilson (1986). In all such work, there is the further problem with data that, traditionally, sentences were units of *langue*, and utterances units of *parole*. But utterances have here become a new genre, neither one thing, nor t'other. The analyst invents not only sentences, but utterances.

In so far as there is one single coherent thread throughout Firth's work, it is the contextual theory of meaning, and the principle that language cannot be studied as isolated sentences: 'the complete meaning of a word is always contextual, and no study of meaning apart from a complete context can be taken seriously' (Firth, 1935, p. 37). Firth makes fun of the isolated sentences on which famous linguists have based arguments: grammatically well-formed, but difficult or impossible to imagine in use, such as: *The farmer kills the duckling*; *Pussy is beautiful*; *I have not seen your father's pen, but I have read the book of your uncle's gardener* (Firth, 1935, pp. 60–1). Yet even Firth, despite his sharp strictures quoted above (perhaps because of the rigour of his own demands?) analyses little text, sometimes merely presenting texts as though their features were obvious (see Firth, 1964, 118–34).

Halliday's arguments often rely on invented sentences about aunts, dukes and teapots, or about Christopher Wren and a gazebo. However, in his major grammar (Halliday, 1985a, 1994), he does provide detailed textual commentary and analysis of real texts. And in his famous article on Golding's *The Inheritors* (Halliday, 1971), he provides an analysis of the stylistic effects achieved by the author's departure from expected frequencies of selections in the transitivity system. More recent articles analyse scientific texts (Halliday and Martin, 1993), and other work on probabilistic grammar (Halliday, 1993) is based on several million words of corpus data.

Especially with reference to data, it is important to check whether linguists do what they claim to do. For example, a major initiative in corpus linguistics, the Survey of English Usage, was begun at University College London in the 1960s. Substantial corpora of written and spoken data were collected, made available to scholars and published, in both book form and computer readable forms, and used as evidence for two major grammars of English, most recently *A Comprehensive Grammar of the English Language* (Quirk et al., 1985). However, the precise relation between the corpus data and the grammatical description is very vague. As Sinclair (1991a, pp. 100–1) points out, only occasional references are made in Quirk et al. (1985) to the Survey corpus. In fact, almost all such references are used to provide frequency data: for example, the frequency of different modals (p. 136), of split infinitives in educated speech (p. 498) or of types of noun phrase in different genres (pp. 1350–2). Only very occasionally is an example sentence explicitly taken from the corpus. The implication is that the example sentences either are invented, intuitive native speaker data, or are modified and idealized from the corpus in unspecified ways. This relation between corpus, example sentences and description is not discussed at all in the introduction to Quirk et al. (1985), and the accountability to data of description and theory is therefore undefined. Francis (1993) gives other examples.

I am emphasizing here cases of linguists not following principle 2. This emphasis is unfortunately necessary, because it is so easy to be blind to the very small amount of data on which contemporary linguistics is based, and this is fundamental to the whole intellectual organization of the discipline: the theories which linguists develop, the types of corroboration they claim, the methods they use and the ways in which students are trained. This unfortunately negative set of comments does, however, usefully bring out two contrasts: between the rhetoric and the reality in much linguistics (where data often means invented data); and between Sinclair and other linguists, even within the relatively homogeneous British tradition of corpus linguistics.

Against a reliance on invented data, Sinclair (1991a, p. 5) counters with the principle that examples are 'not to be tampered with', and talks of 'the absurd notion that invented examples can actually represent the language better than real ones'. The mind plays tricks, and there is no justification for modifying data. Sinclair (1991a) provides a thorough critique of the use of intuitive data, and gives precise examples of its limitations in lexical, grammatical and semantic studies. Intuitive judgements are particularly untrustworthy with respect to the frequency and distribution of different forms and meanings of words, and to the interaction of lexis, grammar and meaning.

In addition, he develops the point above about the essential confusion between data and theory in much work:

> invented examples are really part of the explanations. They have no inde-
> pendent authority or reason for their existence, and they are constructed

to refine the explanations and in many cases to clarify the explanations. . . . Usage cannot be invented, it can only be recorded. (Sinclair, 1987a, p. xv)

And he points out difficulties of perception due to training and warns against the imposition of pre-corpus beliefs on corpus data: 'Linguistics usually operates with . . . abstract categories. . . . But . . . it is good policy to defer the use of them for as long as possible, to refrain from imposing analytical categories from the outside' (Sinclair, 1991a, p. 29). The link between an insistence on authentic data and a preference for surface grammar is here evident.

This discussion raises classic problems of the relation between language and text. The view that the abstract language system is realized in actual instances in concrete text is too simple. When they had only very limited corpus data, linguists studied actual instances, knowing that most were untypical. When the Chomskyan paradigm shift justified studying intuitive data, linguists ignored actual instances entirely, and studied invented instances, knowing that most could never occur, and were also untypical. A large corpus, consisting of at least several million words, searched with computer assistance, provides a way out of this dilemma. One of the main uses of a corpus is to identify what is central and typical in the language (Sinclair, 1991a, pp. 17, 102ff). These points raise questions of the representativeness of a corpus, and as Sinclair (1991a, p. 103) admits, what is required is a theory of typicality which is yet to be fully worked out (see section 9.1).

Authentic language occurs as language-in-text. Firth (1957b, pp. 5, 29) argues that 'the actual language text duly recorded' should be the main concern of the linguist. So a related principle is:

Principle 3.   The unit of study must be whole texts.

The reason for this principle is that few linguistic features of a text are distributed evenly throughout (Sinclair, 1991a, p. 19). One example is that marked lexical and syntactic differences are often found between different parts of a scientific research article, say between abstract, introduction, main argument and conclusion (Swales, 1990).

Work by Halliday (e.g. 1971) and Sinclair (e.g. 1965, 1966a, 1968) includes significant linguistic stylistic studies of literary texts, where the concern has to be with the interpretation of the whole work. And this principle has immediate consequences for the construction of corpora. It rejects the sampling methods necessarily used by the relatively small first-generation computer readable corpora (Brown, LOB and London–Lund), where

2,000- or 5,000-word text fragments are used. The Cobuild corpus (and now the Bank of English corpus) therefore includes whole texts (Sinclair, 1991a, p. 19).

> Principle 4. Texts and text types must be studied comparatively across text corpora.

The heterogeneity of language is a central assumption in Firthian linguistics: 'Unity is the last concept that should be applied to language. Unity of language is the most fugitive of all unities, whether it be historical, geographical, national, or personal' (Firth, 1935, p. 67). And it is widely accepted that an important aspect of language variation is the varying frequency of lexical and grammatical features across different text types: in fact, register variation is usually defined as the systematic variation in such frequencies (e.g. Halliday, 1991, p. 33). Sinclair's analyses of literary style and of distinctive discourse structures in different discourse types (for example, between teachers and pupils, or doctors and patients) document such genre variations.

There are various factors which can disguise the inherent variability of language, but the main one is an exclusive reliance on introspective data. Since such data are consciously invented to illustrate a theory, they are carefully selected and highly edited. But self-conscious editing and monitoring are characteristics of written rather than spoken language. The very fact that it is sentences which are invented biases the data towards written language, since sentences are units of written language, and only, at best, partially relevant to spoken discourse. The common claim that studying intuitive data means studying language independent of its medium of transmission in speech or writing is therefore false.

The view that language varies systematically across text types has implications for interpretation. It follows that texts are interpreted against a background of expectations: and interpreted as much for what they omit as for what they express. As Firth puts it, in an uncharacteristically psychological formulation: '[The] patterns of language in the "unconscious" background are just as important as the patterns of speech we make and hear' (Firth, 1964, p. 183).

This view of language variation also has the methodological implication that text study must be comparative. As Sinclair put it, 30 years ago:

> Any stretch of language has meaning only as a sample of an enormously large body of text; it represents the results of a complicated selection process, and each selection has meaning by virtue of all the other selections which might have been made, but have been rejected. (Sinclair, 1965, pp. 76–7)

This comment expresses the Hallidayan concept of the language potential from which selections are made as the potential is realized in a particular text. And it was published at a time when computer-assisted techniques of corpus study were starting to become feasible (see Sinclair et al., 1970).

A currently fashionable phrasing of this point is that all texts make intertextual references. In what they include or omit, all texts make assumptions about their readers or listeners. Texts are shaped by prior texts, by repetitions or by being oriented to routines and conventions. Therefore all texts are inherently historical (cf. Fairclough, 1992).

Much work in the systemic tradition recognizes that many texts are mixed: for example, there are many mixed modes between spoken and written language. And there are many studies which show that written and spoken genres overlap in their linguistic characteristics (see section 3.9). Biber's work has had a particularly large influence on British work on corpus linguistics. His best known work (Biber, 1988) is a computer-assisted study of 67 linguistic features across a million and a half words of two corpora (LOB and Lund: see notes on corpus data) of written and spoken British English. For the range of genres represented by those two corpora (including face-to-face and telephone conversations, press editorials, fiction, official documents and academic prose), he studied the lexical and syntactic features which correlated with each other, or alternatively which occurred in largely complementary distribution.

In most genres, Biber (1988, p. 180) finds that the majority of texts are grouped tightly around the mean (that is, the standard deviation is small), but some texts are quite atypical (that is, the range is large). Such work provides empirical comparisons of different genres, and can therefore provide a powerful interpretative background for the analysis of individual texts. Such analyses of expected patterns are beginning to document the 'unconscious background' of textual variability against which individual texts are interpreted. However, Biber's analysis is across representative samples of genres and sub-genres, with no analysis of the discourse structure of individual instances of the genres. The most powerful interpretation emerges if comparisons of texts across corpora are combined with the analysis of the organization of individual texts. (See section 1.7 on the studies by Cook, Jucker and Swales.)

Corpus studies show that language in use is characterized by spectacular regularities of pattern with endless variation (Sinclair, 1991a, p. 4). The aim must therefore be a theory of how the language system survives the fuzziness of the variable instances.

2.6 Form and Meaning, Lexis and Grammar

At the same time that Bloomfield (1933) was expressing the view that meaning was the 'weak point' of language study, Firth (1935) was publishing a major article on 'the techniques of semantics' and emphasizing that linguistics without meaning is sterile.

> Principle 5. Linguistics is concerned with the study of meaning: form and meaning are inseparable.

Traditions deriving from Bloomfield and early Chomsky have always had extreme difficulties in combining rigorous distributional analysis of language forms with a theory of meaning. For example, Chomsky (1957, p. 17) asserts that 'grammar is autonomous and independent of meaning', and later (p. 102) only grudgingly admits that 'the fact that correspondences between formal and semantic features exist . . . cannot be ignored'. Later work in generative semantics and work inspired by speech act theory take the debate in different directions, but do not solve the form–meaning problem.

Sinclair takes a different position:

> in all cases so far examined, each meaning can be associated with a distinct formal patterning. . . . There is ultimately no distinction between form and meaning. . . . [The] meaning affects the structure and this is . . . the principal observation of corpus linguistics in the last decade. (Sinclair, 1991a, pp. 6–7, 1991b, p. 496)

It is worth emphasizing that corpus analysis has often been rejected in recent linguistics, on the argument that a corpus cannot give insight into meaning. Yet much British corpus linguistics has been precisely concerned with semantic analysis. The connecting thread has been Firth's notion of meaning as function in context, and more specifically, the concept of collocation, that is, syntagmatic relations between words as such, not between categories. As Firth (1957b, p. 11) puts it: 'You shall know a word by the company it keeps. . . . The habitual collocations [of words] are quite simply the mere word accompaniment.' Collocations must be established in attested texts. They constitute one of the many levels to which meaning is 'dispersed', in Firth's concept. (For detailed development of this definition see section 7.7.)

The main argument is that meaning can best be handled by techniques of text analysis and distributional analysis, rather than by methods of conceptual analysis. This requires detailed examples, which are best given under the next, related principle.

> Principle 6.   There is no boundary between lexis and grammar: lexis and grammar are interdependent.

The concept of lexico-grammar has long been proposed by Halliday. And a major claim in Sinclair's work in the 1980s and 1990s is that if a corpus is used to construct the grammar, then the interdependence of lexis and syntax becomes obvious. But Sinclair's detailed lexico-syntactic studies take the argument considerably further than Halliday's position that 'lexis is the most delicate syntax'.

A central theme in neo-Firthian linguistics is the nature and importance of choices. Two related concepts can be illustrated most easily from phonology.

1   Language is polysystemic (Firth, 1968, pp. 24, 43, 200). (Firth is here opposing the monosystemic principle of Meillet that a language is 'un système où tout se tient'.) For example, there are different systems at different points in English phonological structure. All consonant phonemes except the velar nasal can occur word-initially; and all except /h/ can occur word-finally. The two structural slots, initial and final, permit different closed classes of paradigmatic choices.

2   Units are often co-selected. For example, English has both nasals and plosives at bilabial, alveolar and velar points of articulation. However, in words such as *limp*, *lint* and *link*, the word-final consonant pairs represent not two choices, but one. Due to assimilation to point of articulation, there are two bilabials, two alveolars or two velars, and no other combinations are possible. Firth talked here of prosodies across more than one unit. (For detailed discussion of semantic prosodies see sections 7.7, 7.8.)

A simple lexical example of co-selection of lexis and grammar, which Sinclair (1992a, p. 14) provides, is that the noun *lap* is more likely to occur in a prepositional phrase in adjunct position, than to occur in the subject or object of a clause. I checked this claim on 2.3 million words of corpus data. There were 19 examples of the predicted construction, such as

> he used to sit me on his lap
>
> she supported the dying hero's head in her lap
>
> he threw the doll into the lap of the woman

and only one other:

> my lap full of seventy times seven bundles

Detailed corpus work has now begun to show the ramifications of these concepts for grammatical description. In an elegant corpus-based study, Francis (1991) provides a more systematic demonstration of the phenomenon that all words have their own grammar. She takes a dozen nouns from a specific frequency band of English (e.g. *accident, artist, darkness*). If grammar and lexis were independent systems, one would expect that a given selection of such words (lemmas) would be evenly distributed over different grammatical positions in the clause, such as subject, object, indirect object, adjunct or qualifier. Traditionally, grammarians have been primarily interested in syntactic structure, and lemmas have been used merely as slot fillers in such structures. The distribution of different lemmas in the same syntactic slots is, however, very uneven. For example, *context* and *darkness* are much more common in adjunct position than elsewhere, whereas *impact* and *independence* are much more common in object position than elsewhere. Francis's article contains a careful discussion of the relevant distributional facts.

The explicitly pedagogical Cobuild grammar (Sinclair, 1990) is a stage towards a thoroughgoing lexico-grammar. It associates structures with lexical items, which are provided in the form of lists. These lists are illustrative and incomplete, although they already provide information which is not available from introspection. Examples are the lists of verbs which occur in the passive, either commonly (e.g. *be earmarked, be rumoured, be short-listed*) or rarely (e.g. *elude, get, suit*) (Sinclair, 1990, pp. 407–8). An even simpler example (p. 410) is the set of semantically related verbs (*adore, dislike, enjoy, hate, like, love, need, want*, etc.) which occur in the structure

> *what* or *all* + PRONOUN + VERB + BE + NOUN

as in

> what we want is Watney's
>
> all you need is love

Other work provides analyses of various lemmas and gives a large number of precise examples to document further these claims about polysystemic organization and co-selection of lexis and grammar. A further stage in the argument shows that different forms of a lemma pattern differently. In a paper on 'the nature of the evidence', Sinclair (1991a, pp. 67ff) discusses the lemma SET and in particular its uses in the phrasal verb SET IN. One of the forms, *set*, is much commoner than the others, *sets, setting*. In its verbal uses, therefore, SET is commonest in past tense. SET IN has a tendency to occur in end structures. And its subjects are generally unpleasant and largely abstractions, such as

> where the rot set in

> disillusion had set in

None of these points could be reliably documented from intuition. (See Louw (1993), and see section 7.7 for more detailed analysis of the negative connotations of SET IN and other lexical items, and for examples of different patterns associated with forms of the lemma EDUCATE.)

For a small example, apparently innocent, but far-reaching in its implications, Sinclair (1991b) shows the non-equivalence of singular and plural forms of nouns, by documenting the different patterning of *eye* and *eyes*. 'There is hardly any common environment' between the two word forms, and they 'do not normally have the capacity to replace each other'. The plural co-occurs with adjectives such as *blue, brown, covetous, manic*. The singular hardly ever refers to the anatomical object, except when talking about injury or handicap. For both singular and plural, the phrasal and figurative meanings are not peripheral, but typical: singular and plural occur in different sets of fixed phrases (*all eyes will be on, rolling their eyes; turn a blind eye, keep an eye on*).

Such analyses show that the co-patterning of different forms and senses of lemmas and of syntax is much more detailed than is generally shown in grammars. And new links are being proposed between lemmas, word forms and syntactic patterns. What corpus study shows is that lexis and syntax are totally interdependent. Not only different words, but different forms of a single lemma, have different grammatical distributions.

With reference to lexis, a further stage in the argument is that lexical items are selected more than one at a time. Using data from *The Times*, Sinclair (1992a) shows this co-selection and the consequent delexicalization of what are normally thought of as lexical, content words. Examples include: *physical assault, physical damage* and *physical proximity*, where the meaning of the adjective duplicates a large part of the meaning of the noun; *scientific experiment, scientific analysis* and *scientific study*, where the adjective does little more than dignify the noun; and *full enquiry, full account* and *full circle*: a government is unlikely to announce a *partial enquiry*!

Two important articles (Sinclair, 1991a, pp. 81–98; Renouf and Sinclair, 1991) analyse aspects of highly frequent grammatical words, which receive either a fragmented treatment or no treatment at all in traditional dictionaries or grammars. The word *of* is traditionally regarded as a preposition. But from concordance data, Sinclair (1991a) shows that *of*, and probably other very common words, are members of one-word classes. If we accept the traditional classification of preposition, this leads to the strange conclusion that the word *of* is the most common member of this class (more than twice as frequent as the next), yet is normally used in a structure which is not typical for the class. Prepositions normally form prepositional phrases which are used as clause adjuncts: *in the same week*, *behind the masks*. But by far the most common use of *of* is to elaborate a preceding nominal group: *the back of the van*, *a small bottle of brandy*.

Renouf and Sinclair (1991) discuss discontinuous pairings of grammatical words in collocations such as

a(n) + ? + of

be + ? + to

too + ? + to

They provide detailed statistics on the frequency of such collocations with intervening words. These collocational frameworks, as Renouf and Sinclair call them, are not grammatical constituents. Nor are the triplets which they frame; for example,

a couple of, a lot of, an indication of, an element of, be able to, be ready to, too easy to, too close to

Such items are highly frequent, an integral part of the language, yet lie somewhere between word and group, and are missed both by current grammatical descriptions and by conventional definitions of collocation.

These studies have far-reaching implications for assumptions which are traditionally made about form classes and grammatical constituents: 'even major parts of speech are not as solidly founded as they might be' (Sinclair, 1992a, p. 14). Although a central topic of Chomskyan syntax has always been to motivate sentence constituents, the evidence for the form–classes which are assumed to be the ultimate constituents has been very thin indeed. Sinclair (1987b, p. 114) talks of some of the main noun and adjective classifications crumbling under corpus evidence. And the Cobuild grammar (Sinclair, 1990) gives many examples of the likely convergence of grammatical classes and lexical sets. The traditional parts of speech system is under attack.

It will become clear just how far-reaching are the central conclusions of such work on lexico-grammar if I list them.

1   Any grammatical structure restricts the lexis that occurs in it; and conversely, any lexical item can be specified in terms of the structures in which it occurs. (Note the difference from the Hallidayan position, quoted above. If lexis and grammar are co-selected, then lexis cannot merely be the 'most delicate grammar'.)

2   Such restrictions are typically not absolute, but clear tendencies: grammar is inherently probabilistic.

3   Meaning is not constant across the inflected forms of a lemma. (Traditional dictionaries do not show this.)

4   Every sense or meaning of a word has its own grammar: each meaning is associated with a distinct formal patterning. Form and meaning are inseparable.

5   Words are systematically co-selected: the normal use of language is to select more than one word at a time.

6   Since paradigmatic choices are not made independently of position in syntagmatic chain, the relation between paradigmatic and syntagmatic has to be rethought.

7   Traditional word-classes and syntactic units also have to be rethought.

8   Native speakers have only limited intuitions about such statistical tendencies. Grammars based on intuitive data will imply more freedom of combination than is in fact possible. (See below for a specific example.) Grammar is corpus-driven in the sense that the corpus tells us what the facts are. Some of these facts may seem intuitively obvious in retrospect (this is often the case with findings in the social sciences). But they cannot be predicted in advance and they certainly cannot be exhaustively documented from intuition.

A contrast between Sinclair's work and other British corpus linguistics emphasizes some of these points. Consider an example from Quirk et al. (1985, p. 1393) on the extraposition of the clausal object in sentences [I? M?] such as

>   you must find *it* exciting working here
>
>   I made *it* my objective to settle the matter
>
>   I owe *it* to you that the jury acquitted me

Quirk et al. (1985) imply by omission that such extraposition is possible for any verb. But corpus data show (Francis, 1993) that two verb lemmas, FIND and MAKE, account for the vast majority (over 98 per cent) of such structures. Such strong probabilistic relations between lexis and syntax should find a place in the grammar.

It is easy to underestimate the radical implications of these points for many widely held assumptions of grammatical description. The principle of co-selection means that the linear (syntagmatic) nature of linguistic relations, and therefore the whole syntagmatic–paradigmatic distinction, must be rethought. If this relation between lexis and grammar is rethought, then so must be the whole relation between dictionaries and grammars.

2.7   Routines of Cultural Transmission

A view of language study as a social science, with the consequent observation of authentic language use in texts, leads to the next principle.

    Principle 7.   Much language use is routine.

In a famous passage, Firth (1935) discusses the often routine and stereotyped forms of everyday conversation, and his proposals here are at the basis of much later work on discourse analysis:

> Conversation is much more of a roughly prescribed ritual than most people think. Once someone speaks to you, you are in a relatively determined context and you are not free just to say what you please. We are born individuals. But to satisfy our needs we have to become social persons . . . it is [in] the study of conversation . . . that we shall find the key to a better understanding of what language really is and how it works. (Firth, 1935, pp. 66, 70–1)

Firth's discussion provides a statement of the tension between individual and social, freedom and constraint, creation and routine, and all this thirty years before work in speech act theory and conversational analysis by Austin, Searle and Sacks. Compare the Firth quote with these very similar statements:

> each turn in a discourse [is] a predictive classification of all possible next turns – and even though literally anything can happen next it is not difficult to supply a comprehensive guide to the next utterance. (Sinclair, 1980)

> each utterance provides a framework within which the next utterance is placed. (Sinclair, 1992b, p. 83)

There are several developments in Sinclair's work on discourse between the 1970s and the 1990s: from a description of one rather narrow discourse type (teacher-dominated classroom discourse) to hypotheses about spoken and written text in general; from a rather elaborate rank-scale model of exchange structure to simple and elegant hypotheses about linear prospective and retrospective text structure; and from work on spoken interaction to powerful hypotheses about the different organization of spoken and written language.

At the centre of these general hypotheses is the concept of prospection in spoken interaction. Sinclair (1992b) regards the creation and maintenance of prospections as the defining criterion of exchanges. He considers whether a two-part adjacency pair (such as question–answer) is the basic exchange structure; or whether the three-part IRF structure, identified for classroom discourse, is basic. He concludes that the three-part structure, as in

I   did you wake up late today?

R   yeah pretty late

F   oh dear

is always the option, and that in many types of discourse it is virtually obligatory.

Moves in spoken interaction prospect ahead: speakers cannot remember exactly what has been said, so cannot refer back with accuracy. In contrast, written text is still present, readers can look back at it, and written language may therefore be retrospectively structured. Sinclair (1992a, pp. 10–11) proposes a completely general mechanism for cohesion in written text, that:

> each sentence . . . contains a single act of reference which encapsulates the whole of the previous text. . . . [The] previous states of the text . . . are present in the current sentence in so far as they are needed. . . . In many cases [written text] also prospects forward.

This is a very simple and powerful hypothesis, which is intuitively understandable, but which requires to be documented in detail from corpus data.

Sinclair (1980) and Sinclair and Brazil (1982) also demonstrate some of the relations between the interpretations of initiations and their grammatical structure. They show that the following syntactic forms are progressively less ambiguous in their functional interpretation: declarative, positive polar interrogative, negative polar interrogative, tag interrogative, *wh*-interrogative, imperative. Those earlier in the list can be interpreted as those later, but not vice versa. For example, it is normal to interpret a declarative as a command, but impossible to interpret an imperative as a statement. To take a classic Austin example, a declarative sentence such as *There is a bull in the field* [I] is notoriously ambiguous. It might be used as a statement, warning or request for clarification: indefinitely many interpretations are possible. But sentences in interrogative form (*Could you put the bull in the field*) or imperative form (*Put the bull in the field*) are much less ambiguous, and perhaps not ambiguous at all.

Superficially, the studies on discourse and on lexis seem far apart, but many of the same principles hold in both areas. In particular, the concept of fixed routines and the concept of linear syntagmatic structure and prospection hold for both discourse and lexis. Thus Sinclair (1991a) gives a central place to fixed expressions, such as clichés, recurring collocations and idioms. (See especially Sinclair (1991a, pp. 109ff) on the idiom principle and open-choice principle in lexis. And see section 7.7.)

Again a contrast is inevitable with the Chomskyan position, where the emphasis is on creativity, but where routine can be conceived only negatively, with behaviourist connotations, as mere habit formation. One of Firth's major insights is the need to achieve a balance, in theories of human behaviour, between freedom and constraint, variation and routine, individual and social. Hence the next principle.

Principle 8.   Language in use transmits the culture.

Firth also points explicitly to the importance of studying the transmission of culture, though he does not make quite clear the connection between everyday routine and cultural transmission.

For his 'contextual and sociological technique' of semantics, Firth (1935, p. 40) proposed 'research into the distribution of sociologically important words' (such as *work* and *leisure*: see sections 3.2 and 7.4). Firth, as was often the case, was here making a programmatic proposal for which he never carried out the textual analysis. To be fair, however, he was proposing a study of social change and ideology, and demanding techniques of data collection and analysis, which became feasible only some fifty years later, with computational methods and access to large corpora.

The cultural theme is not developed explicitly in Sinclair's work. His study of classroom discourse provides models of some of the sociolinguistic knowledge that children learn as they become socialized into patterns of classroom behaviour. However, despite its origins in pedagogical concerns, Sinclair's work is strangely detached from any psychological or social theory, and his corpus work is formulated with no discussion of how the linguistic analysis could support 'a linguistically centred social analysis' (Firth, 1968, p. 177). Firth's position is sociological, largely because of his pessimism about our ability to study private psychological states. (He here unfortunately creates another dualism.) The way in which texts instantiate semantic habits and coding orientations is developed in detail by Halliday (e.g. 1978, p. 111), who relates his work to Bernstein's sociological theory.

Observations about the regular distributions of syntactic choices in text are ripe for integration into textual analyses of language and ideology. And in chapter 7, I discuss in detail how fixed expressions and recurrent wordings can be identified and studied to show how the culture is expressed in lexical patterns. Other lines of development are easily imaginable. Miller (1993) shows how detailed observations about the co-selection of lexical items are highly relevant to psycholinguistic theories of language learning. And Baker (1992), with explicit reference to corpus work, demonstrates how work on fixed expressions is relevant to translation theory.

2.8   Beyond Saussurian Dualisms

A general interpretation of such British work is that Firth, Halliday and Sinclair are developing a position which overcomes Saussurian dualisms.

Principle 9. Saussurian dualisms are misconceived.

Firth (1957b, p. 2n) denounces such dualisms as 'a quite unnecessary nuisance', and explicitly describes (1935, p. 53, 1957b, p. 2) his position as monistic. Both Halliday (1978, p. 38) and Sinclair (1991a, p. 103) reject the competence–performance distinction. And I have noted above the Firthian rewriting of the syntagmatic–paradigmatic opposition.

There are many aspects to the Saussurian paradox (Labov, 1972, pp. 185ff). In the tradition of autonomous linguistics from Saussure to Chomsky, *langue* or competence are conceived as systematic and as the only true object of study, although they are abstract and therefore unobservable. *Parole* or performance are considered unsystematic and idiosyncratic, and therefore, at best, of only peripheral interest. But in addition, *parole* is by definition observable only in passing fragments: as a whole, it is also unobservable. Mainstream twentieth-century linguistics has therefore defined itself with reference to a dualism, both halves of which are unobservable. Much of the significance of computer-assisted study of large corpora lies in possibilities for breaking out of this impasse, since concordancers and other software allow millions of words of data to be searched for patterns which could not be observed unaided.

On the relation between the instance and the system, Halliday's (1991, 1992) metaphor of the weather and the climate is helpful. The weather and the climate are the same phenomenon, but regarded from different time depths. If we are thinking of the next few hours, then we are thinking of the weather: and this perspective determines what kinds of actions we might take (for example, going to the beach, packing an umbrella). If we are thinking of the next decade or the next century, then we are thinking of the climate: and this perspective also determines what kinds of actions we might take (for example, legislating against industrial processes which are destroying the ozone layer). If the climate changes, then obviously the weather changes. But conversely, each day's weather affects the climate, however infinitesimally, either maintaining the status quo or helping to tip the balance towards climatic change. Instance and system, micro and macro, are two sides of the same coin, relative to the observer's position.

Halliday is fond of this way of thinking. Thus grammar and lexis are not two phenomena, but one: the same thing seen by different observers. And every instance in a text perturbs the overall probabilities of the system, if only to an infinitesimal extent: the system is therefore inherently probabilistic (Halliday, 1992). It was Saussure who said that it is the viewpoint which creates the object of study for linguistics. Halliday also points out that it is the position of the observer which creates the illusion of different objects of study: thus abolishing the dualism which Saussure's viewpoint created. Chapter 3 discusses in more detail such work, which attempts to overcome Saussurian dualisms, especially with reference to J. R. Firth, Trevor Hill and work by the British sociologist Anthony Giddens on agency and structure.

2.9   Data, Description and Theory

Possibly the most negative effect of the introspective methodology in much recent linguistics was that 'descriptivist' became a term of criticism or abuse (Sampson, 1980, pp. 146ff). Introspection was often regarded not as merely supplementary evidence, but as having an authority denied to observation: despite the fact that a linguist's introspections are private and not open to criticism by others, and that such private data are particularly dubious when the linguist has a vested interest in collecting evidence to support a given theory.

Sinclair's work shows in a precise and concrete way how a large corpus and an associated technology create a viewpoint which can lead to innovations in linguistic description and theory. The essential vision underlying corpus linguistics is that computer-assisted analysis of language gives access to data which were previously unobservable, but which can now profoundly change our understanding of language. As Sinclair says,

> Analysis of extended naturally-occurring texts, spoken and written, and, in particular, computer processing of texts have revealed quite unsuspected patterns of language. . . . The big difference has been the availability of data. . . . [The] major novelty was the recording of completely new evidence about how the language is used. . . . [The] contrast exposed between the impressions of language detail noted by people, and the evidence compiled objectively from texts is huge and systematic. . . . The language looks rather different when you look at a lot of it at once. (Sinclair, 1991a, pp. xvii, 1, 2, 4, 100)

In this vision of the subject, a corpus is not merely a tool of linguistic analysis, but an important concept in linguistic theory (see section 9.1).

This chapter has emphasized the relation between data, description and theory in linguistics. Labov (1975) has analysed the problems with intuitive data in recent linguistics, and has pointed out that every major paradigm shift in linguistics has been led by a shift in the concept of the basic data for the subject. Examples are: differences between words across languages and over time as data for historical comparative linguistics; synchronic rather than diachronic data for Saussurian linguistics; unwritten Amerindian languages for Bloomfieldean structuralism; the native speaker's intuitions for Chomskyan linguistics; phonological variables across a speech community for Labovian sociolinguistics.

The implication of recent work is that the data now available from computer readable corpora will lead to major changes in linguistic theory. This is one sense of the concept of data–driven linguistics. There is a vision, based on textual evidence of a kind not previously accessible, of 'the emergence of a new view of language, and the technology associated with it' (Sinclair, 1991a, p. 1). Such computer-assisted corpus linguistics provides a new way of thinking about some of the classic and recalcitrant questions that linguistics finds new ways of formulating, but never solves, concerning the relations between data and theory, examples and generalizations, rules and tendencies, knowledge and use, and between linguistics and other disciplines. In this concluding section I will try to identify some of these broader implications of such work and some points for development.

1 *Data-driven linguistics.* Discussions of the relation between evidence and theory question many Popperian assumptions in recent linguistics (on 'the cult of the counter-example', see Sinclair, 1991a, p. 99). Work with corpora provides new ways of considering the relation between data and theory, by showing how theory can be grounded in publicly accessible

corpus data. But the concept of corpus-driven linguistics must confront the classic problem that there is no such thing as pure induction. As Firth frequently warns, in this case quoting Goethe, 'The highest truth would be to grasp that everything factual is already theoretical. . . . There are no brute facts. . . . The notion of a mere fact is the product of the abstractive intellect' (Firth, 1957b, pp. 1, 29). The linguist always approaches data with hypotheses and hunches, however vague. It would be useful, thirty years on, and with technological possibilities unforeseen by Chomsky, to have a thorough reassessment of Chomsky's original criticisms of corpus work, and of the relation between intuitive native speaker data and corpus data (Chomsky, 1957, pp. 50ff, 1965, p. 18).

2 *Probabilistic grammar.* Computer-assisted work will revolutionize not only dictionaries but grammars. At the time of writing (1995), a full lexico-grammar of English has yet to be written. And the test of many of the descriptive proposals will be whether such a grammar leads to lasting revisions in the description of English and in the theory of (lexico) grammar. One question is whether this grammar will be a full-blown probabilistic grammar. Halliday (1991, 1992) and Francis (1991, 1993) make precise, but limited, proposals on the form of probabilistic choices in a grammar. And the Cobuild grammar (Sinclair, 1990) provides initial informal statements: for example, which verbs always, frequently, rarely or never occur in the passive. But the production of a comprehensive probabilistic grammar is uncharted territory. Corpus work depends on the interpretation of frequency and distributional data. Statistics provides ways of summarizing complex numerical data, so that inferences can be drawn from them, showing which variation is likely to be significant or random, and which data sets are homogeneous or heterogeneous. As Sinclair (1991a, 3) admits, 'the numerical and statistical side has hardly begun'. And it may well be that the new kinds of language data now available will lead to the development of new statistical parameters, which might look very different indeed from the parameters known from the statistical tradition of work on lexis.

3 *Descriptive and pedagogical grammars.* The connections between an innovative descriptive and a pedagogical grammar – another classic problem – also require to be spelled out. Different descriptions for different purposes would be a Hallidayan formulation (though this formulation explains little). The link between commerce and academia is also important (and a topic of wide significance in contemporary academic life). Without substantial commercial funding, the work would never have taken place. And organizational and intellectual questions are not independent. Dr Johnson notwithstanding, writing dictionaries and grammars, and studying hundreds of millions of words, is not a one-person affair. As Sampson (1987a,b) points out,

people who invent their own data can work alone, but people who work with probabilistic models of corpora tend to work in groups. However, commercial links then place pressures on the work. In the production of comprehensive dictionaries and grammars, the crux of the matter is the relation between descriptive statement and normative authority. Such work is, after all, of considerable political significance in a country obsessed with teaching grammar and Standard English in schools (see section 7.3).

4   *Linguistic variability.* In the work on lexis and grammar, long texts are used as evidence of the language as a whole. The theory emphasizes variability, but the necessary fiction of 'the English language' has to be maintained in preparing dictionaries and grammars. Differences within individual long texts and across text types are therefore averaged away. There is large scope both for studies of genre variation (Biber, 1988), and for analyses of the internal organization of whole texts (Phillips, 1989).

5   *The public nature of science.* An important implication of technology is that even desktop PCs can give access to linguistic patterns in corpora of up to a few million words. Some projects need large resources of machines and people, but individual researchers with modest technology can now check claims on real data. There is no longer any excuse for exclusive reliance on intuitions – the ultimately private data, and the ultimate protection against counter-example and alternative theory.

6   *Linguistic facts.* Then there are questions about the subject matter of linguistics itself. Linguists who work on intuitive sentence data and linguists who work on attested corpus data are regularly either puzzled or dismissive of each other's work. Are such groups studying the same subject from different points of view? Or are they simply studying different phenomena, as Fasold (1992) argues? One group is studying isolated sentences as abstract objects about which speakers have intuitions (about entailment, ambiguity etc.). The other group is studying utterances in context, events in time, which can be recorded, and which are amenable to distributional and statistical description. It is well known that sentences and utterances do not map easily on to each other. And it is arguable that language in use consists of a mixture of sentence-like and non-sentential elements. The position is confused by sentence grammars (such as Quirk et al., 1985) which are based in unspecified ways on corpus data.

7   *The problem of order.* Linguistics is part of the attempt to find explanations for human behaviour and to formulate a theory of social action. A cognitive, intentionalist theory captures some aspects of language behaviour: language is individual, intentional and creative. But this is only half the picture. Language is also social, partly unintentional and routine, based on social conventions which are not open to introspection. There are many linguistic patterns – revealed in collocations and in co-selections of lexis and

grammar – which are due to habit. Intentional behaviour has many unintended consequences (Giddens, 1984, pp. 8–14). We could adapt Sinclair (1965), quoted above, as follows: 'Any instance of intentional, individual language behaviour has meaning only against the background of an enormously large body of conventional, routine social action.' This is the classic problem of how order is possible in the social world, and our theories must be balanced between the individual and the social.

2.10 Description and Theory, Methods and Applications

Halliday and Sinclair are among the few linguists who have genuinely shifted the focus of the discipline. They have made contributions to educational linguistics, to stylistics, to discourse analysis, to lexicography, and to syntax and semantics. Their work has resulted in major developments in: applied linguistics, especially in educational linguistics; linguistic methodology, especially in the analysis of large corpora; linguistic description, in major dictionaries and grammars of English; and linguistic theory, not only in the extension of linguistic concepts from syntax to lexis and discourse, but also in work which has extensive implications for theories of grammar and meaning, and therefore for core mainstream linguistics.

It is perhaps particularly important to emphasize their contribution to linguistic description. They have, quite simply, discovered a large number of new facts about English: not something which can be said of many linguists. As Firth (1957b, p. 32) said, in his blunt Yorkshire way, 'The business of linguistics is to describe languages.' Of course, many linguists do not hold this view, but the detailed descriptive work now being done in corpus linguistics will bring far-ranging revisions to many received ideas in syntax and semantics.

It is a measure of the importance of work in the tradition which Firth started in the 1930s that it provides many new ways of thinking about recurrent and recalcitrant problems at the basis of the discipline.

Appendix: Notes on the Intellectual Background

J. R. Firth (1890–1960) held the first Chair of General Linguistics at a British university, from 1944 at the School of Oriental and African Studies in London. M. A. K. Halliday (1925–) was a pupil of Firth's. He worked at the University of Edinburgh, and then from 1965 he held a Chair of General Linguistics at University College London, and from 1976 to 1987 a Chair of Linguistics at the University of Sydney. Sinclair (1933–) also taught at Edinburgh, and since 1965 has held the Chair of modern English Language at the University of Birmingham. Firth did not leave a tidy and consistent body of writings, and their relation to more recent work is not always clear. But the third generation of linguists is now working out some of the implications of his ideas. Robins's (1961) obituary of Firth is a useful brief account. And De Beaugrande (1991) has useful chapters on Firth and Halliday.

Other related British work is labelled social semiotics (see Halliday, 1978) or critical linguistics, and was done at the University of East Anglia by Roger Fowler, Gunther Kress et al. Kress also moved to Sydney, and with Halliday and others continued such work; Kress has now (1990–) returned to Britain to the Chair of English at the Institute of Education in London (this is the chair which I held from 1985 to 1990). Related work is also being done at the University of Lancaster by Norman Fairclough, who explicitly relates his work to a Hallidayan framework.

The intellectual and personal friendships are much more complex, but major axes are the Universities of Edinburgh, London, Birmingham and Sydney. I cannot in this chapter discuss details of people and influences, but a study remains to be written of the circulation of ideas on real language, speech acts and conversation. As one specific example: Sinclair (1992b, p. 80) regards corpus-based work by C. C. Fries (1952) as a 'forgotten landmark' which made 'major advances in description'; and Sacks (1992, pp. 95, 189) regards Fries's work as 'extremely close' to what he was trying to do, 'the only grammar of English which [is] an attempt to handle actual conversation itself'. Sinclair makes frequent references to Sacks's work on adjacency pairs. A related study would examine changing concepts of evidence and of 'linguistic facts' (see Labov, 1975).

See further notes on the intellectual background in the appendix to chapter 3.

3

Institutional Linguistics: Firth, Hill and Giddens

In chapter 2, I discussed many ideas in Firth's work which have been given substantial new directions since the development of computationally assisted corpus linguistics. As Sampson (1980, p. 235) puts it:

> To the young . . . linguistic scholar of today, the dignified print and decent bindings of the *Transactions of the Philological Society* smack of genteel, leather-elbow-patched poverty and nostalgia for vanished glories on the North-west frontier, while blurred stencils hot from the presses of the Indiana Linguistics Society are invested with all the authority of . . . the billion dollar economy.

Sampson's reference to the *Transactions* is to the British journal in which some of Firth's most influential work appeared. The reference to the North-west frontier is to the military background of some British linguists, and to the fact that Firth spent time in north India.

The dignified print is well worth close study. It contains sharply formulated programmes of research whose far-reaching implications have still to be fully worked out. In chapter 2, I emphasized the more narrowly linguistic developments in neo-Firthian work on lexis and syntax. In this chapter, I will develop some broader sociological points, in particular the concept of institutional linguistics in work by Trevor Hill and M. A. K. Halliday.

3.1 Institutional Facts

A distinction is often drawn between brute and institutional facts (Searle, 1969, pp. 50–2; Lakoff, 1987, pp. 170–1). Brute facts are objectively true regardless of any human institution: the atomic weight of gold or how tall someone is. Institutional facts are true by virtue of some human institution: the value of gold, as measured by its dollar price, or someone's social standing. The distinction is clear enough in general, although it is unresolved whether a sharp boundary exists between these two kinds of facts. And Firth (1957b, p. 29) says simply: 'There are no brute facts.'

But this important and intuitively clear distinction is often made fuzzier by the principle that it depends on your point of view. When Halliday et al. (1964, pp. 16, 75–7) take up the term institutional linguistics from Hill (1958), they point out that the same facts may be studied descriptively or institutionally. For example, one might be concerned with a descriptive account of the lexis and syntax of Standard English, or with an account of how it has come to be prescribed and standardized over the centuries.

Many facts about language are institutional facts. For example, an important type of language event, discussed by Searle, includes contracts of various kinds (such as an appointment to a job, a marriage ceremony), which exist only within the framework of social institutions. A difficult problem for linguistics – and for the social sciences in general – is how to relate institutional analysis and textual analysis. Text types and genres have stability because of the social institutions in which they are used; and social institutions have stability because of the texts which support them (see section 1.6).

A discussion of institutional linguistics poses some exceedingly difficult sociological and philosophical problems, concerning the relation between micro-linguistic events and macro-social structures. These problems relate to the basic task of social science: the problem of order and a theory of organizations. Without claiming to solve these problems, it is possible to provide linguistic analyses which are sensitive to the issues, and this is the main aim of this book. In this chapter, I discuss Anthony Giddens's work as a major attempt in British sociology to overcome such dualisms of micro and macro, individual and social. And I give initial examples of projects for an institutional linguistics. More detailed analyses are then provided in chapters 4 to 8.

3.2   Firth on Social Semantics

Within linguistics, there are still rather distinct styles of work being done in different countries. As I emphasized in chapter 2, over the past fifty years much British linguistics has been deeply empirical, and has been involved in practical language problems: teaching English as foreign language or mother tongue, teacher training, language pathology, dictionary making and so on.

This is certainly true of the tradition developed by Firth, Halliday and Sinclair. For example, Firth (1935, p. 36) states in the opening sentence of a rather technical paper on semantics that 'The origins of this paper are: first, practical experience of linguistic problems in India and Africa as well as more recently in England . . . '.

Here, I will discuss just two articles, which provide precise proposals for an 'essentially social' semantics (Firth, 1935) and for an 'institutional linguistics' (Hill, 1958). As in chapter 2, my discussion is very selective, not a history of people and influences, but a discussion of a cluster of ideas: again the importance of textual analysis in relation to large corpora of data, but also language in the reproduction of social institutions and of ideology.

Firth (1935) is a linguistic and sociological goldmine, and contains explicit formulations of several themes in later British linguistics. The major principle, quoted in chapter 2, is that: 'the complete meaning of a word is always contextual, and no study of meaning apart from a complete context can be taken seriously' (p. 37). In place of a study of isolated sentences, Firth proposes a 'contextual and sociological technique' of semantics based on specific methods of data collection and analysis. One proposal is for 'research into the distribution of sociologically important words' (p. 40), their 'formal scatter' in different contexts:

> The study of such words as *work, labour, trade, employ, occupy, play, leisure, time, hours, means, self-respect*, in all their derivatives and compounds in sociologically significant contexts during the last twenty years would be quite enlightening. (p. 45)

This is a considerable understatement: such a study of language and ideology, based on evidence of language and social change, would indeed be 'quite enlightening'. Moreover, Firth was proposing a technique some fifty years before it became feasible, given computational methods and the access to large corpora. In sections 7.4 to 7.11, I illustrate how such a technique can now be made concrete and used to study cultural key words.

Firth's view of language is functional. Some twenty years before Austin (1962) on *How to Do Things with Words*, he discusses 'ways of behaving' such as agreeing, encouraging, endorsing, blessing, wishing, and, in general, language as 'a way of dealing with people and things'. His comments on such language functions are rather brief and vague. Much more precise and significant are his remarks on the often routine and stereotyped forms of everyday conversation which are at the basis of much later work on discourse analysis (see section 2.7). Here Firth provides a statement of the tension between individual and social, creative and routine. He also points out the importance of studying the transmission of the culture:

[There has been] not enough accurate investigation into the actual mechanisms and channels of culture contacts. . . . Who are the 'carriers' of the
particular cultural tradition . . . or form of speech? What is the mechanism of
'transmission'? (Firth, 1935, p. 72)

Finally, Firth is quite firm on methods. He argues that, because we know so
little about the human mind, semantics must be essentially social. But he
warns that: 'loose linguistic sociology without formal accuracy is of little
value' (p. 71n).

In summary, some of the major themes in Firth (1935) are: sociological
and contextual techniques for the study of meaning; the need for
text-oriented work, based on a significant corpus of discourse; language as a
social institution, which reproduces the culture from generation to generation; and the importance of routine in linguistic behaviour and in cultural
transmission.

3.3   Hill on Institutional Linguistics

Firth (1935) proposes a contextual theory of meaning; Hill (1958) interprets
context in terms of institutions, but (oddly, disappointingly?) makes no
reference to Firth. Both Firth and Hill assume a view of language in which
users make choices between systemically defined alternatives within structural or distributional frames. Hill proposes the study of language varieties
and language communities as social institutions. This would be

> a new branch of systemic linguistics dealing with the types of relations that
> arise in use between tongues, and between them and their users. . . . As its aim
> is to confront tongues and communities as social institutions, it might be
> called Institutional Linguistics. (p. 455)

(*Tongue* is Hill's technical usage for 'a neutral term for any of the entities
commonly styled dialect, language, etc.' *Variety* would be a more modern
term.)

With acknowledgement to Hill, the term institutional linguistics was
taken up by Halliday et al. (1964) and again by Halliday (1990). Although
the term itself has not been widely used in the intervening thirty years,
many studies have attempted to relate forms of language to its uses and
users. On a loose interpretation, such studies of text–context relations
might include much of what is now called sociolinguistics, and certainly
include most ethnography of communication. Hill (1958, p. 455) sees his
new branch of linguistics as 'presumably subsum[ing] dialectology, insofar

as this is conceived as a synchronic study, and some aspects of stylistics' (p. 455).

The label used for an area of work is of little importance. And the concept of institution itself certainly remains very vague in Hill's article. He uses the term to refer both to whole speech communities or indeed countries, and to social relations or the social order or just society or ways of behaving. Hill does not make clear whether he intends the term to refer to concrete institutions (e.g. individual schools or law courts), or to their abstract formations (education or the law), or whether the term should have its everyday use, as when we say 'the institution of marriage' or 'the family'. Nevertheless, even if he does not provide a conceptual analysis of the term *institution* itself, he does give several precise examples of the phenomena he wishes to explain.

A standard language is a clear example of an institutional fact. Languages are standardized by individuals such as Samuel Johnson or Noah Webster, or social groups such as dictionary makers, grammar book writers, school teachers and committees such as language academies. As Hill (1958, pp. 446–7) points out, the distinction between languages and dialects depends on the consciousness of speakers and on the cultural affiliation of communities. For example, the concept of the American language is based on institutional facts: the linguistic differences from British English are small, but there are two standards, and speakers turn to different dictionaries and different norms. It is in this sense that people often speak of English spelling being one of our institutions.

Hill, like Firth, relates his argument to socialization. Language varieties have different institutional characters according to whether they are transmitted from parents to children (as with a native vernacular) or from adult to adult (as with a koine). And he takes heterogeneity of language for granted. It is currently fashionable to quote Bakhtin (e.g. 1981) on the view that language is heteroglot from top to bottom. But a major theme in Firthian linguistics is that 'unity is the last concept that should be applied to language' (Firth, 1935, pp. 67–8) (see section 2.5). And Hill's proposals here have a textual basis. One section (pp. 450–2) discusses mixed texts. He points out the continuum across standard Anglo-English, educated Scottish English and Scots dialect. Dialect interacts with style (formal–informal), genre (e.g. conversation) and topic (e.g. football), and varies according to the social relations between speakers. Some of his statements (e.g. p. 450) propose exactly the kind of variationist study done by Labov in the 1960s:

standard English koine is one pole and the local Scots dialect the other. Colloquial conversational texts contain a high proportion of lexical and grammatical material referable to the latter pole, whereas other types tend towards the standard English pole. . . . [S]tatements about use may have to be in quantitative form, thus: such and such a percentage of Scots forms occurs in a conversation between two natives about football, compared with a smaller percentage if they are talking about union affairs, or if one of them is talking to an outsider, etc., etc.

(Hill worked at the University of Edinburgh: hence his references to Scottish varieties.)

Firth and Hill develop the vision of a text- and corpus-based study of language variation, of language as social institution, and of the role of language in socialization and cognitive orientation, and these themes have been taken up in many ways within British linguistics.

3.4   Dualisms of Subject and Object, Micro and Macro

The work of Firth and Hill in contextual and institutional linguistics addresses major, still unresolved, problems in relating the micro-analysis of individual texts to the macro-analysis of institutions.

Several of the dualisms which trouble linguistics (see section 2.8) are present in Saussure's observation that language is a social institution, and not a creation of the individual speaker. *Langue* is 'la partie sociale du langage, extérieure à l'individu'. This is the classic problem of all sociology: the problem of order. Society consists of individuals, but is external to individuals. As Firth (1957b, p. 29) puts it: 'We are in the world, and the world is in us.' As Bernstein (1990, p. 94) puts it: 'How does the outside become the inside, and how does the inside reveal itself and shape the outside?'

Abstract *langue* can be observed only indirectly via concrete *parole*. But the process of individual *parole* seems idiosyncratic compared to *langue* as a product, a system which belongs to the speech community. Individual speakers choose what to say, but they must accept the pre-existing linguistic system. *Parole* is produced by intentional acts. But *langue* is not created by individual speakers: speakers must follow convention and social agreement. *Langue* is a social fact, external to the individual, who is born into an existing society. A language is a social institution: the *un*intended product of speakers' intentional acts. Speakers are free, but only within constraints. Individual speakers intend to communicate with one another in the process of moment to moment interaction. The reproduction of the system is the *un*intended product of their routine behaviour. Human actors have purposes, but social systems do not.

One of the most famous formulations of this problematic is by Marx (1852):

> Die Menschen machen ihre eigene Geschichte, aber sie machen sie nicht aus freien Stücken, sondern unter unmittelbar vorgefundenen, gegebenen und überlieferten Umständen. Die Tradition aller toten Geschlechter lastet wie ein Alp auf dem Gehirne der Lebenden.

> [Human beings make their own history, yet they do not make it of their own free will, but under directly encountered, given circumstances, which have been handed down to them. The tradition of all the dead generations weighs like a nightmare on the minds of the living.]

As Giddens (1984, p. xxi) points out, attempts to work out the implications of this statement, about individual and society, freedom and constraint, creativity and tradition, change and status quo, have been of profound importance for the development of the social sciences. And linguistics (and other disciplines) has been constantly beset by the dualisms of subject and object, internal and external, agency and structure, process and product, *parole* and *langue*, language use and language system, pragmatics and semantics, communication and language, creativity and rules, intended action and unintended consequences.

Probably the most basic dualism inherent in individual and institution is micro and macro (Bernstein, 1990, pp. 4, 101, 119, 170). Linguistics studies both individual speech acts created from moment to moment in interaction, and the potential of the overall system; both the behaviour of speakers from clause to clause, and changes in the system from century to century. Historical changes seem mechanical: independent of the intentions of speakers, and exterior to speakers in their long time-scale. Yet if historical changes are (all, mostly?) ultimately a question of fashion, of wanting to sound more like a particular social group, then historical change is, after all, driven by human agency. So individual human agency and social structure are different sides of the same coin, not dualism but duality (Giddens, 1984).

3.5 Giddens on the Constitution of Society

The work by Firth and Hill therefore raises the problem of the relation between linguistic and social theory. Sociolinguistics has often been accused of having no theory of social structures and institutions. Autonomous linguistics has no theory of agency, and has not been interested in seeking one. The social sciences in general have lacked a theory of action, and speech act theory has no theory of institutions and power, despite Searle, quoted above, on institutional facts (Giddens, 1979, pp. 2, 256).

These dualisms receive repeated discussion in much twentieth-century linguistics, albeit in contradictory forms. For Saussure, *langue* is social, and *parole* is individual. For Chomsky, competence is individual, and performance is the category to which the social is relegated, then to be ignored. These dualisms have also been resisted: by Hymes (1971), who opposes communicative competence to both performance and competence; by Labov (1970), who discusses the Saussurian paradox; and by Halliday (1978) and Sinclair (1991a), who reject the competence–performance distinction outright (see section 2.8).

Firth and Hill were both trying to find a position which overcomes Saussurian dualisms. A substantial attempt to find such a position for social theory which overcomes the dualisms of subject and object, micro and macro, is by the British sociologist Anthony Giddens, and his work deserves to be studied by all linguists analysing the relations between language and institutions. Giddens's work is based on detailed discussion of linguistic structuralism (though he appears not to be familiar with the tradition of British linguistics discussed here).

Giddens's main theme is the relations between everyday routine social behaviour, as studied by micro-sociolinguistics, and the long-term continuity of social institutions. He devotes detailed attention, for example, to Goffman's analyses of co-presence as a central mechanism of social reproduction. Giddens's argument is that human agency and social structure are logically implicated in each other. Human agency constitutes social structure. Social structure is the medium for human agency. Our activities constantly, routinely, have consequences we do not intend, and which are deeply involved in the reproduction of social institutions. Therefore mundane social activity is implicated in the long-term and large-scale reproduction of social institutions. Conventions are the very stuff of their continuity and fixity.

A key concept is the recursive nature of social life: drawing on convention reconstitutes it. When I produce a grammatical sentence, I intend to communicate something to someone. I do not intend to reproduce the English language: but this is the unintended outcome of all those people out there producing grammatical sentences. Institutions are standardized modes of behaviour, which are reconstituted in day-to-day social activity. The task for sociology is to show how institutional forms are achieved: how the passing interactional moment relates to the long passing of time. This is what Giddens calls duality of structure: social structure is both the medium and the outcome of the behaviour it organizes. Social systems are created by human actions, but provide a context for those actions.

Compare Halliday (quoted in section 2.8) on weather and climate as an analogy for the relation between instance and system as names for different observer depths. A text is never just an instance: it has to be interpreted against the history of the discourse. So text and discourse, in Foucault's sense (see section 7.2), are names for different segments between instance and system. Linguistics is in an increasingly good position to address directly the dualisms of individual and social, small-scale and large-scale, micro and macro.

3.6 Projects for an Institutional Linguistics

I have three theses about the development of such linguistic work (see Giddens 1987, pp. 22ff). First, the concept of institution will become increasingly central to linguistics. The dualism of micro and macro occurs in a sharp form in text and discourse analysis. How can detailed attention to the structure of texts be reconciled with a full appreciation of their context of occurrence and of their hearers/readers, where, due partly to developments in literary theory, context is seen as the historical, ideological and social context of production and reception?

Studying language as communication leads inevitably to analyses of language in social institutions. It is obvious, though contentious, that uses of language support institutions. Institutions are networks of commitments: they are based on contracts, promises, requests, authorizations and other speech acts. And institutions are intimately related to texts and genres. Textbooks, for example, hardly exist outside educational institutions. And texts have stability because of the power of institutions. More concretely, social institutions are always defined and supported by particular text types:

- school, e.g. textbook, dictation, essay, exam, curriculum;
- science, e.g. lab report, research article, grant application;
- religion, e.g. prayer, sermon, baptism, marriage ceremony;
- television, e.g. news, documentary, soap opera, quiz show.

Second, linguistics will take more seriously again the classic problem of how language relates to the world. Halliday has argued that ideas are often initially proposed at the wrong times. One example may be the concept of institutional linguistics itself. Perhaps it was not formulated in the right way, or in the right place, for a successful up-take. Another is the Sapir–Whorf hypothesis, now unfashionable, but now also amenable to alternative and better formulations (see chapter 7 and section 9.2). One alternative approach to institutions, discourse and world view was provided by Firth (1935) in his technique (quoted above) for studying keywords such as *work*, *play*, *time*.

Halliday (1990) discusses the grammatical construction of reality. He conceives of a grammar of a language as a theory of experience: clause by clause, texts code experience, construe it in certain ways, and synthesize a world view. The essential concept is a Firthian–Hallidayan–Bernsteinian one, that the potential of a language in use is taken up in systematically different ways within different discourses: there are different semantic coding orientations. (For detailed examples, see chapters 4, 6 and 7.)

Halliday refers to relatively well studied examples such as the highly nominalized grammar of many scientific texts, and the lexis and syntax of sexist texts where the choices made by users construe the world from the position of the male. He then gives detailed examples of how the environment is grammaticalized in English and how an ideology of growth as good is deeply grammaticalized in English. (For example, one usually asks how *big/wide/long* something is, not how *small/narrow/short* it is.) This immediately suggests a comparative study: how are the meanings "environment" or "Umwelt" grammaticalized in English and German? What are the relevant semantic fields? What are the collocates which build up, clause by clause, our linguistic, conceptual and ideological views of the physical world? How do these coding orientations differ in advertising, television programmes on nature, specialist or general interest magazines and so on? Firth (1935) proposes other significant semantic fields, such as food and drink, entertainments and politics. Another field, which is the focus of significant current ideological debate in both Britain and Germany, centres on the meanings of "British" or "German" versus "foreigner" or "Ausländer".

Here again are small and large, micro and macro, with fundamental implications for linguistic methods. Small texts are observable by the individual linguist, but patterns of language use, including systematic differences in coding preferences, across millions of words, can be documented only with computational methods. This is the link to my third thesis. Individual texts must be related to institutions, but also to corpora.

Third, the use of computer readable corpora for studying lexis and grammar will profoundly change linguistic description and theory. The essential vision underlying corpus linguistics is that computationally supported analyses of language give access to data which were not previously observable. This was discussed in chapter 2, and will be illustrated in detail in chapters 6, 7 and 8.

We can postpone some of the exceedingly difficult sociological and philosophical problems of dualism, while still attempting linguistic analyses which are sensitive to those problems. Linguists are in a good position to do the kinds of language analysis which would give empirical support to Giddens's claims about the constitution of society. I will conclude this chapter with some initial brief examples of projects – on sexist language and written language – which show how corpus based analyses are essential in studying how language constitutes the social order.

3.7 Sexist Language

A widely held view is that language reflects society. Thus social inequalities, for example between the sexes, exist, and language reflects this in its sexist usages. Cameron (1990) criticizes this view, arguing that language does not passively reflect, but actively reproduces, inequalities. She points out that people make their own history: deliberate and sustained feminist campaigns have been successful in changing some significant aspects of language use, and therefore in reconstructing one aspect of gender relations. In addition, routine everyday language use reproduces society: masculinity and femininity are repeated and reconstituted in language use.

A notorious case of sexist language in English is so-called generic *he*, where *he* is said to mean "he or she". It is easy to find examples of specific sexist usages, but difficult without a corpus and computer-assisted methods to get data on the distribution of forms. Using a concordance program, I studied a corpus of half a million words of spoken educated British English (the Lund corpus: see notes on corpus data). The Cobuild grammar (Sinclair, 1990, p. 31), on the basis of attested corpus data, notes that *they* and *them* are 'very common after indefinite pronouns'. I extracted all occurrences of the indefinite pronouns *someone*, *somebody*, *anyone*, *anybody* (over 400) and looked for occurrences of pronouns referring to the same person in the immediate context:

(a)   they, them, their, themselves, i.e. sex neutral;
(b)   he or she, him or her, etc., i.e. explicitly both;
(c)   he, him, his, himself, i.e. male;
(d)   she, her, hers, herself, i.e. female.

Out of 43 relevant cases, examples of each type [all A] are:

(a)   by the age of sixteen *anybody* who is going to be an academic should have done *their* general reading;
(b)   *someone* describing *himself or herself* as a middle-aged viewer;

(c) why should *somebody* move here when *he* has to pay fifty thousand pounds . . . for a house;

(d) when *somebody* gets sufficiently frail – and sufficiently neglectful of *herself* – as my grandmother's now become.

Example (d) refers to a specific and/or named individual person that the speaker has in mind: I will call these *definite* references. Examples (a), (b) and (c) are references to hypothetical or unknown persons, or references to generalized groups: I will call these *indefinite*.

The overall distribution of forms was as follows.

- Indefinite: *they* 19; *he or she* 2; *he* 6; *she* 0.
- Definite: *they* 4; *he or she* 0; *he* 6; *she* 6.

The encouraging finding is that the non-sexist *they* pattern is the most common overall. The forms *they* or *he or she* are much more common in indefinite sentences, though still used in four definite cases. On the other hand, *she* is used only in definite cases, whereas *he* is equally distributed between definite and indefinite. The overall distribution is still sexist.

These data were from the 1960s, before the main feminist campaigns to change usages such as generic *he*. Even so, the non-sexist, sex-indefinite singular *they* is the commonest form. Comparable data from the 1990s could be studied to check for changes in spoken usage, written data could be compared with spoken, more details could be gathered on characteristics of speakers and so on. Any such study would be unrealistically time-consuming or just impossible without a corpus and computational techniques. (And the small numbers of relevant examples show that a corpus of 500,000 words is rather small for such research.)

Bodine (1975) provides a detailed discussion of singular *they*, and its long history in English, despite criticism from prescriptive grammarians. She bases her discussion on a slightly different categorization to the one I have used:

anyone can do it if they try (mixed sex, distributive)

who dropped their ticket? (sex unknown)

either Mary or John should bring it with them (mixed sex, disjunctive)

3.8   Spoken and Written Language
and Linguistic Theory

The relation between written and spoken language is a large field of study, which requires a combination of corpus analysis and institutional analysis.

For simple reasons, written language is better described than spoken language. Written language comprises a body of texts and records: it is product, not process, and it is therefore more easily open to observation than spoken language. Since most written language is standard language, there arises a logical relation between written forms, standard forms and linguistic description. (In section 2.5, I pointed out the additional relation between invented intuitive data and standard written data.) The concept of a language as a fixed objective system has been very productive in the history of linguistics, but it is an ideologically loaded concept. Description is never neutral.

Williams (1977, pp. 26–7) has discussed the influence of written language on linguistic theory. Linguists are highly literate and linguistic studies derive historically from a highly literate tradition. Historical–comparative linguistics was based on a body of written records, and derived from the study of classical European languages. Within linguistics it is changes in the concept of data which have led to profound changes in linguistic theory, and also to profound changes in the theoretical and ideological significance of linguistic variation. For example, when Boas, Sapir and Bloomfield argued for the priority of the spoken language, they were also making highly ideological statements about the value of Amerindian languages and cultures. Within linguistics, statements about speech-writing relations are in the nature of manifestos which go back into the history of linguistics as an academic discipline. Such statements characteristically mix logical, chronological and ideological arguments (Stubbs 1980, pp. 21ff), and are deeply involved in debates over the institutional status of linguistics as separate from the study of classical languages. All theories are value loaded, and books, writing and literacy are central to modern conceptions of language, both lay and professional.

Studies here also allow empirical progress with the problem of order. An institutional view of language recognizes, with Foucault (1980) and Giddens (e.g. 1984, p. 200), that writing is first and foremost a medium of administrative power. Historically, written language has always had predominantly administrative functions in the control of institutions. It facilitates information gathering, record keeping and documentation, and therefore allows the monitoring and control of resources. Modern states and other organizations are inconceivable without the storage and retrieval of information, which allows power to be centralized and surveillance to be intensified. Fields of power, such as the law and academic disciplines, are codified in writing. Writing makes history, since history depends on records, chronicles and narratives. (The control of such historical documents is a major debating point in British government policy on freedom of information.) Literacy, especially mass literacy, is a major influence on modifying tradition: writing facilitates the creation of a public sphere where things are openly debated. This is in turn a prerequisite for science (see section 1.7.3 on Swales's work).

A textual and corpus-oriented view of language shows, *contra* Bloomfield and many others, that written language is not simply spoken language written down: it has different forms and serves different functions (Stubbs, 1980, pp. 24ff). But the distinction between written and spoken language is an extreme idealization. This is demonstrated in a large body of text analysis by Biber (1988) and others.

Speech and writing are polarized terms referring to clusters of characteristics which typically occur together, but which are logically independent. Thus much written language is standard, formal, planned, edited, public and non-interactive, whereas spoken language is typically casual, spontaneous, private and face-to-face. But these clusters of features are not logically necessary: on the contrary, they are socio-cultural constructs which reflect beliefs about the functions of written language. There is a very strong social convention that published written language should also be standard language: but there is no logical reason why novels cannot be written in non-standard English (and a few are).

A main theme in this book is authoritative texts, and I will illustrate these points by discussing various authoritative text types, dictionaries, textbooks and imaginative literature, and the relation between written language, standard language and authoritative language.

3.8.1   Dictionaries

Dictionaries are a major agent in standardizing the language, with a particular place in educational institutions. And they have always been biased towards written language, partly because written data have always been easier to collect. But the higher prestige of written language is evident in dictionaries such as the *Oxford English Dictionary*: this is based on selections from usage which place written language, and especially imaginative literature, above everyday spoken language. Some dictionaries provide a record of usage, based on citations (in the case of the *OED*) or on attested corpus data (the Cobuild dictionary: Sinclair, 1987a, 1995). But, however they are constructed, they are typically regarded as authoritative and prescriptive by users.

In addition, there is no doubt that the definitions found in dictionaries display the bases of the particular social group who constructed them. Their definitions are aligned. Their authority is social and political. In Samuel Johnson's dictionary of 1755, the personal basis of many of his judgements is evident, conscious and witty, as in his definition of *oats*: 'A grain, which in England is generally given to horses, but in Scotland supports the people'. But the view has arisen that dictionaries contain impersonal definitions, free of bias. (Cameron (1992, pp. 114ff) and Kramarae and Treichler (1985) sketch the beginning of a feminist analysis of dictionaries.)

The enormous political significance of the *OED* is evident from a review of a new edition by a major British politician, Roy Jenkins (in *The Independent Magazine*, 8 April 1989). He contrasts the 'decline of British power in the world' with the 'advance of the English language'. Whereas 'the old imperialism sometimes advanced with a bible in one hand and a bottle of whisky in the other, their descendants have replaced them with the *OED* and a glass of British Council wine' (see Phillipson, 1992).

Dictionaries have always had a major function in standardizing the language. Standard English did not grow naturally. It is the product of selections and decisions taken by men and women (usually men), sometimes individual lexicographers such as Samuel Johnson and Noah Webster, and sometimes groups such as teachers, publishers and printers. However, most people have lost sight of the means by which Standard English has been produced and is maintained. This naturalization is an effect of institutional power. People treat Standard English as though it was a natural product and forget the ideological basis of its authority. Standard languages do not reproduce themselves, though they tend to deceive people into believing that they do; and this in turn is an essential part of their ability to operate as means of social control. The actual production of Standard English is mystified, ignored or suppressed, and it is seen as a finished product. For example, despite a certain amount of publicity given to Robert Burchfield, and anecdotes in the press about his very personal decisions which led to the inclusion of some words in the supplement to the *OED*, these are treated as minor and likeable individual deviations: something he deserves after many years' work on an impersonal product. The source of his authority remains implicit, and the personal decisions of dozens of co-workers which pervade the dictionary are ignored.

Closely related to the observer's paradox (you cannot observe people when they are not being observed) is the describer's paradox: you cannot describe people and their behaviour without the description changing the behaviour. Descriptions are likely to become untrue as soon as they are published, because descriptions of social reality become persuasive as soon as people become aware of them. For example, the attention that linguists have given to non-standard dialects of English, community languages in Britain, and British and American Sign Language has changed the status of these languages. Sometimes this has been the overt aim: to attack the notion that such language varieties are in any way primitive. But they mean that description becomes prescription due to dissemination (Andreski, 1974). And this is also the case with dictionaries. What may start out as a description becomes prescriptive. The *OED* starts out by merely recording the facts, but using prestigious written sources. And it ends up as the most authoritative and normative source of prescriptive judgements about the language (Joseph and Taylor, 1990, pp. 22ff). The *OED* has itself, as we say, become an institution.

In section 7.5, I discuss further the kind of explicitly politicized dictionary provided by Williams (1976).

3.8.2   *Literature*

The relation of authority between dictionaries, standard language and literary language is very explicit in the preface to Samuel Johnson's dictionary of 1755. His sources are 'examples and authorities from the writers before the Restoration, whose works I regard as the wells of English undefiled, as the pure sources of genuine diction' (McAdam and Milne, 1963). And quite often 'literature' means 'good literature': the canon of prestigious literature taught in schools and universities.

Gregory (1984, 1986) provides an interesting case study of the relations between written, literary, standard and published language, by looking at working-class writing published by the community, as opposed to writing published within the dominant mainstream culture. He studied a large corpus, of the writing itself, and also of interviews with authors and historical data from earlier periods. His work questions many taken-for-granted assumptions about writing, publishing, social class and their interrelations. He assumes that social class is itself a relation to means of production. Our traditional views of literature are permeated by assumptions about how literature is produced, which social groups write and who publishes writing, and published writing is overwhelmingly in the hands of the middle class. (In a notorious case, a London school teacher, Chris Searle, lost his job because he published the writing of a group of children.) We also tend to make assumptions about the relation between individual creativity and writing, as opposed to collective or group writing. The view of the solitary, individual author was strengthened by Romanticism, but it is not a necessary state. Gregory takes pairs of terms, such as

written	spoken
published	oral
standard	non-standard
individual	group/collective/community
middle class	working class
establishment	resistance

and shows that the traditional configuration on the left is not the only possible one. For example, there is group writing in non-standard English, published by collectives based in the community. Some of this writing is oral history, but the expectation that prose documentary is the appropriate genre for working-class writers is itself a further assumption.

Forms of community publishing challenge mainstream views of the relations between written, standard and published language, and show that the speech–writing relation changes over time. For example, mass literacy has affected our view of the relation; literacy encourages a particular kind of consciousness of language, and affects our view of spoken language along with our prescriptive notions of correctness. Speech–writing relations have been altered by radio, television and film (see section 1.6), and more recently by access to computer-based word-processing and printing technology.

3.8.3   *School textbooks*

The Western education system is thoroughly verbal and textual (van Dijk, 1981; Stubbs, 1986a, pp. 30ff). The place of written texts, writing and literacy have always been central, and in some contexts *educated* and *literate* are synonymous (see Williams, 1976, on these key words in British culture). But the high value placed on written language is a view with its roots in Western culture: it is not universal. An important topic for an institutional theory of language is therefore books used in schools. Written language, standard language, textbooks, teachers and the school all have perceived authority. We therefore require an analysis of the ways in which this authority is expressed in language.

Foucault (1980, p. 118, cf. p. 131) proposes studying 'how effects of truth are produced within discourse'. School textbooks often present information as neutral or objective. Authors are assumed to be corporate or anonymous: there is a lack of an explicitly personal world view, identifiable and fallible. This may be a feature of the books themselves or of the way they are used by teachers. However, writing is always aligned: it always expresses propositions from a certain point of view, and it is possible to show how language is used to convey a writer's attitude to propositions; whether they are taken for granted as the expression of true, certain, neutral, objective authoritative statements, or are hypothetical and tentative, personal and subjective. (Chapter 6 provides a detailed study of two school textbooks.)

The link to institutions is also evident. School texts may be selected by the teacher, distributed for the lesson, interpreted by the teacher or via another text (such as study notes) and then withdrawn. The control over school textbooks, centralized or local, differs greatly in different countries: compare, for example, the regional control in Germany versus the autonomy of examination boards or individual teachers in Britain. The production of books is controlled by publishing houses, who therefore also influence content, form and dissemination. The most extreme commercial control may be exercised by American publishers of basal reading courses: millions of dollars are invested in the market research and production of such reading schemes. Exact figures are not known, since they are not published: the commercial operations are treated as highly secret by the firms involved. We are dealing with officially and commercially sanctioned versions of knowledge. (The same is increasingly true of the production of dictionaries and grammars in Britain, where the production of large corpus-based works involves investment in many people and much technology over many years.)

The authority of textbooks as a source of curricular knowledge is related to the view that the meaning of a book is contained in the text (see section 1.3). However, students' interpretations of texts can be widely different under different classroom practices. Quite different views of knowledge are transmitted by the hidden curriculum of dictation, rote memorization, oral recitation, *explication de texte*, silent reading or small group discussion. A basic distinction is between a student's unmediated reading and a use of a text which is mediated by the teacher's 'expert' interpretation or by study notes. The interpretation of texts in classrooms is inseparable from social relations.

Books are written for, and therefore embody assumptions about, their audiences. And studies of sexism in school books illustrate how text and corpus analysis can be used to study cultural transmission. Freebody and Baker (1985) and Baker and Freebody (1989) have analysed some of the ways in which books for children construct a view of childhood itself. They analyse a corpus of 80,000 words of children's elementary reading books, and compare this corpus with other corpora of school textbooks and children's spoken language. One set of messages conveyed by such reading books concerns taken-for-granted assumptions about social relations in families and schools, and relations between the sexes.

They use frequency data to present the following findings. The word forms *boy* and *boys* appear more often than *girl* and *girls*; singular *boy* appears more often than plural *boys*; but *girl* and *girls* occur equally often; the gender-neutral plural *children* occurs, but the singular *child* never occurs; boys, but not girls, are *sad*, *kind* and *brave*; girls, but not boys, are *young* and *pretty*; fathers *paint*, *drive* cars and *light* fires; mothers *bake* cakes and *pick* flowers; there are verbs which collocate exclusively with *boys*, but no verbs which collocate exclusively with *girls*; 50 per cent of the occurrences of *girl* collocate with *little*, whereas the percentage with *boy* is lower.

They argue (Baker and Freebody, 1989, pp. 140, 147) that such frequencies and distributions convey interpretations about the social world. Gender is an important and usually relevant way of identifying and talking about people; there are regularly differences between people, based on gender; boys are more individualistic and independent. In a word, gender is a social category, which is partly constructed by such linguistic categories. But these categories are never made explicit. They are implicit in the pervasive co-occurrence and repetition. If frequent associations are made between words, then this repetition makes some features of the world conceptually salient. But since the associations are not explicit, they are difficult to discuss and negotiate. Indeed, they will often not be noticed: they are presented as a constant and natural feature of the world. Such a use of language legitimates a concept of childhood. The language system provides the resources which can be used in different ways. It is the choices which are made from the language which are sexist. (See section 4.7.)

The findings presented by Baker and Freebody do indeed appear to be a characteristic of the specialized corpus of initial reading primers which they investigated. I have checked their findings against a corpus of 3.5 million words, consisting of texts from many genres, both spoken and written, and have found a different distribution of occurrence of these words. The lemma GIRL occurred more frequently than BOY (*girl* 608, *girls* 362, *boy* 474, *boys* 323; GIRL:BOY = 1.22:1). The singular occurred more frequently in both cases (*girl*:*girls* = 1.68:1, *boy*:*boys* = 1.46:1). The collocations *little girl(s)* and *little boy(s)* were nearly equal in frequency (41 and 37 respectively). The collocations *small girl(s)* and *small boy(s)* were less equal (5 and 21 respectively). I also checked all main verbs occurring one, two or three words to the right of GIRL and BOY, but could not see any difference in the distribution of verbs after the two lemmas.

This emphasizes the principle that findings should always be compared across different corpora, in order to know what is normal and what is characteristic of a specialized corpus. In this case, Baker and Freebody have isolated patterns which characterize their restricted corpus of reading primers. But note also that some patterns may become apparent only in very large corpora. Even a corpus of 3.5 million words produces fewer than 50 examples of phrases such as *little boy*, and a bias in the frequency of such usages may therefore become apparent only across much larger corpora.

3.8.4   Vocabulary

Studies of the vocabulary of English, and of the lexical variability of texts, also show that linguistic description cannot be separated from institutional analysis.

A simple but useful generalization is that spoken language shows more variation than written language at all levels of description except lexis (Halliday, 1985, p. xxiv). In comparison with spoken language, it is evident both that the lexis of written registers is more elaborated, and that the lexical density of individual written texts is, on average, higher. (See Stubbs (1986a, pp. 98ff) for a detailed discussion of lexical variation and core vocabulary.)

There are correlations, but no more, within English lexis, among the features on the left and right:

spoken	written
everyday	academic
common	specialist
frequent	rare
informal	formal
monosyllabic	polysyllabic
Germanic	Romance/Graeco-Latin
acquired	learned
active	passive
core	non-core

For well known historical reasons – 1066, Norman French, Latin and all that – there is a broad split in English vocabulary, which is institutionalized in several ways (Williams, 1961, p. 40). The language of learning has a social class basis, and speakers in different social class groups have differential access to the non-core vocabulary. This is due to the way in which Graeco-

Latin loan words have been used to build up the vocabularies of institutions such as religion, medicine and the law. In addition, the way in which vocabularies have been elaborated to build up semantic fields in academic disciplines gives differential access to subjects on the school curriculum. Again we have a case of important relations between language variation, social institutions and academic knowledge.

In these various examples from spoken and written language, we have the beginnings of a theory which can relate forms of language use both to the representation of social groups (as in sexist language) and to authoritative text types and authoritative knowledge (as in dictionaries, mainstream literature, school books).

3.9 Lexical Density: an Analysis of Two Corpora

It might be thought that a purely quantitative analysis of text corpora could show nothing of interest about the functions of speech and writing in maintaining social relations between speakers. In fact, it is only by studying certain quite general quantitative characteristics of spoken and written genres that some patterns become visible. I will illustrate this by summarizing findings from 1.5 million words of written and spoken English.

As well as the kind of vocabulary differences discussed above, it is also evident that written texts are, on average, more lexically elaborated than spoken texts. It is intuitively clear that many written texts, such as published academic articles, are densely packed with information; whereas much spoken language, such as casual conversation, is not. Many studies (such as Biber, 1988) have found this to be a fundamental parameter of variation among texts. An important early corpus study which showed that spoken and written language typically differ in their lexical density was carried out by Ure (1971), and this concept is developed by Halliday (1985b).

The lexical density of a text is its relative proportion of lexical to grammatical words. In English and in many (if not all?) other languages, there is a fundamental distinction which divides the whole vocabulary into two rough categories: lexical words which express content, and grammatical words which relate lexical words to each other. The distinction is made in most modern grammars of English, but since many linguists make the same basic distinction, there are several terms in use. Lexical words are also referred to as major, full and content words; and grammatical words as minor, empty, structural and function words. A very explicit discussion was provided by Henry Sweet in his famous grammar of 1891:

> In a sentence such as *The earth is round*, we have no difficulty in recognizing *earth* and *round* as ultimate independent sense-units. . . . Such words as *the* and *is*, on the other hand, though independent in form, are not independent in meaning: *the* and *is* by themselves do not convey any ideas, as *earth* and *round* do. We call such words as *the* and *is* form-words, because they are words in form only. When a form-word is entirely devoid of meaning, we may call it an empty word, as opposed to full words such as *earth* and *round*. (Sweet, 1891, p. 22)

These two categories divide the traditional parts of speech into two broad sets:

- lexical words – noun, adjective, adverb, main verb;
- grammatical words – auxiliary verb, modal verb, pronoun, preposition, determiner, conjunction.

This two-way categorization represents a very substantial division in the vocabulary of English. And lexical and grammatical words have strikingly different characteristics. Briefly, lexical classes have large numbers of members (there are tens of thousands of nouns, but only a couple of dozen pronouns). Lexical classes are open to new words (for example, new nouns and verbs are being constantly invented; it is very rare for new pronouns to enter the language). And only lexical words take inflections (such as plural inflections on nouns, person endings on verbs).[1]

The lexical density of a text is the proportion of lexical words expressed as a percentage. If N is the number of words in a text, and L is the number of lexical words, then

$$\text{lexical density} = 100 \times L/N.$$

Briefly, one would expect a high proportion of lexical words in written texts, which can be more highly packed with information. Ure (1971) reports on corpora of 42,000 words of spoken and written text. She shows a strong tendency for written texts to have a lexical density of over 40 per cent (range 36 to 57) and for spoken texts to be under 40 per cent (range 24 to 43). My data below, from a larger corpus, agree with Ure's finding for written language: most written texts are above 40 per cent. But for spoken language, my corpus contained a much wider range.

There are simple functional interpretations for such findings. On average, a written text is shorter and has fewer repetitions than a comparable spoken text. It is permanent, highly edited, redrafted and rehearsed, rather than being unplanned and spontaneous as most casual conversation is. A written text is relatively context-free, though never entirely so, whereas a spoken text can rely to a large extent on the immediate physical context. We would therefore expect the information load to be higher in a written text: since it is permanent, readers can re-read obscure sections. Spoken texts must, on the other hand, be understood while they are being produced: they must be more predictable.

So, on average, written texts are less predictable, and spoken texts are more predictable. In turn, lexical words are less predictable: there are thousands of them. Grammatical words are more predictable: there are small numbers of them. In the case of conjunctions, for example, there are only half a dozen frequent items. We would expect, therefore, that written texts have a higher proportion of unpredictable lexical words, and that spoken texts have a higher proportion of more predictable grammatical words.

As Ure (1971) points out, lexis is not always equally necessary. Some texts can have 100 per cent lexical density: a shopping list, for example, can be just a list of lexical words. But the intelligibility of a text is a function of situation and group membership. Texts are differently understood by insiders and outsiders, and a high degree of shared information and shared context can lead to very low lexical density, in supportive, cooperative language use. (See sections 8.4, 8.7 and 8.8.2 on the wide range of ways of indicating shared assumptions and group membership.)

Interesting findings come from a comparison of text types across written and spoken corpora. I have carried out a computer-assisted analysis of the lexical density of texts in two corpora totalling nearly 1.5 million words, and comprising 587 samples from different genres of written and spoken English. (The data comprised the London–Lund and the LOB corpora: see notes on corpus data.) Figure 3.1 displays the main findings and shows the systematic variation of lexical density across different text types represented by the 587 samples.

3.9.1 Interpretation

One general finding is expected: written texts are, on average, more lexically dense than spoken texts. However, there is no absolute difference. On the contrary, the ranges are: 34 to 58 per cent for spoken texts; and 40 to 65 per cent for written texts. Some spoken texts are less dense than any written text; and some written texts are more dense than any spoken text. But there is a large overlap. This immediately disposes of any notion that written and spoken English are two separate varieties.

Within written texts, there are differences between 40 and 54 per cent for

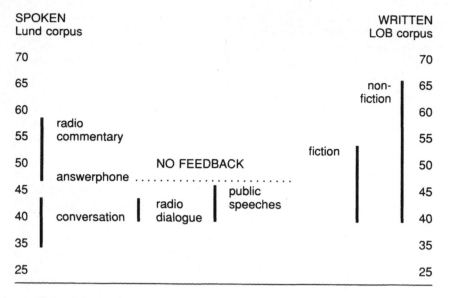

Figure 3.1   Lexical density of 587 samples of written and spoken English.

fiction, and 40 and 65 per cent for non-fiction (including academic articles and bureaucratic reports). Non-fiction has a wider range. Fiction is restricted to lower densities: perhaps at least partly because it includes representations of spoken dialogue, which lowers the percentage of dense written language.

However, the most interesting finding is perhaps the following. The clearest difference is not between written and spoken language, which overlap considerably, but the absolute difference within the spoken language genres. Those uses of spoken language where there is no possibility of feedback from other speakers – radio commentary and telephone answering machines – vary between 46 and 64 per cent. And those uses where there is feedback (conversation, radio discussions) and those where the audience is physically present and where there is at least the possibility of feedback (lectures and speeches) vary between 34 and 44 per cent. Here, there is no overlap at all.

Note, however, that there are varieties of written language (where there can be no immediate feedback) which have lower densities than the spoken genres with feedback. In such analyses, we are dealing with tendencies. Linguistics has largely ignored such quantitative properties of language in use.

3.9.2   Text samples

In order to make such abstract quantitative characteristics of text types a little more concrete, it would be useful to give brief examples of the text samples analysed above. Lexical (content) words are italicized.

1   Radio horse racing commentary. From Lund corpus, text 10-4. Among the highest lexical densities (58 per cent) of the spoken texts. The high density results from the listing of names.

> it's *Northern Circuit* over on the *far side* the *leader* from *Marche d'Or Non Proven* under *pressure* on the *stand side* with *Sea Shanty* then *comes Princess Shumar coming* to the *final furlong* and it's *Northern Circuit* from *Marche d'Or Non Proven* on the *stand side* then *Sea Shanty* then *Princess Shumar* then *Courts of Love* then *Canute's Courtier* they're inside the *final furlong* and it's *Northern Circuit striding* away . . .

2   Political speech. From Lund corpus, text 12-5. Among the highest lexical densities (48 per cent) of the spoken texts apart from radio commentaries.

> *provides* a *basis* on which the *whole party* can *rally* the *great debate* to which I *called* the *party* in the *summer* of *nineteen seventy one* and which was *resolved* by the *clear decision* of *last year's conference* and by the *vote* in the *Parliamentary Labour Party* . . .

3   Conversation. From Lund corpus, text 1-8. Among the lowest lexical densities (36 per cent) of the spoken texts.

> oh no those are just my *scripts* I just *saw* the *note* and I *know* that's *all right*

> just *put* my *glasses* on I can't see a *thing* without them well after *all* they're too *dark* to be *inspiring* aren't they

> I don't *want* one I'm *afraid*

4   Belles lettres, etc.: art. From LOB corpus, text g44. Among the highest lexical densities (58 per cent) of the written texts.

> *Quarrels* and *dissensions ensued* among the *cast*, most of whom *hurriedly* and *shamefacedly handed* over their *parts* to *understudies* in *various pretexts*, and on *November 10th*, *Don Giovanni* was *quietly removed* from the *repertoire*, and *Les Mystères d'Isis substituted*. There was, *admittedly*, an . . .

5   Religious pamphlet. From LOB corpus, text d16. Among the lowest
lexical densities (41 per cent) of the written texts.

> One of the *duties* of *religion* is to *teach men* to *keep* the *law* of *God*. The
> *law* of *God* has a *great deal* to *say* about *things* which have nothing to *do*
> with *worship*. Thou shalt not *steal*. Thou shalt not *kill*. Thou shalt not
> *commit adultery*. There are *three examples* of *religious matters* which
> have nothing to *do* with *praying*. If it is the *job* of the *Church* to *see* . . .

In general, measures of richness of vocabulary, such as lexical density,
provide a robust method of distinguishing genres. A closely related
method would be to calculate the percentage of common words in different
texts and genres. For example, one could calculate what percentage of
the text consists of the 200 most frequent words in the language, as
established for some reasonably large corpus. (Most of these 200 words
will, of course, be grammatical words.) Or one could calculate the percentage of core or basic vocabulary, as opposed to more specialized words.
(Many lists of such basic vocabulary have been published; see Stubbs,
1986a, pp. 98–115.) Texts with high lexical density will have low
percentages of common words and of basic vocabulary. Even such
broad quantitative methods, based on just two categories of vocabulary
(grammatical versus lexical, common versus less common, or basic versus
specialized) can provide clear findings about stylistic variation. (See also
Hudson (1994) on the stability of such quantitative characteristics of text
types.)

I will mention briefly one potential, and very practical, application of
such quantitative analyses of vocabulary. There have been many cases in the
news recently where it is alleged that the police have attempted to fabricate
verbatim interview transcripts of suspects in criminal cases. Such fabrication
is very difficult to carry out convincingly, since it requires the simulation, in
writing, of a spoken conversation which has been recorded under stress.
When people attempt this, they tend to write things down as if in a drama
script. But people do not naturally speak as if they were in a stage play, and
fabricated confessions therefore tend to contain features of written rather
than real spoken discourse (Coulthard, 1992a). Knowledge of the norms of
spoken and written language, such as I have provided above, could be of very
practical value to a linguist called to testify in court as an expert witness that
such fabrication of evidence has taken place. (See chapter 5 on language and
the law, and chapter 7 for other analyses of norms of occurrence for lexical
items.)

3.10   Conclusion

Such empirical, corpus-based studies of how language is used in the construction of gender and other social relations, of educational knowledge and of authoritative texts show some possible contributions of linguistics to Giddens's project. In the spirit of Firth and Hill, such studies reveal the relations between conscious, individual speech acts and the unconscious characteristics of larger stretches of discourse. They therefore provide empirical evidence about the relationship between individual human agency and the long-term structure of social institutions.

Appendix: Further Notes on the Intellectual Background

In the appendix to chapter 2, I gave brief biographical details on Firth, Halliday and Sinclair. Trevor Hill worked in Edinburgh at the same time as Michael Halliday and John Sinclair, and his article acknowledges other Edinburgh colleagues. Basil Bernstein was Professor of the Sociology of Education at the London Institute until 1990. When Halliday held the chair at University College London, he worked closely with Bernstein, and wrote a sympathetic foreword to volume 2 of Bernstein's *Class, Codes and Control* (1973), at a time when Bernstein's work was misunderstood and attacked by many British linguists and educationalists. Ruqaiya Hasan, Halliday's wife, was a research associate of Bernstein's. As I pointed out in chapter 2, the Edinburgh–London axis, with its intellectual and personal contacts, has been an important one for the development of British linguistics.

There is a close relationship between what Firth calls focal or pivotal words and what Raymond Williams (1926–88) calls keywords, nodes around which ideological and political battles are fought (Williams, 1976; and see sections 7.4 and 7.5 below). Williams does not appear to have known the work of Firth or the London School of Linguistics. And Anthony Giddens (1938–) (personal communication) was unaware of Firth's work on developing a monistic position for linguistic theory, when he (Giddens) was writing his important studies of dualisms in social theory. It is also possible for major theorists to be producing closely related work, although unaware of each other's thought.

Sometimes ideas seem just to be in the air. As Kress (1993) points out, developments in linguistics are not independent of wider social changes.

Changes in social circumstances have made it more difficult to maintain an a-social, a-historical, autonomous linguistics which takes as its starting point a homogeneous language. Firth was arguing against the assumption of homogeneity in the 1930s. But, nowadays, many factors make heterogeneity very difficult to ignore: the fact of multilingualism, the shift from an industrial to a service base in Western economies, the political prominence of language questions, and the issues of language and power raised by the feminist movement.

Sometimes, also, the history of linguistics is a history of ideologically motivated misreadings: consider Bloomfield on Saussure, or Chomsky on Port Royal (Joseph, 1990). However, in this book I cannot provide a history of British linguistics, merely occasional brief background notes on work originating in Edinburgh and London. A serious study of the sociology of ideas in British linguistics is sadly lacking.

Part II
Text and Corpus Analysis

4

Baden-Powell: a Comparative Analysis of Two Short Texts

We are born individuals. But to satisfy our needs we have to become social persons. . . . Who are the 'carriers' of the particular cultural tradition . . . or form of speech? What is the mechanism of 'transmission'? (Firth, 1935, pp. 66, 71–2)

The next five chapters present analyses of texts and corpora. These analyses progress from short texts (of a few hundred words) to much longer texts (whole books of tens of thousands of words), and from small corpora (of a million words or so) to larger corpora (of many millions of words), using increasingly powerful computer-assisted methods. In order to make this progression more visible, and to facilitate the use of the book for teaching, I will summarize at the beginning of each chapter

- the main data analysed – individual texts and/or collections of texts in a corpus;
- other data used for comparative purposes;
- the main linguistic features analysed in these data;
- the main purpose of the analysis and the main findings.

This chapter is intended for readers with no previous knowledge of text analysis, and provides an introductory example of how lexical and grammatical analysis can contribute to a critical analysis of the social world. The chapter shows how choices of words and grammar represent events from an identifiable point of view.

4.1 Organization of the Chapter

The main data analysed in this chapter are two short texts, of about 330 and 550 words each: Baden-Powell's last messages to the Boy Scouts and Girl

Guides. They are reproduced in an appendix to the chapter. To most readers of this book, these texts will probably seem very old-fashioned. Some of their presuppositions now seem patronizing, some aspects of their sexism seem glaringly obvious and some of these features need little comment for a modern reader. However, other patterns are perhaps less obvious and require methods of lexical and grammatical analysis to reveal them.

I discuss the use of individual words in the texts. However, the main point of the analysis is to show that certain words occur within different collocations and different grammatical structures. Some of these patterns are compared with data from corpora of 1.5 million words of written and spoken English. In the analysis of two short texts, computer-assisted methods are not necessary. However, I will show that, even here, concordances can be useful in order to display conveniently and clearly the repeated patterns. Computer searches are required to find comparative data in large corpora. And in following chapters, computer methods will be necessary in order to identify such patterns across longer texts or corpora.

The main purpose of the analysis is to show how ideological (in this case sexist) positions are conveyed, not just by individual words, but by patterns of vocabulary and grammar. Some sexist imbalances are inherent in the English language, but others are constructed by the way language is used in individual texts.

4.2   Baden-Powell

Baden-Powell (1857–1941), henceforth BP, was a British general. His main fame in late Victorian society was due to his role as commander in the defence of the town of Mafeking, in the Cape Province of South Africa, during the Boer War, in which the British defeated the Boers of the Orange Free State and the Transvaal. The Siege of Mafeking was a celebrated event which lasted 217 days from October 1899 to May 1900 before the town was relieved.

The fact about his life which is of immediate relevance here is that he was the founder of the Boy Scouts Association. This was a movement which he set up in 1908, to develop boys' character and practical outdoor skills such as camping and hiking. BP's principles of self-reliance and healthy living, based on love of God and country, and also on his military experience in southern Africa, are set out in his *Scouting for Boys*. Following on the immediate success of the Boy Scouts movement, he founded the Girl Guides movement in 1910.

4.3   The Texts: Production and Reception

The two texts for analysis are BP's last messages to the Boy Scouts and Girl Guides. The Girl Guides text was published in 1941 in *The Guide Magazine*, which was sold to nearly every girl in the movement. It appears to have been reprinted only once in 1942, and not at all since that date. The Boy Scouts text was published in the 1942 memorial edition of *Scouting for Boys*, has been reprinted in subsequent editions and is still available printed on a postcard which is sold in Scout Association shops. The two texts, for girls and boys, show striking differences, and it is these differences which I will analyse here.[1]

It is important to bear in mind the context of production of the texts. Their author was a man born in the middle of the nineteenth century, and probably in his late sixties when he wrote them. He was a famous British military commander, who founded and became the leader of worldwide movements, based on partly military principles. The texts were written over sixty years ago, and published over fifty years ago. The English language has changed perceptibly in this time, not only in vocabulary (and to a lesser extent in syntax) but also in its discourse conventions.

It is also important to consider the context of reception of the texts. A principle of text analysis is that texts should be located institutionally. Who produced them? Who reads them? Adults or children? A single individual or hundreds or millions of people? How are they distributed? What genre do they represent? W. N. Francis (1979), in an influential article on corpus linguistics, proposes that what he calls the reception index should be taken into account in the interpretation of a text. Texts are not all equivalent as regards the number of times they are heard or read. A presidential address or major sports event might be heard by tens of millions of people. Some texts (for example, religious texts) are studied intensively, constantly repeated and learned by heart by hundreds of millions of people over centuries. It is exceedingly difficult to know how to estimate such readerships, but evident that we use different interpretative strategies in reading a private letter written to us by a friend, a public letter to the editor of a newspaper and so on.

The two BP texts have been very widely circulated, must have been read by hundreds of thousands of children and adults, and one of the texts (but not the other!) is still in print. There are traces of many genres in the texts: advice to one's children, the speech of a leader rallying the troops, a sermon and the dying speech of a famous person: indeed BP is rather self-mocking about this last genre, in his reference to the dying pirate chief in the Scouts text.

4.4   Content Analysis

I start from the assumption that the sexism of the two texts is now largely obvious to us, reading the texts over fifty years after they were published. They express, quite explicitly, the view that women and men have very different places in the world, and many aspects of these views would now appear deeply objectionable, or perhaps just ridiculous, to many people. Their tone strikes us, over fifty years on, as patronizing and naive. And there is no reason to suppose that Girl Guides down the years have passively absorbed BP's message. They may have actively contested it, given it subversive readings, laughed at it or just ignored it. There is no direct way to investigate this, although one indication is that the Guides text has long been out of print.

So, I start with some differences between the two texts, which I will now refer to as G (for Guides) and S (for Scouts). Assumptions about their different readerships are conveyed by some quite superficial aspects of the two texts. Text G is longer and more complex in various ways. The Guides seem to be credited with being able to understand a text which is considerably more complex, lexically and syntactically, than are the Scouts. Text S is shorter and simpler. Perhaps the Scouts are credited with a more limited attention span. Even in such respects as length, readers are positioned by the text. (Compare, for example, how school textbooks are often divided into short sections.)

Text G is full of references to men. Guides are defined in relation to home, husband and children, and text G contains several words (*husband, parents, comrade, servant*) which refer to relations between people, or between people and God: Guides are *comrades* to men, and the *chosen servants* of God. Conversely, text S makes no mention of women. There is one abstract reference to *other people* and one reference to a fictional male character, the pirate chief. If anything, Scouts are defined by reference to their *career* (mentioned once), but such relationships remain vague and abstract. (See section 7.10 for more detailed analyses of the connotations of words such as CAREER, WORK and HOME.)

The two texts express a 'separate spheres' ideology. Text G is about the duties of wives and mothers. Being a 'comrade' is defined explicitly as *taking an interest in your husband's work*. Women belong to the private sphere of home and family, not to the public sphere of career, business, commerce and politics. And both texts express the preservation of this status quo. Text S encourages boys explicitly to *be contented with what you have got and make the best of it*. And text G is full of references to God's plan for the world, to what

God wants, to what God *means us to be*, to where Guides fit in to this plan and to the inevitability of things: happiness *comes by itself* and hard work *brings its own reward*.

It is obvious, when we read such texts so many years after their production, that concepts of women, men and children are historically variable. The BP texts seem dated precisely because such categories are not natural, but are historically constructed and reinforced by texts such as BP's and many others. Such ideas may seem natural to people at a certain time, but this is because they are produced, maintained by their constant repetition in texts such as these, and thus naturalized, not natural. A major component of sexism (as of racism) is the social stereotyping of categories, whereby a part stands for the whole. The best example of "mother" is often assumed to be "housewife and mother", and this category contrasts with working mother, unmarried mother, stepmother, surrogate mother and so on. Such categories are used in constructing arguments, defining expectations, and jumping to conclusions. "Working mother" is itself a stereotype in which an individual who is labelled by the category may be assumed to have other characteristics (Lakoff, 1987, pp. 79ff).

4.5   HAPPY and HAPPINESS

It is relatively easy to see how words such as HOME, WORK and CAREER have social significance. The content and connotations of such words are ideologically loaded, and their meanings are often openly contested. For example, many women point out that "housework" is not regarded as "proper work", and that a "working woman" or "working mother" is not a woman who works in the home, doing "housework", but someone who is "in work", that is in paid employment. The word WORK is ambiguous in contemporary English (see section 7.10). However, my comments so far relate to the content of the texts, but say nothing about how patterns of lexis and grammar contribute to such meanings.

It is less obvious that words such as HAPPY can also have ideological uses and connotations. I will study two related word forms in the two texts: *happy* and *happiness*. In both texts the word *happy* is the most frequent lexical (content) word (see section 3.9 on lexical versus grammatical words). The four most frequent lexical words, with their text frequencies, are:

- text G, happy 11, children 6, happiness 5, world 5;
- text S, happy 6, die 4, happiness 4, life 4.

These very simple lexical statistics already indicate some important differences between the two texts.

We can ask both what *happy* means in the English language as a whole, and what *happy* means in these texts. All words are indeterminate in meaning. But the word has a history in the two texts, with particular distributions and collocations. BP makes the word mean something, and, by the combinations in which he uses it, he does his own small piece of semantic engineering. By using *happy* in combination with other words, he selects some connotations rather than others, and, if ever so slightly in the overall history of English, he puts pressure on the collocates and on the grammatical constructions in which the word occurs. Consider how the distribution and collocations of the two word forms differ in the two texts.

4.5.1   Text G: Guides text

There are ten instances of the adjective *happy* in the first third of the text, no occurrences at all in the middle third, then almost exclusively instances of the noun *happiness* in the last third. There is a shift, with a break in the middle, from adjectival to nominal uses, from *happy* as a quality to *happiness* as an abstract thing. That is, the word forms *happy* and *happiness* have a micro–history in the text.

hat your business in life is to be happy and to make others happy. That soun
is to be happy and to make others happy. That sounds comfortable and easy,
it? You begin making other people happy by doing good turns to them. You ne
not worry about making yourselves happy, as you will very soon find that th
itself; when you make other people happy, it makes you happy too. Later on,
e other people happy, it makes you happy too. Later on, when you have a home
y one you will make your husband a happy man. If all homes were bright and c
hy and clean and busy they will be happy. Happy children love their parents.
clean and busy they will be happy. Happy children love their parents. There
hild. I am sure God means us to be happy in this life. He has given us a wor
happiness into the world by making happy homes and by being yourselves good,

who pass away; secondly, to bring happiness into the world by making happy
nt of life. By giving out love and happiness in this way, you will gain for
ind that Heaven is not the kind of happiness somewhere up there in the skies
your own home. So guide others to happiness and you will bring happiness to
rs to happiness and you will bring happiness to yourselves and by doing this

Concordance 4.1   Happy and happiness in Girl Guides text.

Approximate synonyms and semantically closely related words which occur are: *bright, cheery, joy, enjoy*. And collocates, which imply a particular view of happiness, include: *busy, clean, healthy, reward, work*. The meaning of the word WORK is, of course, also being constructed by such collocations within the text.

The syntactic contexts in which the words are used can be most easily studied in concordance lines: see concordance 4.1. The lemma occurs in these constructions and phrases:

MAKE NP happy (6); MAKE happy N (1); BE happy (4)

BRING happiness (2); GIVE OUT happiness; GUIDE to happiness

Happy and *happiness* occur in particular grammatical frames. One can simply BE *happy*. But in most of the cases, happiness involves other people. The grammar of *happy* in this text implies that it is something one can be, or be made by others, and that *happiness* is an object which one can give to someone, or a place to which one can guide someone.

Such comments show one major flaw in the kind of grammar which many people remember from school. Vague memories of school grammar are filled with definitions such as: nouns are the names of persons, places and things; and verbs are the names of actions. Such correspondences are often accurate, but these are merely the relations which might be expected. When it is said that nouns are the names of persons and things, verbs are the names of actions and adjectives are the names of states, such statements appear to be definitions. However, it would be more accurate to regard them as disguised statements about how we expect the words to be used. States are typically encoded as adjectives: *happy, poor, intelligent*. But states can be re-coded as nouns: *happiness, poverty, intelligence*. A state can be grammaticalized as a thing. Thus one can both *make people happy* and also *guide people to happiness*. Halliday (1985a, p. 319ff) calls this grammatical metaphor. The traditional use of the term metaphor means substituting one word for another (as in *He is a lion in battle*). Grammatical metaphor means substituting one grammatical class for another.

4.5.2   Text S: Scouts text

The patterns in text S are quite different. There is no shift from adjectival *happy* to nominal *happiness*. The two word forms are mixed throughout. Approximate synonyms and semantically related words are: *contented, enjoy, jolly, on the bright side* (versus *gloomy*). And collocates include: *healthy,*

o think it over. I have had a most happy life and I want each of you to have
and I want each of you to have as happy a life too. I believe that God put
d put us in this jolly world to be happy and enjoy life. Happiness doesn't c
our turn comes to die, you can die happy in feeling that at any rate you hav
'Be prepared' in this way, to live happy and to die happy – stick to your Sc
this way, to live happy and to die happy – stick to your Scout Promise alway

world to be happy and enjoy life. Happiness doesn't come from being rich, n
self-indulgence. One step towards happiness is to make yourself healthy and
loomy one. But the real way to get happiness is by giving out happiness to o
to get happiness is by giving out happiness to other people. Try and leave

Concordance 4.2   Happy and *happiness* in Boy Scouts text.

strong, useful. Every instance of *happy* collocates, within three words to left
or right, with *life, live* or *die. Happy* is a feature of lives and deaths; *happiness*
is an object or a place.

Again the syntactic contexts can be most easily displayed in concordances: see concordance 4.2. The uses are:

happy life; be happy; die happy; live happy

step towards happiness; get happiness; giving out happiness

Only one of these constructions (*give out happiness*) implies that other people
are involved.

4.6   Comparative Data

It is important to emphasize that there is nothing unusual about BP's use of
the words *happy* and *happiness*, in the sense that he does not construct
strange lexical and grammatical combinations. His usage is not atypical, but
he makes selections from the potential of the language, and this selectively
reinforces different patterns in the two texts.

There is little point in looking at usage as recorded in most dictionaries,
since this is not based on a corpus. However, the Cobuild dictionary
(Sinclair, 1987a) is based on a twenty million word corpus of varieties of
English, and all citations in the dictionary are attested in the corpus. Under
the entry for *happy*, these citations show the same collocations as occur in the
BP texts (even though these are sixty years old):

this will make the children happy [A]

money did not bring happiness [A]

the happiest day of my life [A]

In order to discover some facts about the frequency of different uses of *happy*, I also studied a corpus of 1.5 million words of spoken and written English (LOB plus Lund: see notes on corpus data). In this small corpus, the most frequent lexical collocates of *happy* in the three words before and after were *life* and *make*. The next most likely lexical collocates were

> entirely, marriage, days, looked, memories, perfectly, sad, spent, felt, father, feel, home

(In section 7.7, I discuss in detail methods for discovering significant collocates of a given node word.)

The words *happy, happier, happiest* and *happiness* occur in 125 texts (out of 500) in all the main genres in the LOB corpus of one million words of written English: they are both frequent and evenly distributed. And if we compare texts G and S further with LOB, it becomes clearer which selections BP has made from the potential of the language. Relative to this general corpus, BP uses nominals much more frequently. (BP's percentage of nominal versus adjectival or adverbial use of HAPPY is 31 to 69 per cent in text G, and 40 to 60 in text S. The LOB percentages are 18 to 82.) And texts G and S use collocations with MAKE and LIFE more frequently. BP uses specific collocations relatively more frequently than they occur in the general corpora. (MAKE-*happy* accounts for 44 per cent of collocations in text G, but only 4 per cent in LOB. *Happy*-LIFE accounts for 50 per cent of collocations in text S, but only 5 per cent in LOB.)

The argument so far is as follows. From the potential available in the language, these texts use particular actual selections, which attach particular connotations to the lemma. Meanings are conveyed not only by individual words and grammatical forms, but also by the frequency of collocations and by the distribution of forms across texts. There are general expectations in the language as a whole as to how words will be used: for example, which collocations will typically occur. Texts may fit such expectations, or deviate from them. In addition, texts create their own patterns and expectations, which they can then either maintain or break. The meaning of words is created in texts: the instance has a history in a text. And ultimately, words change in meaning because their use in texts changes.

4.7   Practical Implications: Sexist Language

Such analyses have important practical implications. One conclusion is pessimistic. A common line of thought is that it is possible to clean up a language by removing sexist expressions from it. At least it should be possible to clean up texts, by writing them in non-sexist ways. Such a verbal hygiene view of language works in some cases, and Plain English campaigns and feminist campaigns against sexist usages have had much success. It is possible at least to rid texts of usages which are blatantly asymmetrical and/or insulting to women. But it is possible to legislate in advance only with respect to relatively self-contained sub-systems of the language, such as the pronoun system (see section 3.7 on false generic *he*) or asymmetric morphological forms (such as *actor, actress, master, mistress* and *bachelor, spinster*). However, although there is nothing inherently sexist about the word *happy*, it can be used in sexist ways. As I have shown here, it can be used asymmetrically in texts, and language comes in texts, not in isolated words.

It is often claimed that language reflects society. But, as Cameron (1990) shows, this view is faulty. It is not that society first exists, and is then reflected passively by language Language is itself a social practice, and language actively reproduces and transforms society In the case of sexist language, feminist campaigns have had considerable success in changing some language usages. For example, pressure has led to institutions changing the ways in which women are referred to, to publishers producing non-sexist style sheets for authors and so on. Language can, perhaps in relatively modest domains, be actively changed by human agency. And these changes restructure social relations.

However, my analysis shows that sexist language can operate at different levels. This is one area where linguists should be able to help with analysing an important issue of language in society, because they are good at analysing patterns at different levels. If concepts are lexicalized, and represented in individual words, then they are usually relatively easy to recognize. And many of the asymmetries in the vocabulary of English have been well analysed and are now well known. It has often been pointed out that *bachelor* and *spinster* have strong tendencies to collocate with very different sets of words, and this can be quickly confirmed from corpus data. Examples of frequent collocations from a 120 million word corpus included, respectively,

carefree, confirmed, eligible, young; degree, arts, science

aged, aunt, old, shelf (*as in* left on the shelf)

Once such lexical examples have been pointed out, they are usually fairly easy to see, and successful feminist language engineering has mostly been at this lexical level. Terms such as *chairperson* or *sexual harassment* do not create new phenomena: but they draw explicit attention to phenomena which previously existed. The name does not create the practice, but the practice can be more easily identified if it is named. [Names bring actions into consciousness, and actions with names become social.]They can more easily be talked about, and if necessary made subject to laws.

Slightly deeper in the language, and slightly more difficult to perceive, are fixed phrases and collocations involving such individual words or pairs. A (male) author, whose article I recently commented on, readily accepted that the words *master* and *mistress* were asymmetrical and therefore sexist. But he would not accept that the expression *to master a language* was in any way sexist, and was unwilling to change the expression to, for example, *to become fully competent in a language.*

Words and phrases are easier to recognize than aspects of meaning which are encoded in syntax. Even outer layers of the grammar, such as the asymmetrical use of *he* and *she*, are more abstract and are part of automatic behaviour which is difficult to see or to bring under conscious control. More abstract still are probabilities of occurrence and patterns of usage: see my analysis, in section 3.7, of the use of *he* and *she* in definite and indefinite expressions. Such choices are probabilistic tendencies, and can be observed only indirectly, with quantitative computational techniques across large amounts of corpus data.

4.8   Theoretical Implications:
Meaning in Texts and in Language

In section 7.7, I will discuss in detail a method for studying some of the patterns of lexical collocation which help to form social stereotypes. These techniques derive from Firth's (1935) proposals for 'a contextual and socio-logical technique' of semantics, for studying words in socially significant contexts (see section 3.2). The techniques involve studying the formal scatter (including what I have here called distribution) of the use of words in different contexts. In the meantime, this chapter has provided a small example of a textual approach to studying meaning, and a small example of how language use reproduces the culture from generation to generation. All texts make assumptions about their readers or listeners. All language is intertextual: it is shaped by prior texts, oriented to conventions and interpreted against the background of a very large corpus of linguistic experience (see section 2.5).

This brief analysis also gives examples of several important concepts: the nature of word meaning, grammatical metaphor and the relation between instance and system. It illustrates the principle that words do not have determinate meanings which can be defined in advance of their use. The word *happy* does not have a proper, fixed, stable meaning, entirely independent of its use in texts. All words are open to new uses and are flexible in their meanings to some extent. There are therefore changing relations between occurrences in a text and the underlying language system. In several articles, Halliday (1991, 1992, 1993) has discussed how the local micro occurrences in a text either maintain the status quo of probabilities in the language as a whole, or, however infinitesimally, shift these probabilities. The instance and the system are names for different observer depths.

Too much weight should not be placed on individual texts. But if particular lexical and grammatical choices are regularly made, and if people and things are repeatedly talked about in certain ways, then it is plausible that this will affect how they are thought about. The argument is about semantic habits, and about habitual ways of speaking. This argument has been developed in detail by Bernstein (1975) and Halliday (1990). They talk of coding orientations: systematic tendencies in the selection of meanings. It is the continuous reinforcement, through massive repetition and consistency in discourse, which is required to construct and maintain social reality. And in order to specify the linguistic mechanisms of the system which has this power, we need grammar as a tool of analysis (Halliday, 1978, p. 170).

There are patterns which contribute to the meaning of texts, but which are not open to direct observation. The patterns are not in the individual words, but in the grammar, and they therefore require abstract descriptive categories to state them. The descriptive, formal and technical cannot be avoided. You cannot understand the world just by looking at it. Language cannot be analysed simply by exhibiting individual samples of it (Gellner, 1959). It is necessary to identify the linguistic mechanisms which convey ideologies.

The view that you can talk about the world by displaying examples of it was the mistake made by the Sages of Lagado, and exposed by Jonathan Swift in *Gulliver's Travels*. These sages thought that words were merely the names of things, and that they might as well carry round the things themselves and use those in their conversations in place of words:

which hath only this inconvenience attending it, that if a man's business be
very great, he must . . . carry a greater bundle of things upon his back . . . I
have often beheld two of these sages almost sinking under the weight of their
packs.

But language in use is not transparent: it does not display for us its
underlying meanings. To expose these meanings, methods of description
and analysis are required. As Gellner (1959, p. 296) says, in parody
of Wittgenstein: 'That which one would insinuate, thereof must one
speak.'

Such analysis shows how grammar can help to explain the discourse of a
society: how different points of view can be expressed by stylistic choices,
and how such choices can embody different ideologies. Ideology need not
function at the level of conscious or intentional bias. But ways of expressing
things are not natural. Once it is realized that choices have been made, it is
also realized that other choices could be made, and that reality could be
differently presented.

4.9   Educational Implications

These points have educational implications for teaching pupils and students
how to read texts critically, and to consider systematically questions such as:
Whose point of view is expressed in texts? How are readers positioned? How
are social relations represented (if at all)? How is the potential in the grammar realized by choices in the text?

The view of language illustrated briefly in this chapter is that language
organizes experience. Therefore language is part of experience. Therefore
language is never neutral. My interpretation of the texts uses lexical and
grammatical analysis as part of a programme of critical cultural analysis:
critical in the sense of showing up connections which are often hidden from
people (Fairclough, 1989, p. 5). This is probably the most important reason
for teaching grammar: it helps people to understand how meanings are
expressed. (Though there is often shamefully scant attention paid to analytic
skills in English language work in secondary schools in Britain – and in
universities, which have a large responsibility here.)

Since my view of text analysis is explicitly concerned with changing
perceptions, it follows that language study is political: not in the sense of
indoctrinating students into a particular point of view, but in the sense of
providing them with ways of analysing points of view and deciding for

themselves on their own position. There is a very widespread view that unquestioning acceptance of the status quo is a-political, and that a critical view is indoctrination. I reject this view. Analysis allows people to discuss how points of view are expressed in any text, and then to make up their own minds. It is the view that language is natural and transparent, and that texts merely record rather than interpret, which conceals ideology and leads to indoctrination. All texts use grammar to persuade. (The present book is no exception.)

Many educational arguments suffer from the Mulberry Bush problem: they just go round and round. Sometimes for a depressingly long time. One such argument concerns whether grammar should be taught in schools. In an article published fifty years ago in a book called *The Teaching of English in Schools*, Gradon (1946) presents a very explicit defence of teaching grammar:

> Too many teachers reject grammar because they are only familiar with the grammar which was taught when they themselves were at school. Geographers do not teach children the cosmography of Ptolemy or scientists the doctrine of the humours although the heavens and the human body are unchanged. . . . Yet how foolish to cease teaching geography or physiology altogether because the mediaeval doctrines are no longer palatable.

I would argue that grammar is essential in the English curriculum: but what I mean by grammar is a long way from many people's stereotypes. For example, grammar is a major theme in discussions of English teaching (see section 7.3). But I presume that my concept of grammar in this chapter is very far from what various Secretaries of State for Education have had in mind when they have insisted on the importance of grammar in the English curriculum. It is a very long way from a position which relates grammar to etiquette, manners and morals, or to Standard English and the nation.

4.10   Other Analyses

I have shown how the Baden-Powell texts represent women and men differently. There are many other analyses of this topic. In section 3.8.3, I summarized work by Baker and Freebody (1989) which shows that girls and boys are differently represented in initial reading books: they analyse the different distributions of the lemmas GIRL, BOY and CHILD and their collocates. In another study, Clark (1992) compares how women and men are differently represented in newspaper accounts of violent crimes (typically by men against women); she studies how both lexis and grammar are used to convey blame. And Nair (1992) also shows how social ideologies and cultural presuppositions are conveyed by forms of discourse; she discusses how women and men are classified and represented in matrimonial advertisements in newspapers from India, UK and USA.

Other studies are of different social groups. For example, the articles in Meinhof and Richardson (1994) discuss how poverty is represented in the British media; the analysis by Kress (1994) on the grammar of the noun *poverty* is similar in many ways to my analysis above of the grammar of *happiness*.

I have elsewhere (Stubbs, 1990) analysed a newspaper text which represents Blacks and Whites differently. I looked at an article from a British tabloid newspaper, which reported violence in South Africa on the occasion of Nelson Mandela's release from prison in February 1990. Although the article reported violence by both Blacks and Whites, the vocabulary and the grammar used to talk about the groups was distinctly different. First, the words *Black* and *White* occur with different accompanying words. Blacks act in *mobs*, *crowds*, *factions* and *groups*. They constitute *millions* who live in *townships* and *tribal* homelands. They *mass* in *thousands*, and are *followers* of *nationalist leaders*. But Whites (also reported as committing violence) are individuals or *extremists*: by implication different from other (normal?) Whites. Second, the grammar of the text represents Blacks and Whites differently. When Blacks are reported as committing violence, they are in subject position, and at the beginning of the clause, as in the following examples [all A]:

> mobs of [Mandela's] followers ran wild and looted shops
>
> Mandela supporters knifed a man repeatedly
>
> jubilant Blacks . . . clashed with police
>
> ANC supporters have been feuding with . . .
>
> elements of the 50,000 crowd began rioting
>
> the youths hurled bottles and rubbish at the police

The point of view from which events are reported becomes particularly clear when verbs are used which allow subject and adjunct to be reversed. For example, the following sentences might refer to the same event:

> Blacks . . . clashed with police [A]
>
> police . . . clashed with Blacks [M]

It is the first version, with *Blacks* in subject position, which occurs in the article. However, when Whites are reported as committing violence, grammar is used differently. Events are presented in passives and nominalizations:

> a . . . black ANC follower was . . . killed by an unidentified white man [A]
>
> there was also bloodshed by white extremists [A]

In this second example, violent action by Whites is nominalized (*bloodshed*) and presented as a state (*there was* . . .), and reference to the victims is omitted. The violence is made more abstract and less brutal by the grammatical choices which are made. There is a connection between the grammar used and the perspective adopted.

Other analyses provide evidence that such linguistic features are not restricted to this single text, but are widespread techniques of representation, across many different contexts. For example, Said (1978), in his discussion of representations of the Orient in Western literature, points out that Arabs are regularly represented in large numbers, not as individuals. And Lee (1992, pp. 91ff) provides an analysis of a 1976 newspaper article about South Africa, in which he identifies many of same features as I have done, including the use of passives and nominalizations to refer to violence, the presentation of events from a White, not a Black, perspective and human actions presented as uncontrollable natural forces such as volcanoes and rivers:

> tension was already boiling over (my text)
>
> the situation . . . was highly volatile (my text)
>
> the black township . . . erupted (Lee's text)
>
> the marchers . . . swept through a roadblock (Lee's text)

These various studies of the ways in which lexical and grammatical choices differently represent different social groups might provide ideas for student projects on the use of language in the media, and more generally on ways in which lexis and grammar are used (often unconsciously) to represent events from an inexplicit but identifiable point of view. For example, with the availability of newspapers on CD-ROM, it is a simple task to extract all occurrences of the lemmas WOMAN and MAN in a year's edition of a given newspaper, and to study whether their use is symmetrical or not.

The analytic questions which can be addressed in concrete ways by such analyses include: How is discourse organized to appear factual, literal, objective, authoritative and independent of the author, rather than appearing to be expressed from a particular point of view? What are the rhetorical processes which are used to produce widely accepted versions of reality? How do people organize accounts of events? Why are some versions of reality remembered? To answer such questions requires ways of analysing patterns in texts and in the language, and therefore requires grammar as a tool of analysis.

Foucault (1980, p. 118) talks of how effects of truth are produced within discourses. 'Each society has . . . types of discourse which it accepts and makes function as true' (p. 131). The task is to make visible 'what was previously unseen' (p. 50). Such analysis is often simpler than it might seem, since there is a relatively small set of grammatical features which tend to be significant for expressing power relations and for expressing what is taken for granted (Fairclough, 1989, pp. 110ff). These include whether sentences are positive or negative, or active or passive, whether verbs are nominalized, how pronouns (especially *we* and *you*) are used, and how modality is expressed (see chapter 8). These are the grammatical features which express whether participants, agency and causation are explicit or hidden (see section 6.8), and whether claims are being made as factual, certain, taken for granted, authoritative, categorical and part of the status quo, or as tentative and open to change (see section 6.10).

All these things are expressed in the grammar. Analysis therefore depends on an understanding of both the potential of the language and its realization in texts: both how the English language expresses such meanings and how this grammar is used in particular texts. This is why Halliday (1990) talks of grammar as a theory of human experience.

4.11 Summary

My argument in this chapter has been as follows.

1   Meanings are conveyed directly, by the choice of particular words, but they are also conveyed indirectly by patterns of co-occurrence: which

words collocate, and which words occur in which grammatical constructions. Such patterns are not directly observable, since they depend on abstract categories. But the analysis is not especially difficult: I have not used elaborate concepts or terminology in this chapter.

2   A language has a range of grammatical forms for encoding experience: grammatical analysis is therefore essential for analysing certain kinds of meanings.

3   Such analysis involves knowing how English grammar in general expresses these meanings, and also analysing which lexical and grammatical patterns have been selected (consciously or not) in particular texts.

4   Changing the words may not change the world. But drawing people's attention to such grammatical patterns can sometimes help to change their perceptions of the world. There is a potential for change. Grammar is choice. Different choices produce different meanings. The political nature of such choices is evident when analysis is applied to texts which represent relations between groups of people.

Appendix: Baden-Powell's Last Messages

Text G: Baden-Powell's last message to the Girl Guides

My Dear Guides, This is just a farewell note to you, the last that you will have from me. It is just to remind you when I have passed on that your business in life is to be happy and to make others happy. That sounds comfortable and easy, doesn't it? You begin making other people happy by doing good turns to them. You need not worry about making yourselves happy, as you will very soon find that that comes by itself; when you make other people happy, it makes you happy too. Later on, when you have a home of your own, by making it a bright and cheery one you will make your husband a happy man. If all homes were bright and cheery, there would be fewer public houses and the men would not want to go out to them but would stay at home. It may mean hard work for you, but it will bring its own reward then, if you keep your children healthy and clean and busy they will be happy. Happy children love their parents. There is nothing can give you greater joy than a loving child. I am sure God means us to be happy in this life. He has given us a world to live in that is full of beauties and wonders and He has given us not only eyes to see them but minds to understand them if only we have the sense to look at them in the light. We can enjoy bright sunshine and glorious views. We can see beauty in the flowers. We can watch with wonder how the seed produces the young plant which grows to a flower which in its turn will replace other flowers as they die off. For, though plants, like people, die their race does not die away but new ones are born and grow up to carry on The Creator's plan. So, do you see, you women are the chosen servants of God in two ways: first to carry on the race, to bring children into the world to replace the men and women who pass away; secondly, to bring happiness into the world by making happy homes and by being yourselves good, cheery comrades for your husbands and children. That is where you as Guides especially come in. By being a 'comrade', that is, by taking an interest in your husband's work and aspirations, you can help him with your sympathy and suggestions and so be a guide to him. Also, in bringing up your children, by strengthening and training their minds and characters as well as their bodies and health, you will be giving them to the better use and enjoyment of life. By giving out love and happiness in this way, you will gain for yourselves the return love of husband and children, and there is nothing better in this world. You will find that Heaven is not the kind of happiness somewhere up there in the skies after you are dead but right here now in this world in your own home. So guide others to happiness and you will bring happiness to yourselves and by doing this you will be doing what God wants of you. God be with you. Baden-Powell.

Text S: *Baden-Powell's last message to the Boy Scouts*

Dear Scouts, If you have ever seen the play 'Peter Pan' you will remember how the pirate chief was always making his dying speech because he was afraid that possibly when the time came for him to die he might not have time to get it off his chest. It is much the same with me, and so, although I am not at this moment dying, I shall be doing so one of these days and I want to send you a parting word of goodbye. Remember, it is the last you will ever hear from me, so think it over. I have had a most happy life and I want each one of you to have as happy a life too. I believe that God put us in this jolly world to be happy and enjoy life. Happiness doesn't come from being rich, nor merely from being successful in your career, nor by self-indulgence. One step towards happiness is to make yourself healthy and strong while you are a boy, so that you can be useful and so can enjoy life when you are a man. Nature study will show you how full of beautiful and wonderful things God has made the world for you to enjoy. Be contented with what you have got and make the best of it. Look on the bright side of things instead of the gloomy one. But the real way to get happiness is by giving out happiness to other people. Try and leave this world a little better than you found it and when your turn comes to die, you can die happy in feeling that at any rate you have not wasted your time but have done your best. 'Be prepared' in this way, to live happy and to die happy – stick to your Scout Promise always – even after you have ceased to be a boy – and God help you do it. Your friend, Robert Baden-Powell.

5

Judging the Facts: an Analysis of One Text in Its Institutional Context

There are no brute facts. (Firth, 1957b, p. 29)

There is a great field for practical semantics in the contextualization of crucial words in judicial remarks and judgements. (Firth, 1935, p. 69)

In this chapter I discuss various principles which underlie people's interpretation of language, especially language which is ambiguous and complex. My examples are from language in courtrooms, where such interpretation can have important consequences.

5.1   Organization of the Chapter

I discuss several examples from the large literature on legal language, especially examples concerning the connotations which words can convey. Other examples are then taken from the transcript of a judge's summing-up (about 5,800 words) at the end of a criminal trial. I have selected for analysis four linguistic features which are widely discussed in general textual studies or in studies of courtroom language: modal verbs (used ambiguously in English to express possibility or permission), presuppositions (central to the representation of innocence or guilt), syntactic complexity (relevant to the comprehensibility of spoken language) and the connotations of individual lexical items. Comparative data on the individual lexical items are drawn from a corpus of 120 million words of written and spoken English. Again in this chapter, concordances are used to show patterns of language use more clearly.

The main purpose of the analysis is to discuss whether lexical and grammatical features of a judge's style could influence a jury. That is, could linguistic factors affect a legal decision? I cannot prove that a jury did interpret a summing-up in a particular way: I cannot look inside their minds. But I can attempt to show that patterns of language are likely to be interpreted in a certain way, because that is how they are likely to be interpreted in everyday life. The linguist has to try and show how a reasonable person, doing his or her best to understand, is likely to interpret language.

I will show that, while the summing-up is very careful and explicit about some aspects of the jury's required decision, there are nevertheless instances where the language is unclear. A basic principle of the analysis, already illustrated in chapter 4, is that meanings are conveyed not only by individual words and their combination in sentences, but also by patterns of discourse and by breaks in those patterns.

The transcript of the judge's summing-up is from a case in which I was employed as an expert witness to prepare a report for a hearing in the Appeals Court. The defendant had been found guilty, and had appealed on the grounds that the summing-up had been biased against him.[1] The use of linguistic analysis in the courtroom provides striking examples of linguistics being applied to important social issues, often in circumstances where the outcome of the analysis could have considerable practical consequences, especially for a defendant. (See appendix for references to many such studies.) When linguistic analysis is applied in such circumstances, the standards of proof attainable in text analysis require a very careful statement.

In addition, courtroom language provides striking examples of the mediation of reality by language. It is a commonplace to lawyers that criminal cases are not tried on the 'facts', but on the spoken testimony of witnesses. The only access which the jury, judge and lawyers have to the facts is via the accounts which different witnesses give, and there are always at least two competing versions of these facts, from prosecution and defence.

5.2   Interactions in Social Institutions

Much discourse analysis studies face-to-face casual conversation between social equals, since this is arguably the most frequent and most basic kind of social interaction. However, many of the interactions which are crucial to people's lives take place within social institutions – such as schools and universities, doctors' surgeries and hospitals, police stations and courtrooms – where very different language conventions operate. And much of this talk, in meetings, examinations (of many kinds), consultations, interviews, negotiations and so on, has the purpose of reaching a decision. In such settings, the Gricean cooperative principle (Grice, 1967/1975) may not always hold. There may be confrontation and conflict, as well as co-operation. This is the case in the courtroom, where Gricean maxims (be truthful, be informative, be relevant, be clear) are supplemented by other conventions.

There is an increasing amount of such institutionalized discourse in modern highly industrialized societies. And it is within such institutions that strangers, from different social classes and language backgrounds, are in interaction with each other. There are therefore likely to be misunderstandings in precisely those encounters which lead to important decisions in people's lives.

5.3 The Linguistic Encoding of Facts

In a court of law, the utmost social significance of language is evident. Language is action, and under certain circumstances, speech acts themselves may be criminal acts: consider slander, libel and defamation, threats, blackmail, bribery or perjury (Kniffka, 1981; Shuy, 1993). But speech acts in the courtroom itself are also social action. For example, a defendant's *admission* of guilt will have real consequences. And the *verdict* given by a jury and the judge's *sentencing* are speech acts in the strong sense of utterances which create a state of affairs in the world.

Furthermore, courtrooms are highly institutionalized and depend on special rules of language use: not only elaborate forms of address and ultra-politeness (such as *M'Lud, My Learned Friend*), but rules restricting leading questions (in examination-in-chief, though not in cross-examination) and restricting what may be said (for example, rules about hearsay evidence). Such rules may be at variance with everyday conversation. For example, it is common for casual conversation to consist of repeating and commenting on what other people have said: witnesses in a trial are not allowed to repeat such hearsay evidence, and many witnesses find this restriction difficult to understand and very difficult to obey.

A trial is aimed at resolving a dispute between two versions of reality, and language counts for everything. In the British adversarial or accusatorial system (sometimes also called the sporting theory of justice), truth is expected to emerge from opposing representations. The defence and prosecution prepare their cases separately and in secret, and resolving the conflicting accounts depends largely on the linguistic skills of those involved on the day in question. Very little is cut and dried beforehand, since no independent legal mind has looked at the case as a whole before the trial (Berlins and Dyer, 1989, p. 125). Witnesses and lawyers attempt to present, in the language they use, an unambiguous definition of past events. And what the jury (and others) have access to is not the facts themselves, but multiple definitions of the facts expressed in language: a case is always tried on facts as they are made to appear in testimony. For a jury, the crucial courtroom audience, it is therefore not possible to separate what happened from the words used to talk about it (O'Barr, 1982, p. 97, provides a good statement of these points).

Furthermore, the presentation of these versions is carried out at an abstract and formalized level. There are various links in the chain which the jury does not see, since the defendant will have instructed solicitors who have in turn instructed barristers. The lawyers themselves also have no access to the facts except via their interviews with their client and possibly other people involved. And, in the court itself, the plaintiff and defendant are not allowed to confront each other directly. Their versions are presented via barristers to the judge and jury, with many constraints on the permitted form of evidence. In American courts, members of the jury are forbidden to make independent visits to the scene of an incident: they may consider only facts as they are presented in court (O'Barr, 1982, p. 42), and this is generally also true of cases in Britain.

The underlying propositional structure of all the discourse in a jury trial, even if it lasts days, weeks or months, is very simple. There are just two conflicting propositions:

> The prosecution says: "You did it."

> The defence says: "No, I didn't."

This is a very clear case of the linguistic and social construction of reality. A jury always has to contend with conflicting versions of reality, at least two, from the prosecution and the defence, but possibly many more. The evidence is mainly what witnesses say in the witness box (and also what expert witnesses may have reported in writing). And at the end of a trial, the closing speeches from prosecuting and defending counsel and the judge's summing-up are further interpretations of these interpretations, conflicting summaries of original testimony and so on.

The basic discourse sequence of a jury trial (at least the parts which take place in the presence of the jury), which shows the sequence of conflicting versions of events, is as follows:

The jury are sworn in.

The Clerk of Court reads the indictment and says: 'To those charges the defendant has pleaded not guilty, and it is your task to say whether he (or she) is guilty or not guilty.'

Prosecuting counsel's opening speech.

Evidence:

Prosecuting counsel's examination of witness.

Defending counsel's cross-examination of witness.

Prosecuting counsel's re-examination of witness.

Repeated for witnesses 1 to *n* . . .

'That is the case for the prosecution.'

Defending counsel's opening speech.

Defending counsel's examination of witness.

Prosecuting counsel's cross-examination of witness.

Defending counsel's re-examination of witness.

Usually starting with the defendant, then repeated for witnesses 1 to *n* . . .

'That is the case for the defence.'

End of evidence.

Prosecuting counsel's closing speech.

Defending counsel's closing speech.

Judge's summing-up.

The jury retire to consider their verdict, then return, and the foreman/woman gives the verdict.

If guilty:

Prosecuting counsel's presentation of defendant's 'antecedents': personal details and previous convictions, if any.

Defending counsel's plea in mitigation.

Judge's sentence.

There can be variations on the pattern: for example, there may be more than one barrister on each side; defence counsel usually does not make an opening speech unless the case is complex; prosecuting and defending counsel do not always cross-examine and re-examine; the judge may ask questions, and so may the jury in written form.

Because the law relies on interpretations of language, the standards by which words are interpreted are inevitably different for the legal profession and the lay public, and it is inevitable that judge and jury will use language differently. People interpret discourse according to their own conventions, and it is therefore very likely that the jury are not always able to suspend their common-sense interpretations of language in ways the court may require of them. This is another potential source of misunderstandings.

5.4   Words and Connotations

It is a general principle of language use that the same event can be referred to in an indefinitely large number of ways. If witnesses or counsel talk about events using certain terms, it is likely that the jury will also use these terms to think about them.

Danet (1980) analyses an American case where a doctor carried out a late abortion which led to his being convicted of manslaughter, and where vocabulary was an explicit concern in the trial itself. In such a case, one might say: *the fetus was aborted* or *the baby was murdered*. Although each phrase can be used to refer to the same external reality, very different moral points of view are encoded, and different assumptions about offence and guilt are implied. During the trial, the lawyers negotiated the different connotations of terms such as *products of conception, fetus, male human being, male child, baby boy* (and many others). When, as here, the meaning of an act is itself ambiguous (When does life begin? What do we mean by a person?), then it is impossible to separate what happened from the language used to talk about it. And such semantic choices, with their presuppositions, are crucial to the outcome of the trial: if no person existed, then no manslaughter could have occurred.

There is always a category shift when one moves from ways of talking to ways of thinking. And it is impossible to discover what effect such lexical choices actually had on the jury. But one can analyse the points of view from which such lexical choices are made, the incommensurable frames of reference they assume and the presuppositions they make. For example, *baby boy* connotes helplessness, in a caring frame of reference which presupposes that there is a life to be ended. Words such as *fetus, abortion* and *termination* assume a medical frame of reference, rather than a criminal one. No terms are neutral. Choice of words expresses an ideological position.

In a much cited experiment, relevant to courtroom cases, Loftus and Palmer (1974) provide empirical evidence that lexical choices can influence perception and memory. They showed people a film of a traffic accident, and then asked questions such as *How fast were the cars going when they hit each other?* But they varied the question by using different verbs, and this influenced people's estimates of the speed. Higher estimates were given with verbs such as SMASH and COLLIDE than with BUMP and CONTACT. Furthermore, when they were asked *Did you see any broken glass?* (there was none in the film), people who had been asked about the cars *smashing* into each other were more likely to say "yes". That is, using the word SMASH triggered preconceptions both about speed and about likely consequences (broken glass). Individual words evoked a frame of reference in which various assumptions were made.

In this experimental case, subjects had direct access to the event itself, in the form of the film, yet language still influenced their perception and memory. In a real trial the jury have no such access: they have nothing but the words used in the courtroom, which makes it even more plausible that words will influence assumptions.

Such connotations can be seen in characteristic collocates. In a 120 million word corpus, I studied the collocates of the simple past tense forms in the semantic field of "hit". HIT itself has a wide range of uses, often metaphorical and/or in fixed phrases (*hit for six, hit rock bottom*). Collocates show this wide range:

> areas, badly, bottom, car, earthquake, flooding, hard, hardest, jackpot, recession, sales, six, target

BUMP has connotations of clumsiness. *Bumped* collocates with

> accidentally, car, head, lurched, stumbled

COLLIDE is used predominantly with large vehicles. *Collided* collocates with

> aircraft, car, jet, lorry, mid-air, plane, ship, tanker, train, trawler, vehicle

SMASH has connotations of crime and violence. *Smashed* collocates with

> bottles, broken, bullet, car(s), glass(es), looted, police, windscreen, window(s)

STRIKE has more metaphorical uses or is used with natural disasters. *Struck* collocates with

> blow, disaster, earthquake, lightning, tragedy

5.5   The Data

I will now take examples from the summing-up by the judge at the end of a case of assault occasioning actual bodily harm. This is the technical name for an offence which can cover serious incidents, and can carry a prison sentence of up to five years (Clarkson, 1987, p. 119). In common-sense terms, the present case concerned a minor incident. One man was accused of hitting and slightly bruising another man, and the jury found the defendant guilty. Following O'Barr (1982), I will discuss whether apparently minor differences in presentational style may make major differences in the evaluation of accounts of events.

The data are the written transcript of the judge's spoken summing-up. During a trial, the judge takes detailed long-hand notes of testimony, and uses these notes to sum up at the end. Short-hand records and/or audio-recordings of everything that is said in court, including the summing-up, are made by official court reporters, and these can later be used to prepare transcripts. I have had no access to the testimony given in the case, and cannot therefore comment on the fairness of the summing-up in the sense of how accurately it summarizes what witnesses said. I can look only at internal features of the summing-up itself.

I also have no way of evaluating the accuracy of the transcript. Court reporters are supposed to transcribe verbatim what is said in court, but Walker (1990) studies how they transform in many ways what is said, by prescriptively tidying up features of normal spoken language. However, since it is the transcript itself which is considered in any appeal, that is what is relevant to my analysis here.

5.6   Analysis of the Data

O'Barr (1982, pp. 16ff) provides good examples of legal language of various kinds. Some legal language is highly formal. Examples from the summing-up include a material inconsistency; learned defence Counsel

It is also often repetitive. Examples from the data include

> wholly separate and distinct; you and you alone; thinks or seems to think; well and good; the first and most important; honest and genuine mistakes; a statement or statements; unless and until; untruthful and deliberate lying; reliability and accuracy; how far you can or ought to or do rely

Some examples are tautologies: lying is, by definition, untruthful and deliberate. But such pairs or lists of near synonyms are a common general characteristic of legal English. Compare well known examples such as

> without let or hindrance; null and void; to have and to hold; each and every; breaking and entering; rest residue and remainder

These double or triple constructions derive partly from early legal English, where French/Latin and Anglo-Saxon terms were used alongside each other. Clerks were not sure if the terms meant the same, so they put in both for safety, on the belt and braces principle (O'Barr, 1982, p. 16).

However, on occasion, the judge uses doublets or triplets where the words do differ significantly in meaning:

> *intentionally or recklessly* applied *unlawful* force

> *unlawful* and *intentional or reckless* application of force

These are everyday words, but they have technical legal meanings which are discussed at length in books on law. For example, Clarkson (1987, pp. 58ff, 64ff) discusses: *intentional, malicious, negligent* and *reckless* (as in *reckless driving*). But the judge gives no warning to the jury that they have technical meanings: they may assume that this is part of his stylistic habit of being verbose. On the other hand, it would be dangerous if their meaning in the law departed too far from everyday meanings, since it is juries of ordinary men and women who have to interpret such phrases. Jury cases are designed for those who are not legally trained, and who are therefore dependent on everyday language and how it is understood.

Jurors also have to use common-sense reasoning to assess the credibility and plausibility of competing interpretations of events. (O'Barr (1982, pp. 42–6) discusses the centrality of such demeanour evidence, but the complete lack of guidelines to evaluate it.) In interpreting the summing-up, jury members will therefore be asking themselves, just as they do with everyday conversation: The judge said X, but what did he mean? What was he implying? Why did he phrase it in that way? What was he trying to tell us?

Counsel for the prosecution and defence give, in their closing speeches, accounts which are inevitably in opposition: interpretations which explicitly attempt to show the defendant in a bad or good light. But the judge's summing-up should be from an independent, impartial source. The judge's role is to decide legal issues, not to express views on the facts or on the witnesses, and certainly not on the result (Berlins and Dyer, 1989, pp. 102ff; Jones, 1983, pp. 121ff). In terms of content, a summing-up has essentially two parts: directions and explanations of the law, and a summary of the main points of evidence, concentrating on what is in dispute or seems contradictory. The judge is the judge of the law, and gives the jury directions on how they must interpret the law. If he or she gets this wrong, this could be the basis of an appeal. But the jury are the judges of the facts, and they must make inferences about who is to be believed about what happened. This basic distinction accounts both for things which a judge says and for the way in which they are said.

The judge in the present case made explicit to the jury several problematic aspects of language use in the courtroom. He drew the jury's attention to the inevitably selective nature of his summing-up. He recommended the jury to disregard his comments if they did not find them helpful. He directed the jury to disregard the content of what witnesses had previously said in statements to the police, even if this contradicts what they said in court. He distinguished between everyday interpretative principles (such as there's no smoke without fire) and the more rigorous interpretative principles required by the court. He directed the jury that, if they were not sure of the defendant's guilt, then they must find him not guilty. He commented on the technical, legal meaning of several terms. He repeated several times that it is for the prosecution to prove guilt, not for the defence to prove innocence. He pointed out that the defendant is inevitably under stress, and that this could affect his perceived credibility.

Some of these instructions, as the judge himself is pointing out, are at variance with how language is interpreted in everyday life. For example, it is probably a legal fiction that words can be 'struck from the record'. It is unlikely that a jury can simply forget some parts of what has been said to them. In fact, asking that they be ignored may, on the contrary, draw attention to them. So, the judge's remarks show that he is very sensitive to discrepancies between court procedures and everyday communication (O'Barr, 1982, pp. 6, 41, 94, 102).

5.6.1   Length and discourse markers

The summing-up covers 11 pages of official transcript: about 5,850 words. It probably took between 35 and 45 minutes to deliver. The jury could not possibly have retained all the details, and would therefore be susceptible to overall impressions created by the language used. Many research studies have been done on lectures (which are typically similar in length to this summing-up): Bligh (1972) reviews over 60 studies on how successfully listeners can retain material presented as lectures. One finding (Bligh, 1972; Beard, 1972) is that listeners' attention is typically high at the beginning of a lecture, and falls, with local peaks and troughs, until just before the end, when it rises somewhat. In addition, audiences experience micro-sleeps which result in temporary complete loss of attention.

The judge is doubtless aware of this, and marks the beginning of sections in his summing-up, to attract the attention of the jury to significantly new points, usually by saying: *Well, members of the jury.* . . . Such markers are, however, less frequent in the second half of the summing-up, when the jury's attention is likely to be flagging. The two cases which do occur in the second half both preface comments on alleged inconsistencies in the defence testimony. The judge marks clearly when he is coming to the end:

Well, members of the jury, there we are. At the end of the day, . . .

The jury are most likely to have retained points made at the beginning, after such markers of discourse organization, and right at the end, when they realize the concluding points are being made.

5.6.2   Connotations of individual words

The case involved two men. It was not in dispute who was involved, but only whether or not one had struck the other. Words which convey connotations of emotion or violence are therefore particularly relevant to interpretations of conflicting testimony.

The words *aggravate, aggravated, annoyed, irritation, mad* and *temper* occurred several times (see concordance 5.1). Such repetition is likely to make an idea salient for the jury. A similar case occurs with *reeled* (quoted from a prosecution witness): this occurs several times (see concordance 5.1), with reference to the plaintiff falling backward after he had been allegedly assaulted by the defendant. The word carries an implication that the plaintiff was struck or pushed, and/or became giddy, etc., and is likely to be

All personal and place names have been changed in these data.
Mr P = plaintiff. Mr D = defendant.
Mr DWA = defence witness A, etc.

ar what was said. I saw Mr D lift his arm up and the other man reeled, his hat fell off and he fell against the wall." Mr D seems to have gesticulated. "I think his hand caught Mr P because he reeled. He did catch him. Mr P reeled against the wall." Now, his hand caught Mr P because he reeled. He did catch him. Mr P reeled against the wall." Now, members of the jury, it was put to tep and went backwards towards the shop, P was in the mews and reeled around saying, "I've been hit, I've been hit." I said, "Don't t. What else would I do with it? The man was clearly trying to aggravate me. He didn't aggravate me at all." And then Mr D with it? The man was clearly trying to aggravate me. He didn't aggravate me at all." And then Mr D said this, and you may it was perhaps a rather curious answer for somebody who wasn't aggravated at all. Taking off Mr P's hat, he said, "It was my way s was this just the last straw for Mr D? Had he been wound up, aggravated as he put it, by Mr P and did he lose his temper and he said, "It was my way of showing that I wasn't particularly annoyed." Now, you're going to have to ask yourselves was knock his hat off when striking Mr P's head in an explosion of irritation over this petty matter? "P was walking out and I was u are satisfied so that you are sure that this man allowed his irritation to boil over and he lost control of himself and struck to have their special little bin and it has been driving Mr D mad for a long time that everybody roundabout uses it as if it were wound up, aggravated as he put it, by Mr P and did he lose his temper and knock his hat off when striking Mr P's

Concordance 5.1 REEL, AGGRAVATE, etc. in Judge's summing-up.

remembered by the jury, both because of the repetition and because it paints a small dramatic picture. The verb has connotations of staggering, unsteadiness, dizziness, jerky movements, and of violence and disaster.

Examples [all A] from a general corpus show that the word connotes confusion and/or violence due to some outside force:

> sends the pulse racing and the senses reeling
>
> reeling from shock
>
> blood trickled into his mouth as he reeled backward
>
> bashing X on the ear and sending him reeling backward
>
> the man was reeling drunk
>
> the markets reeled under the uncertainty
>
> the shipping industry is still reeling from last March's Exxon Valdez disaster

I also checked the most frequent and typical collocates of REEL in a large (120 million word) corpus, using methods which I will discuss in detail in section 7.7. These connotations are confirmed by characteristic collocates of the word forms *reeled* and *reeling*. (I omitted *reel* and *reels* to avoid irrelevant phrases such as *Scottish reel* and *reels of cotton*.) The collocates included

> blow, blows, drunk, mind, senses, send, sent, shock

5.6.3   Modal verbs

Meanings are conveyed not only by individual words, but by patterns of words used by a speaker. Words take part of their meaning from the context in which they occur.

Concordance 5.2 provides a concordance of all examples of the words *may* and *might* (24 plus 7 instances). The majority occur in phrases such as:

you may think (that)	12 instances
you may feel (that)	2 instances
you may remember	2 instances
you may/might find	3 instances
you may/might ask/say to yourselves	4 instances

evidence to remind you of what was said here. When I sum up I may very well make comments upon the evidence. If you agree

that resulted in bruising. That is what it comes down to, you may think. That is the prosecution's case. And let me make this

hat is no offence and the verdict is not guilty. However, Mr P may have suffered an injury, whether because he was shocked by

it the defence, not for the defence to prove its case. And you may think that there are three different types of witnesses. The

e doctor. He examined me." Well, there was some confusion, you may think, as to whether Mr P spoke just to Mrs PWA or to some

that is a material inconsistency, pay attention to it, but you may think really it doesn't matter a great deal. She said, "I

. I saw Mr P sway and fall against the wall of the close." You may think this is a rather more emphatic description of her evi

in her statement. The reason I remind you of this is that you may feel that this helps you in deciding whether there might have

n Mrs PWA and Mr P to trump up a case against Mr D because you may think to yourselves, if there was such a conspiracy, one thing Mr

interviewing Mr DWA and Mr DWB, the defence witnesses, and you may think that there is some force in this criticism, that a thorough

right eye. And, members of the jury, one of the questions you may care to ask yourselves is this: if Mr D did not cause any y

ed when I give evidence on oath." That is the first point. You may also take it into account as part of the evidence as a whole b

side him and said nothing because there was no point." And you may remember that is rather different from what his Counsel sug

didn't aggravate me at all." And then Mr D said this, and you may think it was perhaps a rather curious answer for somebody

nce to swearing and so forth. And then Mr D was asked what you may think a pertinent question: "Well, why didn't you tell that to th

ver made by Mr D to any bad language by the defendant, and you may ask yourselves if this was the reason why Mr D returned the

Land Rover and was carrying a computer to the shop which, you may remember, was totally different from what both Mr D and Mr

bin, but they take no notice." Then he said this which is, you may think, a quite significant and important piece of evidence: Mr

laughing and continued working." And, members of the jury, you may think that is slightly different from the general picture given b

the end of the day, if you think that is what happened or what may have happened – because it is not for this defendant to prove

ause it is not for this defendant to prove his innocence; what may have happened is that the defendant just removed Mr P's hat

if you are satisfied so that you are sure as to that, then you may feel that the prosecution has proved its case and it will be

number, either a lady or a man, who acts as your foreman. You may find it very helpful for you to appoint a foreman at the

er, guilty or not guilty, on which you are all agreed, and you may think that in this case you will be able to do so. However,

ct according to the evidence and that is the true verdict. You might find yourselves in the opposite frame of mind. You might

. You might find yourselves in the opposite frame of mind. You might say to yourselves, "We are satisfied so that we are sure that

circumstances, no problem – verdict, decision not guilty. You might say to yourselves, however, somewhere in between. You

You might find yourselves, however, somewhere in between. You might say to yourselves, "Well, maybe he's guilty and maybe he

ou come to the conclusion that that is what did happen or what might have happened – because it is not for Mr D to prove that

that n a review of all the evidence, that all this defendant did or might have done was simply thumb and forefinger to lift off Mr

hat you may feel that this helps you in deciding whether there might have been a conspiracy between Mrs PWA and Mr P to

Concordance 5.2   MAY and MIGHT in Judge's summing-up.

Because it is the jury who are the judges of the facts, and because therefore the judge cannot pass judgement on those facts, it is almost inevitable that a summing-up will contain phrases of the kind *you may think, . . . and it is entirely for you to decide . . .* [A], when discussing inconsistencies in testimony. However, the modal verb *may* is ambiguous in English. It can denote permission (*you may go now: I've finished* [I]), or possibility (*he may go, or he may not* [I]). Further, it is well known that there is significant social class variation in speakers' uses of modal verbs. *May* is largely restricted to middle class Anglo-English (e.g. Brown and Miller, 1980).

In the following cases, *may* is used as a true modal of possibility. Mr P is the plaintiff. Mr D is the defendant.

> Mr P *may* have suffered an injury . . . because . . .

> but *you may think* really it doesn't matter a great deal

> that is what happened or what *may* have happened . . . what *may* have happened is . . .

In one case, the judge expresses a proposition in the *may*-clause, and then denies it:

> *you may think* that x, . . . but the fact is that y

In one case, it is unclear whether the intended interpretation is *may* of permission ("this would be permissible evidence") or *may* of possibility ("it is possible that x"):

> *you may* also take it into account

But in the majority of cases there seems to be no tentativeness intended at all. In these cases, *may* is used without its literal meanings of permission or possibility:

> when I sum up I *may very well* make some comments upon the evidence

It is surely certain that he will.

> what the Crown has to prove is x . . . that is what it comes down to, *you may think*

In context, this seems a definitive summary of the essential issue.

> *you may think* that there are three different types of witnesses

The categorization which follows seems comprehensive.

> there was some confusion, *you may think*, as to . . .

In context, it seems clear that there was.

In several cases, because of the evaluative adjectives and adverbs (italicized), the judge appears to be telling the jury what he himself thinks:

> *you may think* this is a *rather more emphatic* description
>
> *you may think* it was perhaps a *rather curious* answer
>
> Mr D was asked what *you may think* a *pertinent* question
>
> which is, *you may think*, a *quite significant and important* piece of evidence
>
> and, members of the jury, *you may think* that is *slightly different*

(These adverb–adjective constructions seem to me to have middle class connotations, but I admit I have no corpus evidence of this.)

In contrast to *may*, all occurrences of *might* are genuine modals of possibility (see again concordance 5.2). This is further evidence that *may* is used in a different way.

In summary, because of the structure of a summing-up, phrases such as *you may think* almost inevitably occur frequently. However,

- *may* occurs only in some social dialects of British English;
- it has two main meanings, permission and possibility;
- it is used in different senses in the summing-up;
- it sometimes signals possibility, but more often, it signals what the judge himself thinks.

The last case occurs because a pattern is established within the summing-up: the pattern has a micro-history in the text (see sections 1.4 and 4.5), and becomes part of the judge's style. Uncertain instances are likely to be interpreted in line with the pattern. Thus, the implication of phrases such as *you may think that x* can become: "it would be reasonable or natural for you to think that x, (or even) I am instructing you to accept that x".

A key instance is therefore a comment towards the end of the summing-up:

you may feel that the prosecution has proved its case

I comment further on this example below.

5.6.4 Presuppositions

In discussions of guilt and innocence, presuppositions about the defendant's actions and emotions are important to the messages conveyed. I use the term *presupposition* in a linguistic, not psychological, sense. I cannot know what was in the judge's mind, but I can identify presuppositions in the words he used. It would then be natural for a jury to conclude that these presuppositions were actually held by the judge. If, for example, I say

John's brother has been abroad for years [I]

then my sentence presupposes that "John has a brother". And it would be natural for you to conclude that I actually believe that he has a brother.

In simple cases, a test for a presupposition is that it remains constant in negative or interrogative versions of the clause. Consider this example: the first version is attested (but see below) in the summing-up.

this man allowed his irritation to boil over [A]

this man did not allow his irritation to boil over [M]

did this man allow his irritation to boil over? [M]

All three versions presuppose that "this man was irritated". The attested version further asserts that "he allowed his irritation to boil over". (On definitions of presuppositions, see also section 8.7, and Levinson, 1983, pp. 167ff.)

Almost any sentence at all contains presuppositions, usually several. But the following are cases where presuppositions imply that the defendant is guilty of an offence, and that this is a natural thing to think or is taken for granted. I identify presuppositions in the italicized sections of the judge's remarks [all A], and make them explicit between double quote marks. Mr D is the defendant.

Some presuppositions are conveyed by tense forms of the verb, as in it has been *driving Mr D mad for a long time* (presupposition: "Mr D has been mad/annoyed for a long time, and is still mad/annoyed")

or by individual verbs, as in

had he [Mr D] been . . . aggravated *as he put it?* (presupposition: "Mr D had said he was aggravated")

what Mr D *admits* is that he did it twice (presupposition: "Mr D did something wrong and/or he did something which he or someone else had previously denied")

he [the defendant] *starts off* entitled to be believed (presupposition: "the situation then changes")

Contrast a formulation such as *He is entitled to be believed* [I], which would convey no such presupposition.

Sometimes the presuppositions are difficult to interpret, because they are embedded in hypothetical constructions. A fuller context for the first example above is

but on the other hand if you are satisfied so that you are sure that this man allowed his irritation to boil over . . . [A]

The presupposition is embedded under the projecting clause (see section 6.10) *you are sure that*.

any offence, *let alone one as unpleasant as this*

The presupposition ("an unpleasant offence has occurred") is embedded under the hypothetical *any*.

he is likely to be convicted of *this assault upon that old man*

whether it is likely that a person with such a character would have committed *this offence*

The presuppositions ("an assault on that old man occurred"; and "this offence occurred") are embedded under projecting clauses containing a hypothetical *likely*.

Such presuppositions are crucial in the present case, since what is at stake is the definition of certain events. If it is assumed that an act did occur, and was thereby an offence, then there is only one possible actor.

5.6.5   *Syntactic complexity*

O'Barr (1981, p. 395; 1982, p. 27) discusses American research on jury instructions which shows that they are 'poorly understood by most jurors'. In particular, he discusses one syntactic construction as 'the basis of the incomprehensibility of typical jury instructions'. Most sentences in English have the main verb early, followed by qualifying clauses. Sentences which consist of complex qualifying clauses, followed by the main verb, are more difficult to understand.

Consider this example from the summing-up:

> . . . a verdict of guilty . . . *and* that is the true verdict

This occurs at the end of a complex sequence of qualifying clauses, concerning hypothetical states of affairs:

> if you are in that state of mind, then, although obviously it is unpleasant to find any fellow human being guilty of any offence, let alone one as unpleasant as this, it will be your duty to return *a verdict of guilty* because you have sworn to return a true verdict according to the evidence *and that is the true verdict* [A, italicization added]

In outline, the sequence is:

> if you [the jury] are in that state of mind
>
> then, although *a*
>
> let alone *b*
>
> it will be your duty to *c* [main clause]
>
> because *d*
>
> and that is the true verdict [main clause]

In addition, the syntax is ambiguous. The final clause could be taken to mean: "the true verdict is guilty". The ambiguity results from the use of *and*, which stands in an unclear relation to the preceding conditional. (Contrast: "*If* you are in that state of mind, *then* that is the true verdict.")

Another case of syntactic ambiguity is this:

> however, Mr P may have suffered an injury . . . because he fell back and hurt himself

Again, the intended logical link with the preceding point is unclear. Is the judge directing the jury that if this is what happened, then this *would* count as assault, or *would not*? This point seems crucial to the jury's decision. In this connection, the phrase *occasioning actual bodily harm* is used three times. Again, the implication of causality is unclear. It is unclear (to me) whether *occasioning*, in this technical phrase, is intended to include both direct and indirect causation. (In fact, the jury requested clarification from the judge on precisely this point about causation. The judge clarified that direct causation was meant.)

Almost the very last thing the judge says, before he refers to arrangements for lunch, and likely to be remembered for that reason alone, is

> *you may feel* that the prosecution has proved its case and it will be your distasteful duty to return a verdict of guilty

Again this occurs after a complex sequence of *if*-clauses:

> Well, members of the jury, there we are. At the end of the day, if you think that is what happened or what may have happened – because it is not for this defendant to prove his innocence; what may have happened is that the defendant just removed Mr P's hat by lifting it off between his thumb and forefinger and dropping it to the ground – verdict not guilty. But, on the other hand, if you are satisfied so that you are sure that this man allowed his irritation to boil over and he lost control of himself and struck out at P's head, hitting his – knocking his hat off and then striking his head, and that resulted in that bruising about which we have heard, if you are satisfied so that you are sure as to that, then *you may feel that the prosecution has proved its case and it will be your distasteful duty to return a verdict of guilty* [italicization added]

Here the sequence is

> at the end of the day, if you think *x*
>
> because *a* . . . ;
>
> what may have happened is *b* . . .
>
> but . . . if you are satisfied that *c* and *d*
>
> and that resulted in *e*
>
> if you are satisfied so that you are sure as to that
>
> then *you may feel* that . . .

The clauses also follow *you may feel*, as discussed above. It is therefore easy to interpret this as a direction or suggestion to the jury to find the defendant guilty.

5.7 Conclusion

Linguists should always be prepared to state what degree of confidence they have in their analyses, and this responsibility is particularly important when the analysis could have important social consequences. I will therefore draw attention to some aspects of my analysis.

I think it likely that members of the jury interpreted utterances in the summing-up in line with the interpretative principles which I have set out. In particular, features of the language are likely to have led the jury to believe (correctly or not) that the judge thought that the defendant was guilty, and that this was a natural thing to think.

I am very aware that there are many features of the data which I have not analysed. Even for a text as short as 5,000 words or so, there are no methods of comprehensive text analysis: a listing of all presuppositions in all clauses would be very many times longer than the original text, and less comprehensible. However, it is possible to select for analysis features (such as modal verbs) which many different studies have shown to convey important social meanings.

As I emphasize elsewhere in this book, there are always interpretative jumps when one moves from ways of talking to ways of thinking, and from normal strategies of interpretation to actual interpretations of a given text: it is impossible to discover how a jury actually understood a given summing-up. However, I can identify principles and strategies (also demonstrated in other studies) which reasonable people will use, when they are trying to be cooperative and to understand what is being said to them.

Such analysis certainly involves selection, but it makes use of empirical evidence in other comparable studies. In addition, comparative corpus data can provide direct empirical evidence about the connotations of words. Chapters 6 and 7 propose methods of making more systematic comparisons between what occurs and what might be expected to occur, and between individual instances and norms.

This chapter has provided examples, from one social context, of how language mediates our understanding of past events. Such mediation is very widespread. For example, historians also try to understand past events which can no longer be directly observed. Like participants in a courtroom, they have no unmediated access to the past, but must rely on contemporary witnesses and on various forms of documentation. Their primary sources of evidence are predominantly written documents (plus other forms of statistical material and so on). And secondary sources take the form of contemporary commentaries or more recent interpretations by other historians. (For detailed case studies on language and history see Corfield, 1991.)

Students will be able to think of many other cases where the 'same' past event is represented differently in different texts, such as history books for children of different ages, or newspapers of different political persuasions. Analyses could provide interesting student projects on how facts are represented in texts.

Appendix: Other Studies of Courtroom Language

Language and the law is now a major area of applied linguistics, and a substantial literature shows how linguistic analysis can be important for social issues. Useful reviews are provided by Tiersma (1993) and Gibbons (1994). Some studies particularly relevant to my analysis are as follows.

Levi and Walker (1990) locate work on language and the law within the tradition of legal realism. A formal tradition holds that correct decisions are reached in court cases if purely rational and deductive procedures are followed. However, a realist tradition argues, as I have done in this chapter, that the law is inseparable from society, and therefore accords importance to empirical reports of social behaviour, including language.

Probably the best known work on the language of the court itself is by O'Barr (1981, 1982), one of the creators of the field of language and the law. Particularly relevant to my chapter is his discussion (1981, pp. 395ff, 402ff) of research on whether juries can reliably understand jury instructions. Walter (1988) studied closing speeches by lawyers in American courts. She emphasizes the low average formal education of jury members and the very mixed cross-section of society which an average jury represents. This is traditionally held as a strength of the jury system, but it can lead to the problems of communication across social groups which I have mentioned above. And Levi (1992) discusses the language of jury instructions in an American murder trial. She found vague and confusing language, syntactically complex and containing words which the jurors probably would not understand: they were misunderstood when tested on college students.

Other work studies cross-examining strategies (Atkinson and Drew, 1979), or other aspects of courtroom language, such as plea-bargaining, small claims courts and lawyer–client interaction. Harris (1984a, b) analyses audio-recordings from British magistrates courts, to study how decisions are reached when largely working class defendants have to negotiate with largely middle class magistrates.

One of the most important studies is Berk-Seligson's (1990) careful linguistic and ethnographic analysis of Spanish–English interpreting in American courts. The accuracy of such interpreting is an area of crucial public concern, and her book has important implications for the administration of justice. Her main data comprise 114 hours of audio-recorded courtroom proceedings involving 18 interpreters. She studies the differences between English and Spanish in the expression of causality, agency, responsibility and blame: inevitably a substantial part of the meanings expressed in any court. Any language has a variety of ways of talking about causation and agency. For example, English provides transitives, intransitives and passives with and without agent, to talk about the same event, but variously foregrounding or omitting the agent. Possibilities include

the defendant broke it

it was broken by the defendant

it got broken

it broke

Spanish provides an overlapping but different set of possibilities, including two different reflexive constructions with no direct equivalent in English. The passive is common in spoken English legal usage. Although it is syntactically possible in Spanish, it is very formal, and hence rare in spoken language. These differences force interpreters to take decisions (possibly unconscious) in an area of meaning crucial to court cases. Often no one-to-one translation equivalent exists. If, in addition, the interpreter is sympathetic or unsympathetic to the defendant or witnesses, there is considerable scope for skewing what is said. This is all thoroughly documented from the book's audio-recordings. And Berk-Seligson concludes that the language used by interpreters can affect judicial proceedings in subtle or dramatic ways. In chapter 6, I provide a more detailed analysis of such verb forms in English, and their implications for the expression of agency and responsibility.

Other work relevant to my chapter includes analyses of how an average person interprets language. Johnson (1990, pp. 300ff) discusses how texts are interpreted by that strange legal fiction, the ordinary reasonable person. Specific cases have involved whether advertising is 'legal, decent, honest and truthful', and how ordinary people might understand information on consumer products, such as health warnings on cigarette packets (see papers in Levi and Walker, 1990). A similar analysis was carried out by Prince (1982), who was an expert witness in a dispute over the meaning of a questionnaire for applicants for an insurance policy. The insurance company claimed that an applicant had lied in answering questions; Prince claimed (successfully) that he had followed reasonable principles of interpretation. The type of argument used by Prince is very close to my analysis above: it depends on the various principles and strategies which a cooperative hearer or reader has at his or her disposal in order to understand language in use. In particular, Prince illustrates the parallelism principle: sentences are interpreted on the basis of preceding sentences, when the sentences exhibit parallel structure. Gumperz (1982b, pp. 173ff) discusses a case in which features of the defendant's language may have detracted from his credibility, irrespective of the actual truth of what he said in evidence (see also O'Barr 1981, pp. 396, 403). It is one of the responsibilities of juries to assess the credibility of witnesses and to draw inferences from this.

Milroy (1984) summarizes the role of expert linguistic evidence in cases in the UK and USA. He points to 'the general ignorance (shared by the public and some experts alike) of the complexity of language' (p. 53), particularly with respect to structural differences between language varieties. His point that 'abstract systematic differences . . . are never obvious to ordinary speakers' (p. 68) is central to my analysis above of how language patterns are interpreted.

Work on language and the law has not been merely descriptive and theoretical. Linguists have been increasingly employed as expert witnesses in court cases, and have carried out analyses of such diverse data as: confessions alleged to have been fabricated by police (Coulthard, 1992a); misunderstandings between non-standard dialect speaking witnesses and police; and clandestine recordings made by law enforcement agencies and used in court as evidence of drug dealing, bribery, etc. (Shuy, 1993). Linguists have also been involved in many other aspects of forensic linguistics, which are less relevant to my discussion here. These include other aspects of speaker or writer identification, for example in cases of threats, blackmail or extortion.[2]

In addition to such work on legal cases, other relevant work includes analyses of the 'linguistics of blame': including Clark (1992) on how British tabloid newspapers report and represent crimes of violence, and Goldman (1994) on the grammatical expression of accident, chance, causation, responsibility and excuse in different languages and cultures.

6

Human and Inhuman Geography: a Comparative Analysis of Two Long Texts and a Corpus

Marx (1852) and Giddens (1984, p. 363) make points about representation:

> Human beings make their own history. (Marx)
>
> Human beings make their own geography. (Giddens)

6.1 Organization of the Chapter

The main data analysed in this chapter are two school books of 80,000 and 30,000 words. Comparative data are drawn mainly from a corpus of written English of one million words. For a few lexical items, comparative data are drawn from a much larger corpus of 120 million words.

Two main syntactic and semantic features are analysed, which concern, respectively, whether events and knowledge are attributed to agents:

- the expression of causativity in ergative constructions;
- the expression of modality in projecting *that*-clauses.

The main finding is that there are large (statistically significant) differences in the distribution of these syntactic patterns in the two books.

The analysis has three main aims. First, I discuss these differences as evidence of the different ideological stances expressed in the books. Second, I show some problems in the analysis: the use of corpus data for the stylistic analysis of long texts requires more detailed semantic analyses of verb classes than are currently available. The necessary baseline data on the use of such verbs can, in turn, come only from corpora. Third, I provide a criticism of work in critical discourse analysis, and argue that work which studies the relationship between grammar, text and ideology can be given a firmer descriptive and methodological basis with the help of computational methods.

6.2   Introductory Discussion

A basic principle of much of the discussion in this book is that the same events can always be talked about in different ways. Consider the following two paragraphs from a section on Scotland in a school geography textbook:

> The area covered by the HIDB [Highlands and Islands Development Board] lost population every decade between 1851 and 1961. Young people moved away to seek work in the industrial areas of lowland Scotland and England. Many emigrated to North America, Australia and New Zealand. There were few incentives to stay in the scattered farming and fishing communities.
>
> Since 1966, the population has increased slowly, helped by many types of development in the area. Big projects such as oil, aluminium and paper offered large numbers of jobs, although many were lost when the industries cut back or closed.

In this short fragment, different grammatical choices are made in talking about the same events. In some cases, the people involved are represented grammatically as being agents:

> young people moved away
>
> many emigrated

In other cases, there is no explicit mention of the people involved, as though things were natural events perhaps:

> the area . . . lost population
>
> the population has increased slowly
>
> many [jobs] were lost
>
> the industries . . . closed

All language in use shows variation, and it may simply be that the authors were trying (consciously or not) to vary their grammatical choices for stylistic reasons. However, if these choices tend in a particular direction, then these tendencies may nevertheless convey meanings to readers.

6.3   The Importance of Comparative Data

It would be quite wrong, however, to imply that such phrases in themselves mean that the book is somehow biased. Comments on individual words and phrases should always be made against the background of comparative data from a corpus. In order correctly to interpret such uses in a particular text, we require findings on how such words are used in the language in general. Using methods which I will describe in detail in section 7.7, I studied the typical collocates of LOSE across a corpus of 120 million words. The lemma is predominantly used in abstract and metaphorical meanings (this is a common finding for frequent words in the language). The most frequent collocates of LOSE are abstract nouns, including

> battle, confidence, control, election, interest, job(s), lives, sight (*as in* lose sight of), temper, touch, weight

Even other frequent, and more concrete, uses, such as *lose hair* and *lose money*, do not show a fully literal meaning of the word as in "to lose and not be able to find again".

Even if such abstract and metaphorical uses are very common in the language as a whole, this is no reason for authors to take them over uncritically. Analysis shows how such phrases can code reality repeatedly in familiar and reassuring ways, which come to seem natural or inevitable. The metaphors may be dead, in the sense that their implications are no longer conscious. But therein may lie their power to construct objects of thought.

In the 120 million word corpus (of which a large proportion consisted of texts from British newspapers), the word form *losses* occurred 8,795 times: 10 per cent of these occurrences were in the collocation *job losses*. Looked at from the other end, JOBS are *created*, but they are also

> axed, cut, eliminated, lost, shed

> Similarly, EMPLOYEE collocates with

> compensate, dismissals, layoff, relocate, retrain, sacking, severance

When an area is overlexicalized in such a way, it is often a sign of a socially taboo or delicate area (Halliday, 1978, pp. 164–82). Section 7.10 presents many further examples from the semantic area of "work, jobs, employment".

In the remainder of this chapter, I discuss how the use of grammatical constructions can be systematically compared across long texts and corpora.

6.4   Criticisms of Discourse Analysis

Since the mid-1970s, text and discourse analysis have been major areas in linguistics, with proliferating conferences, articles and books. Such work has also developed into substantial sub-areas, notably critical discourse analysis, which argues that all linguistic usage encodes ideological positions, and studies how language mediates and represents the world from different points of view. Fowler (1991a, p. 89), one of the originators of critical linguistics, provides this definition:

> Critical linguistics proposes that analysis using appropriate linguistic tools, and referring to relevant historical and social contexts, can bring ideology, normally hidden through the habitualization of discourse, to the surface for inspection.

My main concern in this book is with the 'appropriate linguistic tools'.

There are several recent books whose titles relate 'Language' and 'Discourse' to terms such as 'Ideology', 'Social Reality', 'Perspective' and 'Point of View' (e.g. Fowler, 1991b; Hodge and Kress, 1993; Lee, 1992; Martin, 1985; Simpson, 1993). Yet, although critical discourse analysis is now embodied in textbooks and undergraduate courses, there are major unresolved criticisms of its data, methods and theory.

One criticism questions the uncertain relation between discourse and grammar. In a thorough and severe review of discourse analysis in general, Frawley (1987, p. 361) has pointed out that 'the field has a negative identity'. By this he means that work frequently attacks formal linguistics, but thus derives its strength only negatively, from its criticisms of formal grammar. It 'blow[s] loud calls on the neo-empiricist, contextualist trumpet' (p. 361), but is often mere fact-gathering with no clear methods and theories. Frawley praises Halliday's work as the best in the selection he reviews, and Halliday (1985a, p. 345) has argued that 'the study of discourse . . . cannot properly be separated from the study of grammar that lies behind it.'

A second criticism questions the inadequate linguistic basis for many cultural and ideological interpretations of texts. For example, Bell (1991, p. 215) has criticized the 'lack of sound basic linguistic analysis' in much work on media language (a central topic in critical linguistics).

He argues that 'most studies [have] leapt past the groundwork to premature conclusions about the significance of poorly described linguistic patterns.'

A third criticism is very simple indeed: not much data is analysed. For example, Phillips (1989, p. 8) points to a limitation not only of sentence linguistics but also, ironically, of much text analysis, namely that it rarely analyses whole texts: 'Linguistics has traditionally been restricted to the investigation of the extent of language which can comfortably be accommodated on the average blackboard.'

So, in this chapter I discuss the descriptive and methodological bases of the linguistics of representation, as Fowler (1991b, p. 8) calls it. I will develop these criticisms of discourse analysis, by arguing the inseparability of grammar and discourse, and by providing a comparative analysis of grammatical patterns across two whole books and a small corpus.

6.5   Texts and Text Fragments

The main focus in this chapter is on methods of analysing long texts. At many recent conferences on applied linguistics and sociolinguistics, analyses of spoken and written texts have been increasingly common, but such analyses are often based on short texts or text fragments. For example, papers at recent conferences of the British Association for Applied Linguistics (Clark et al., 1990; Graddol et al., 1993) have analysed, *inter alia*, extracts from school textbooks, student writing, speeches by a government minister, simulated business conversations and magazine advertisements. Features of lexis, syntax and discourse have been analysed from various points of view; for example, as expressing a particular ideological stance (in a school textbook), as communication failure (in multi-cultural business meetings), or as semantic engineering (in political speeches).

Such analyses can provide insightful and plausible observations on textual organization. They almost always point out textual features which I, for one, would otherwise not have noticed. But the restriction to data fragments poses problems of evidence and generalization. And criteria for evaluating analyses often receive little explicit discussion; for example, how analyses of different texts can be replicated and compared, and how this can lead to cumulative progress in the field. The analyses in my own previous book on discourse analysis (Stubbs, 1983a) do not escape such criticism: they are of short texts and text fragments and lack a comparative basis. And the same points hold also for a wide range of other work on text analysis. Indeed, so far in this book, I have analysed only short texts. The longest text analysed in detail has been the judge's summing-up (chapter 5), although I have made some use of comparative data from larger corpora.

These are generalizations about a broad range of work, and it would be unfair to imply that all work is open to these criticisms. To take just two examples: Atkinson (1992) provides a detailed comparative syntactic analysis of the diachronic development of the genre research article across a substantial corpus of medical English; and Hunston (1993a, b) analyses syntactic features in small corpora of spoken and written English (see below).

6.6   Data and Hypotheses

The data for this chapter are two books and a small corpus.

- Text G (Geography) is a secondary school book, of about 80,000 words, on the physical and human geography of Britain. It is not presented as having any ideological axes to grind, but simply as factual: more on this below.
- Text E (Environmentalist) is a secondary school book, of about 30,000 words, on the damage being caused to the environment by industrial processes. It is written with explicitly persuasive purposes.
- As comparative data, I will use the LOB corpus: one million words of written (published) British English, divided into 500 samples from a range of genres, including newspaper articles and editorials, fiction and non-fiction, academic and non-academic (see notes on corpus data).

Much recent text analysis, especially within critical linguistics, starts from the Hallidayan assumption that all linguistic usage encodes representations of the world. It is always possible to talk about the same thing in different ways, and the systematic usage of different syntactic patterns encodes different points of view. As in chapters 4 and 5, I again start from this assumption, and will test whether the difference of ideological stance in the two books is expressed in their different use of the grammatical resources of English. More specifically, my hypotheses are that the environmentalist text – because of its explicit orientation to the responsibility for environmental problems and solutions – attributes both events and knowledge more frequently and more explicitly to their agents. These hypotheses, formulated more precisely below, will be strongly corroborated, though I will also draw attention to problems in such interpretations.

And as in previous chapters, unless otherwise stated, all linguistic examples cited are attested in the data, and are cited in an unmodified form. Upper case indicates lemmas: for example, the lemma CHANGE is realized by the word forms *change, changes, changed, changing.*

6.7   Computer-assisted Comparative Analysis

A major criterion for text analysis is that individual texts or text fragments must be analysed in ways which allow comparisons to be made to other texts and text corpora. The reason is stated clearly by Sinclair (1965, pp. 76–7) in a quote which I gave in chapter 2:

> Any stretch of language has meaning only as a sample of an enormously large body of text; it represents the results of a complicated selection process, and each selection has meaning by virtue of all the other selections which might have been made, but have been rejected.

This quote raises major issues of scale, comparison and interpretation. And the principle of comparative analysis has implications for methodology. Some patterns of language use are not directly observable, because they are realized across thousands or millions of words of running text, and because they are not categorical but probabilistic. Such patterns may be discernible, in a rough way, via intuition. But in order to describe such distributions systematically, significant amounts of text must be stored in a computer and searched, and quantitative methods must be used to describe the patterns.

Such methods bring immediate advantages. Subjective decisions are always involved in the choice of texts and of linguistic features for analysis. But computer assistance means that exhaustive and objective searches may be possible for all examples of a feature.

6.8   Example 1. Ergative Verbs:
the Syntax of Key Words

Every clause encodes a representation of the world. A language makes available various resources, but different selections are made from this potential in different texts.

Transitivity has frequently been studied within critical linguistics (e.g. Fowler, 1991b, pp. 70ff; Lee, 1992, pp. 59ff; Simpson, 1993, pp. 86ff), since it places agents, actions, processes and patients in various relations to each other. Transitivity is often discussed with reference to passives, and to the possibility of expressing or ignoring agency. But the passive is only one way of avoiding mention of agency in English, and omission of agent is only one reason for using passives or intransitives. Other ways of constructing agentless clauses include non-specific subjects and impersonal constructions (e.g. *somebody* . . . ; *there was* . . .), and ergatives, which are discussed in detail here.

My first analysis of the two school books concerns lexical and syntactic patterns which express change, causation and agency, since these are inevitable topics for books on physical and human geography and on the environment. Consider these examples [all A] with the lemmas CONCENTRATE and EXPAND. In their subject, verb and object, clauses which are active and transitive encode a chain of agent, action and goal:

> management *have concentrated* investment in a few yards

> the company *expanded* their labour force

Passive structures allow the agent to be omitted:

> services *will be concentrated* at category B airports

> the refinery *was expanded* in 1981

And when combined with inanimate subjects, intransitive structures do not allow the agent to be expressed, since there is no available syntactic slot:

> works *have concentrated* at these sites

> Britain's cities *have expanded* outwards

6.8.1　*Definitions and terminology*

Following Halliday (1985a, p. 145) and Sinclair (1990, p. 155), I will refer to such verbs as ergatives. Ergativity is an important area of English syntax, though it is not identified as such in major grammars of English (e.g. Quirk et al., 1985). When it is discussed, this is usually (e.g. Lyons, 1968, pp. 350ff) in relation to other constructions (including passives) which express causation, agency and animacy. Ergatives are verbs

- which can be transitive or intransitive; and
- which allow the same nominal group as object in transitive clauses and as subject in intransitive clauses.

(Other verbs, such as EAT – *Gill is eating, Gill is eating oranges* [I] – can be both transitive and intransitive, without being ergative.)

This is the definition of ergativity used by Sinclair (1987a, pp. 1620–1; 1990, pp. 155ff). Or as Sinclair (1990, p. 155) puts it, such verbs 'can describe an action from the point of view of the performer of the action or from the point of view of something which is affected by the action'. For example, in the following [all A, not M] clauses from text G,

several firms *have closed their factories* [transitive]

factories *have been closed* [passive]

factories *have closed* [intransitive]

factories is both object and subject: but in all three cases the closing happens to the factories. Other structures can also be used with the same lemmas; for example [also A]

. . . caused *the closure* of many factories [nominal]

The essential point is that ergative verbs have agentive and non-agentive uses. Halliday (1985a, pp. 144ff) points out that after a passive, but not after an intransitive, it is possible to ask: who by, or what by? Thus even agentless passives have an underlying agent; intransitives do not. Halliday analyses ergativity semantically as a pattern of transitivity which is based on one variable of causation: whether the process is represented as being caused from without, or from within, as self-caused. He claims that this pattern has come to prominence as part of a far-reaching process in modern English, which has left the transitivity system in a particularly unstable state, and that the majority of verbs in common use in English are ergative.

This area of English grammar is terminologically confused: see the appendix to this chapter. However, Lyons (1968, pp. 350ff), Halliday (1985a) and Sinclair (1990) all use the term ergative for such verbs in English, and I will continue this practice here, since it labels an interesting verb class for which no other term is conveniently available.

So, ergativity is an essential structure in the assignment of semantic roles. (See the appendix to chapter 5 on the important empirical analysis by Berk-Seligson (1990) on verbal structures in the attribution of blame and responsibility.) Such facts are often discussed in critical linguistics, but usually on the basis of short illustrative fragments, not with reference to the distribution of patterns across long texts.

6.8.2   Data analysis

Sinclair (1990, pp. 155ff) points out that many verbs of change are ergative: for example, CHANGE, CLOSE, DEVELOP, FORM, IMPROVE, INCREASE. In text G, CLOSE occurs 80 times, all in collocations with *factories, plants, works, firms, mines, mills, docks, schools, railway lines*, etc. Occurrences are: transitives (6), passives (9, all agentless), intransitives (41) and nominals (24, all agentless). In the few transitives, the agent is never an individual, always an organization (*ICI, BSC*, etc.) or a more abstract metaphor; for example (with reference to a British Minister of Transport who ordered the closure of railway lines)

the 'Beeching axe' *closed* hundreds of lines

There is a similar pattern with DEVELOP (276): transitives (19), passives (11, all agentless), intransitives (51) and nominals (189), e.g., respectively,

Birmingham *developed* a jewellery quarter

Aviemore *has been developed* as an all-year centre

air links *have developed* between the mainland and islands

the stages of *development* for western economies

6.8.3   Comparison of texts G and E

In order to compare texts G and E, all the ergative verbs (about 430 lemmas) were extracted from the Cobuild dictionary (Sinclair, 1987a), the only English dictionary to code such verbs explicitly. Using concordance software, I then extracted all occurrences of all forms of these lemmas from the two school books, and studied their occurrence in concordance lines of 132 characters. This provides a span of about ten words to left and right, which is usually sufficient to identify the syntax co-selected with the verb. See sample lines in concordance 6.1.

I studied just three patterns:

[Tr] transitive (VERB + NP)

ing. In the mid-1970s, the rich Icelandic fishing grounds were closed to all except Icelandic vessels. The so-called 'cod war' showe Thames Valley, they can be dredged. Quarries and gravel pits close down when their profitable deposits have been exhausted. Do the than Britain's ageing expensive shaft mines. 4 Many coalmines closed because the most easily and cheaply mined coal was exhausted. ed coal-cutting caused unemployment. Many small pits had to be closed because the large machines were unable to operate in them. Co processing coal to produce synthetic oil and natural gas. The closure of old mines will continue, until by the year 2000 a small nu elby will be from older Yorkshire collieries which are soon to close. Selby should achieve a productivity of 13 tonnes per manshift had to be modified. Many older coalfield-based ironworks were closed because they were unsuitable. Stage D: The move to the coal teelworks is home-produced. The old coalfield-based steelworks closed as large coastal works opened. The economics behind this are s over 6000 kilometres by sea. Stage E: Rationalisation : The closure of the coalfield-based steelworks has meant the disappearance nable to sell the steel they produced, the corporation rapidly closed its old plants, causing severe unemployment. Even the sites ch ace was opened at Redcar and the three Cleveland furnaces were closed. The Redcar site was chosen because it was close to a new deep ops, cafes and pubs. There were few other industries. When BSC closed the iron and steelmaking part of the plant in 1980, 6000 men l tube-steel plant remains open, employing 5000. Following the closure, Corby was declared a development area and an enterprise zone BSC (Industry), to help create jobs in areas affected by steel closures. Corby is seriously affected by closure of the steelworks. as affected by steel closures. Corby is seriously affected by closure of the steelworks. The unemployment rate is over 20 per cent. e is no hospital or railway station. The technical college has closed and shops are closing. Hundreds of council houses stand empty. ailway station. The technical college has closed and shops are closing. Hundreds of council houses stand empty. Some new firms have ynes, but its situation is more encouraging than that of steel- closure areas such as Consett in north-east England and Ebbw Vale in te for a steel-works in the 1930s? 4 Why was Corby steelworks closed? 5 The table below shows the population of Corby between 1931 e British steel industry between 1840 and 1980? 3 Why did the closure of the steelworks have such a dramatic effect upon the commun ing prices and the economic recession. Six oil refineries have closed. QUESTIONS A1 What processes take place at an oil refinery en. The resulting overcapacity has caused job losses and plant closures. QUESTIONS A1 How important is the chemical industry for easy to compete with foreign imports. The Invergordon smelter closed in 1981, a victim of the economic recession. The smelter's own ropped, workforces were reduced and three assembly plants were closed (Linwood in Scotland, Speke on Merseyside and Abingdon in Oxfo as 7000 separate firms contributing to the Metro. If BL was to close, the British industrial economy might face disaster. British L es disappeared as companies merged. Rationalisation caused the closure of many factories. Today, one company dominates the industry; ately available in many declining manufacturing areas. Factory closures can leave whole communities without work (Fig D). Certain gr n West Yorkshire, population began to fall after textile mills closed. The town council made efforts to stop the town dying. Its pol

Concordance 6.1 Verb and noun CLOSE in one school book, sample only.

ow and inefficient methods. In 1963, Dr Beeching proposed the closure of unprofitable lines and the improvement of money-making rou

and the improvement of money-making routes. The 'Beeching axe' closed hundreds of lines and thousands of stations. The closures have

g axe' closed hundreds of lines and thousands of stations. The closures have not been spread evenly throughout the country. More of

tem as shown by the statistics below: 2 Suggest some uses for closed railway lines. 3 (a) Describe the Tyneside Metro system. (b)

large ships has meant that fewer are needed. Ports have had to close their older, smaller docks and reduce the size of their workfor

me of the larger east coast ports have declined becaus e of the closure of old and inadequate dock systems. 3 A select group of seap

was completed when the City Docks in the heart of Bristol were closed to commercial traffic in 1980. Today, only pleasure craft use

ands of England. When industrial premises and shops were being closed elsewhere, and city populations were falling, Milton Keynes wa

as grew fast with early industrialisation. Now, factories have closed and the housing is old. People and industry have been attracte

rkets on price or range of stock, and many have been forced to close. Village schools have closed as the number of children has decl

tock, and many have been forced to close. Village schools have closed as the number of children has declined. Village clinics, post

he end of the nineteenth century, Cornish mines were forced to close because of low-cost ores coming from abroad, for example tin fr

ng and trade in wines and sherry. The inner Bristol docks have closed to commercial traffic but trade continues downstream where the

ppropriate areas of the coalfield, write: Many small mines now closed; A few large mines; Mines extending under the sea-bed. 2 Why

neering products has declined and many jobs lost as firms have closed. QUESTIONS A1 Look at Fig B. Measure the sections of the

first phase has been completed. Meanwhile, smaller works have closed at Skinningrove, Cargo Fleet and Hartlepool. There have been r

Cargo Fleet and Hartlepool. There have been redundancies and closures in the shipbuilding and heavy engineering industries. Durin

0. In places like Consett, County Durham, where the steelworks closed in 1980, the rate of population fall is much greater. Small mi

cheduled as 'D villages') have declined to zero because of the closure of the coalmines. The decline in population is not the only

7 mines remain, employing 27,000 miners. Older mines are still closing. However, a number of new mines are opening in response to th

s than 20,000 today. The last inland steelworks, at Ebbw Vale, closed in 1978. Only the coastal works at Port Talbot and Llanwern ar

1 Figure C shows the Nine Mile Point colliery in Gwent which closed in 1964. It left behind old pithead buildings, rusting railway

ing equipment is old and inefficient. In 1972, the South Docks closed. Many of the other docks are being used less and less. Ferries

Concordance 6.1 Continued

[Pa] passive (mainly BE + VERB-*ed*)

[In] intransitive (VERB)

Here are further examples for three lemmas from text G:

ICI *closed* its Carrickfergus plant [Tr]

industrial premises and shops *were being closed* [Pa]

most of the quarries *have* now *closed* [In]

British Shipbuilders . . . *have concentrated* investment [Tr]

services *will be concentrated* at category B airports [Pa]

works *have concentrated* at these sites [In]

Brazil *has expanded* its steel production [Tr]

the refinery *was expanded* in 1981 by the construction [Pa]

Britain's cities *have expanded* outwards [In]

Table 6.1 gives the summed figures for all forms of all ergative verbs in texts G and E.

Table 6.1 Two school books, all ergative verbs, all forms

	Transitive	Passive	Intransitive	n
Text G	179 (23%)	204 (26%)	403 (51%)	786
Text E	147 (52%)	30 (11%)	107 (38%)	284

$\chi^2 = 88.22$; d.f. = 2; $p < 0.001$.

6.8.4 Interpretation

Relative to text length, texts G and E have almost exactly the same number of ergative verbs: slightly fewer than one per 100 words of running text. However, the distribution of transitive, passive and intransitive choices is significantly different ($p < 0.001$). Text E has many more transitive forms, with correspondingly fewer passives and intransitives. Consistent with explicit orientation to the responsibility for environmental damage, text E expresses causation and agency more frequently through more frequent transitives. The relative percentages of transitives and intransitives are reversed in the two books, and this reversal is in the intuitively expected direction. The hypothesis that explicit causation would be more frequently expressed in text E is strongly corroborated.

More accurately, it is the combination of intransitivity and inanimate subjects which leaves agency unexpressed. For all sentences in text G, only 2.5 per cent have named and identifiable persons in subject nominal position. Other subjects are: organizations (12.2 per cent) and unidentifiable groups of people (29.5 per cent). The largest set is non-human: 55.8 per cent. Stubbs and Gerbig (1993) give details.

6.8.5   Comparison of texts G and E and LOB

However, without comparative corpus data, we are limited in how we can interpret such figures. We do not know whether such distributions are within a typical range for English: does text G have relatively few transitive uses, or is it text E that has relatively many? Furthermore, although the two books are on comparable topics, their content differs, and they use different vocabulary, including overlapping, but different, sets of ergative verbs.

To ensure that I was comparing like with like, I therefore selected the five ergative verbs which are most common in both texts and which also occur in all three forms (transitive, passive and intransitive) in one or both texts. These lemmas are CHANGE, DEVELOP, FORM, IMPROVE, INCREASE. Table 6.2 gives the summed figures for the three verbal structures across these five lemmas.

Table 6.2   Two books and LOB, five ergative verbs, all forms

	Transitive	Passive	Intransitive	n
Text G	97 (31%)	54 (17%)	161 (52%)	312
Text E	53 (55%)	12 (13%)	31 (32%)	96
LOB	395 (49%)	156 (20%)	249 (31%)	800

χ^2 G by E = 18.48; d.f. = 2; p < 0.001.
χ^2 G by LOB = 43.06; d.f. = 2; p < 0.001.
χ^2 E by LOB = 2.86; d.f. = 2; not significant at 0.2 level.

6.8.6   Interpretation

The frequency of these five lemmas together relative to 1,000 words of running text is: text G, 4; text E, 3.2; LOB, 0.8. This is straightforward enough: as one might expect from the content of the books, the lemmas are four to five times as frequent in texts G and E as in the samples in the corpus.

Again, for these five summed lemmas, the percentages of transitive and intransitive forms are almost exactly reversed in texts G and E. And again, this reversal is in the expected direction. The differences between texts G and E, and also between text G and the corpus, are statistically highly significant ($p < 0.001$). However, text E and the corpus are very similar on this feature. That is, it is the environmentalist text which is very close to the norm for the language, as represented by the corpus. And it is text G which represents agency infrequently, in comparison to the (small) corpus.

6.8.7 Variation across verbs

It is sometimes objected that the concept of global frequencies of occurrence across the language (for example, as here, averaged patterns on ergative verbs across LOB) is meaningless. Such frequencies vary across different text types: indeed, such systematic variation defines register. Every text is in some specific register. *Ergo*, global frequencies represent a meaningless averaging. Halliday (1992, pp. 68–9) answers this objection sharply as follows. 'Global probabilities are just that: global probabilities.' It is always spring, summer, autumn or winter. But this does not mean that it is meaningless to talk of an average annual rainfall. It usually rains less in Scotland in May and September than in other months, and on some days it doesn't rain at all [*sic!*]. But Scotland is still wetter, on average, than the south of England.

However, such figures do hide variation: that is what average figures do. And there can be interesting variation across different verbs within one text. For example, table 6.3 gives the figures on OPEN and CLOSE in text G. When things get opened (usually an optimistic, more positive event), then there is at least an implicit agent there somewhere to take the credit (most occurrences are agentless passives). When they get closed (not so positive), then intransitivity prevails! Closing is represented as something that just happens. Examples include

the reservoir was . . . officially opened by the Queen

the first power station in Great Britain was opened in 1882

when the aluminium works closed, unemployment . . . rose

most of the quarries have now closed

Table 6.3   One school book, two ergative verbs

	Intransitive	Other	n
OPEN	7 (16%)	36 (84%)	43
CLOSE	41 (76%)	13 (24%)	54

$\chi^2 = 34.07$; d.f. $= 1$; $p < 0.001$.

Averaging across a corpus can make sense, but it is also important to remember that every lemma has different syntax. (See section 2.6 on co-selection of lexis and syntax.)

6.8.8   Comparison of texts G and E: passives

The figures above show that, for ergative verbs, text E has fewer passives than text G. It is widely reported that passives are frequent in genres such as scientific articles and school textbooks. Nevertheless, many studies give no quantified findings, and many studies do not define passive explicitly. These two facts often make comparison between studies impossible. Such errors in presentation are serious, because they prevent readers from re-analysing findings or replicating them. Comparisons between different studies and cumulative research become imprecise or impossible.

About thirty years ago, Svartvik (1966) carried out a computer-assisted study of passives in a 320,000 word corpus. This corpus is small by present-day standards, but the study was carefully done and still provides useful comparative findings. Svartvik studied passives in eight text types. He found, per 1,000 words of running text, an average of 11.3 passives overall; with a range from 3.0 in advertising to 23.0 in science. Active was more frequent than passive overall, but this frequency varied from about 3 to 1 to 9 to 1. (Svartvik (1966) is usefully re-interpreted by Halliday (1991).)

Independently of the study of ergative verbs above, I identified all passives, with all verbs, ergative and non-ergative, for both texts (see concordance 6.2). Text G has 20 passives per 1,000 words: almost as many as Svartvik found in scientific writing for adults. Text E has fewer, 13.5 per 1,000 words: something above Svartvik's average for his corpus.[1]

Further, Leech and Svartvik (1975) estimate that 'about 4 out of 5 English passive clauses have no agent.' (This estimate is much rougher: they do not specify their corpus.) In Text G, more than 7 out of 8 passives have no agent. Text E has the same percentage of *by*-passives with agents, but holera and typhoid killed thousands of Britons. These diseases were caused by infected water. Now all the water supplied to homes ca Wells: Permeable rocks such as chalk, limestone and sandstone are called aquifers because they bear water. The water usually remain can be artificially pumped out through wells. When the aquifer is sandwiched between two impermeable rocks, pressure can build up at supplied to the water system. Water in the storage reservoirs is purified naturally and is readily available in times of shortage. rally and is readily available in times of shortage. The water is passed through filter beds before it can be used. Figure E shows t ary Reservoir which is over twice the size of Hyde Park. Water is pumped into the Thames from the ground water stored within the lim system linking rivers by pipelines and tunnels (Fig E). Water is transferred from the wetter areas to the drier areas of the countr sewers and eventually to the local sewage works. Sewage works are located beside rivers in or near towns. The water discharged into the water you drink comes from C 500 million litres of water are used in Greater London every day. Discuss the problems associated , England's largest natural lake. One and a half million trees were felled to make way for it, and a hamlet, several buildings and t r it, and a hamlet, several buildings and the main valley road were drowned by the rising water. Why was this remote Northumberland lopment Fund and the British government. A further £43 million was loaned by the EEC at reduced rates of interest. Kielder Water wi ng permits are sold direct to the public. Worm and fly fishing are permitted and motorboats are available for hire. Water sports: ion of the water takes place further downstream. The reservoir is used by small boats of all kinds, and water skiers. Boat trips: e a farmer in the Kielder Valley when the Kielder Water Scheme is announced. You learn that half your land is to be flooded. What ar demand for consumer goods increased. The new industrial growth was concentrated in the Midlands and south. In the older industrial a e distribution of old people. (c) How do you think old people are distributed in your area? (d) Are some areas especially attracti because there was little money available. 1930s More success was achieved through the creation of trading estates such as Trefores three-tier system shown on Fig D. 1982 The three-tier system was retained but the size of the assisted areas was greatly reduced. ze of the assisted areas was greatly reduced. Enterprise zones were established. Figure F lists the incentives provided by the gove of investment costs for industry in the assisted areas, which is used to top up national regional development grants. Between 1975 as crops are continuously grown. Nutrients and minerals which were replaced by roots and fallow years are now replaced by soil cond uch 'free range' chickens are rare. Most eggs and chicken meat are produced on factory farms like that illustrated. There are thousa completely sterile so that no disease can enter. The chickens are fed on concentrated feed pellets and may be injected with drugs t y per cent of the EEC's budget is spent on the CAP. The farmer is guaranteed a price which is fixed each year. An intervention price et is spent on the CAP. The farmer is guaranteed a price which is fixed each year. An intervention price is set up for each product, often surplus production within the EEC. The surplus products are stored (butter 'mountains' and wine 'lakes') or sold cheaply with ectares were grown and the rape sold for cash. The black seeds are crushed to extract oil which is used for cooking oil, margarine a old for cash. The black seeds are crushed to extract oil which is used for cooking oil, margarine and salad dressing. The residue of

Concordance 6.2 Passives in one school book, small sample only.

g? B1 Study Fig A. (a) What percentage of farmland in the UK is used for (i) arable crops, (ii) temporary grass, (iii) permanent grass with dairy cattle, cereals and fodder crops. Seventy people were employed. By 1984, the farm had taken over several neighbouring farm with dairy cattle, cereals and fodder crops. Seventy people were employed. By 1984, the farm had taken over several neighbouring farm and barley which are grown in vast fields. Only fifteen people are employed on the farm in 1984.' Account for these changes. 2. In England. Soft wheat is not suitable for bread production; it is used in the making of cakes and biscuits. 'Hard' wheat for bread imported from the USA and Canada. The dramatic decline of oats is explained by its inferiority to barley: oats have a lower average. The geography of cereal production is shown on Fig B. Wheat is limited to the east of the country, barley and oats can be grown ing has become highly mechanised. The first combine harvesters were introduced on British farms in the early 1930s, but it was not until lines worked most efficiently in large fields because less time was wasted in turning and manoeuvring, so cereal farmers have removed refinery where the sugar content (about 20 per cent by weight) is extracted; the pulp and the green tops are used for animal feed. S per cent by weight) is extracted; the pulp and the green tops are used for animal feed. Sugar beet has precise climatic requirement e liberal use of nitrogen fertilisers, and agrochemical sprays are needed to combat weeds and disease. The high yields possible each em in the future. QUESTIONS A1 What areas of arable land were used for barley in 1937 and 1982? Explain the increase in area. nt crops in certain areas. The intensive growing of vegetables is called market gardening. Market gardens are usually less than ten nsist mainly of greenhouses. Heating, ventilation and humidity are controlled automatically and the greenhouse crop may be watered a Many of the apples grown in Somerset, Devon and Herefordshire are used in the production of cider. Another important crop is the f and Cox's Orange Pippin. Conference pears are grown. The trees are raised in a nursery and then planted at 5 m × 2 m intervals. They sed in a nursery and then planted at 5 m × 2 m intervals. They are pruned annually but it is four or five years before fruit can be five years before fruit can be harvested. The apples and pears are picked by local casual labour during August and September, and th local casual labour during August and September, and the fruit is stored in cool airtight chambers. During the winter, the fruit is stored in cool airtight chambers. During the winter, the fruit is graded and packed as required. Strawberries: Strawberry plant h a central marketing office in Paddock Wood. The strawberries are marketed throughout Britain and some exports are arranged. The ap strawberries are marketed throughout Britain and some exports are arranged. The apple co-operative consists of ten farmers combinin There are fourteen women in the packhouse. Extra casual labour is employed for the fruit harvest from mid-June through to October. U

Concordance 6.2   Continued

fewer abstract agents. (Stubbs and Gerbig, 1993, provide further details of these analyses.)

These various differences between texts G and E, in the frequency of ergatives, passives and agents, all tend in the same direction as regards the representation of agency. A useful methodological strategy, seldom used in text analyses, other than very informally and intuitively at best, is to compare analyses of different features, to see if they corroborate or contradict each other.

6.9 Interpretative Problems

The above comparisons are very striking and the levels of statistical significance are very high. But stylistic interpretations are less straightforward than such figures may suggest.

6.9.1 *Further notes on ergatives*

First, ergative is not a well defined verb class. The class of verbs which can be ergative is increasing in contemporary English. Examples from text G, which are probably relatively recent ergative usage, are

why these companies *relocate* in development areas

organizations that have *located* in Milton Keynes

The Cobuild dictionary (Sinclair, 1987a) records RELOCATE but not LOCATE as ergative. I heard the following instance recently on British radio. The manager of a large nationalized concern was discussing privatization. With reference to staff likely to lose jobs, he said

they will be able to *relocate*

That is, staff were grammatically represented not as being sacked, but as having an opportunity to be the cause of their own relocation. Other examples, all from one letter to the editor of a newspaper (*Times Higher Education Supplement*, 8 April 1994) are

X cites women's reluctance to work overtime or *relocate* to gain promotion . . . there will indeed be many women who cannot offer . . . the

> capacity to *relocate* . . . I cannot be alone in noticing men who achieve promotion . . . without *relocating*

Sinclair (personal communication) has suggested that intransitive uses are probably intelligible with almost any verb, although such uses may initially need an evaluative adverb, as in these examples from a wine club advert and an applied linguistics textbook:

> [this wine] will continue to improve although it *is drinking well* at the present time
>
> subjects who . . . do not *test well* (who become over-anxious)

In summary, ergativity is a productive feature of English. However, the verbs coded as V-ERG in the Cobuild dictionary occur relatively frequently as ergatives in the 20 million words corpus used for the dictionary, and therefore provide a good sample for my purposes. This provides a good example of a case where intuitions do not provide reliable data. Trask (1993, p. 93) regards ergatives as 'far from fully productive in English'. This is almost certainly wrong, but only a corpus could provide data on which verbs are frequently ergative, on diachronic changes in such ergative usage and on productive and idiosyncratic(?) uses with evaluative adverbs.

Von Polenz (1988) suggests – with reference to German, but the same point seems to hold for English – that there has been a shift, on many verbs, from two-place to one-place predicates, and that this is part of a long historical shift towards more compressed syntactic constructions.

6.9.2   Probabilistic patterns

A more serious problem is that such stylistic patterns are probabilistic. There is no absolute difference between the two texts, and stylistic interpretation of frequency and probability data is very uncertain. One might ask, simplistically, why intransitive uses occur at all in text E. One reason is that intransitives with inanimate subjects can express events which have no agent: they are out of control. This is an important theme of the book: that processes have been started which cannot easily be stopped. Consider these uses of ergative ROLL and STOP, both transitive and intransitive, in text E:

> it's like trying to *stop* [transitive] a truck that's *rolling* [intransitive] down a hill with bad brakes . . . we have so much momentum that it takes a long time to *stop* [intransitive]

Intransitives in text E often refer to physical processes, which are beyond human control:

> chlorine atoms *bond* with the free oxygen atoms

> free oxygen atoms which would otherwise *combine* with oxygen molecules

> grasslands and desert will *expand*

> these chemicals *float* up into the stratosphere

> mortality rates from skin cancer are now *increasing*

> if the earth's surface warms up, some snow and ice will *melt*

6.9.3   Another analysis: unexpected findings

This area of meaning – animacy, human and non-human agency, causation, control – has been studied in related work by Gerbig (1993). Starting from the findings above, Gerbig carried out an identical analysis of ergative verbs on a different corpus, consisting of texts about ozone depletion, written in connection with pending international industrial legislation: 20,000 words from each of industrial, research and environmental organizations, and 10,000 words from the press. In their texts, industry is attempting to slow down legislation and to spread the responsibility for environmental damage, while environmentalist groups are attempting to speed things up and to sharpen the focus of responsibility.

However, contrary to expectation, Gerbig found environmental organizations using slightly more intransitive constructions than industry. How could this be explained? Explanations might lie both in what is taken for granted in the texts and in the different meanings expressed by ergativity. Texts G and E are school textbooks, and they cannot assume too much prior knowledge in their readers. Gerbig's texts, however, show different interest groups responding differently to a common theme. Everyone knows who is responsible for ozone depletion: this is the whole point of the legislation. There is therefore no need to focus explicitly on agency and causation. But, in addition, Gerbig argues that different meanings are expressed by ergatives in different sets of texts. In the environmentalist texts, a central meaning encoded by intransitives is that the destruction caused by industry is out of control:

> the crisis *deepens*

the size of the Antarctic ozone hole *has increased*

the rate of ozone loss *has been accelerating*

In the research texts, intransitives are also frequent, perhaps because the one–participant-only construction allows the focus of the clause to be on the event itself. As in other scientific writing, human agency is in the background:

the Arctic polar vortex *forms* each winter

ozone levels *are* now *dropping*

not only *has* the surface *warmed* but . . .

In the industry texts, the "blame avoidance" meaning may be relevant, along with the "objective scientific findings" meaning. It is in the press that transitive constructions, and therefore agents, are more frequent: perhaps in line with the well known tendency of the press to personalize events.

Gerbig's analysis shows the following. First, the comparison of her analysis and mine is possible only on the basis of quantified and replicable findings. Second, a study of global frequency patterns must be combined with a study of the corresponding concordance data from individual texts. Neither analysis is sufficient on its own. In particular, one must take into account the assumptions with which readers approach texts. Third, classes of verbs, such as ergatives and reporting verbs, require much corpus based work (see Hunston, 1993a,b; Francis, 1993) before the range of meanings which they convey will become clearer.

One type of probabilistic information which is starting to become available from corpus-driven grammar is what is to be expected syntactically with various lexical items; for, example which verbs are likely to be passive or intransitive, or to have impersonal subjects (for examples, see Sinclair, 1990; Francis, 1993).

6.10   Example 2. Projecting Clauses

In the analysis of ergative verbs, I discussed whether events are attributed to agents. The second analysis, of projecting clauses, concerns whether factual knowledge is attributed to agents. I take it for granted that there are no brute facts (Firth, 1957b; Martin, 1985; and see chapters 3 and 5). However, textbooks are repositories of what we believe to be accredited facts. So one can study the linguistic means used to present them. Are they encoded as reliable and objective knowledge, obvious to common sense and independent of the persons who discovered or formulated them? Or are they presented as hypotheses for which some named source is responsible, and which are open to different interpretations? Textbook writers are interested in facts. Linguists are interested in factivity. Textbook writers, teachers and pupils should be aware of some of the relations between the two.

The modality system of a language provides ways of indicating the speaker/writer's commitment to propositions; for example, how certain or reliable they are. All languages have evidential devices (Chafe, 1986) which encode epistemological considerations, such as the degree of reliability the speaker/writer attributes to a proposition and the source of the knowledge (for example, direct personal experience, hearsay, inference). Languages differ considerably, however, in which kinds of evidence it is obligatory to encode. And within languages, genres differ considerably in which kinds of evidentials are frequently used. (Chapter 8 discusses evidentiality in detail.)

It is tempting to look at how degree of reliability of knowledge is encoded, by studying the use of factive predicates (which presuppose the truth of the proposition) and non-factive predicates (which make no such presupposition). An informal check showed that texts G and E do not differ significantly in their uses of factive and non-factive predicates. That is, there are no obvious differences in how certain the knowledge is presented as being. But I did not code this systematically, because distinctions between factive and non-factive are not easy to make reliably. Even expressions such as *the fact that* are not necessarily factive: for example, *the fact that Eileen might have been* . . . [A] from Francis 1993, p. 154).

6.10.1 Definitions

Instead, I studied systematically how the source of propositions is encoded, with reference to just one evidential device: projecting clauses. In English, modality can be encoded within a clause, for example by a modal verb and/ or adverb. A bald statement, expressing certainty by a simple present verb form (*CFCs destroy ozone*), can be explicitly modalized (*CFCs can destroy ozone* or *CFCs certainly destroy ozone*). But Halliday (1985a, p. 332) and Hunston (1993a) point out that modality can also be encoded as a separate projecting clause:

scientists have discovered that CFCs destroy ozone [M]

many people now recognize that CFCs destroy ozone [M]

I will discuss only such projecting clauses which precede *that* (and which have been identified via a concordance of the word *that*).[2] All the following examples are attested in one of the two texts. Most occurrences involve VERB + *that*:

scientists *discovered* in 1974 *that* . . .

scientists *say that* . . .

many people *feel that* . . .

the electricity boards *point out that* . . .

But projecting clauses are also introduced by adjectives and nominal groups:

several local people were *afraid that* . . .

it is *possible that* . . .

there is still *no scientific proof that* . . .

it is now *scientific fact that* . . .

The lexico-semantic classes of words associated with these structures encode thought processes or their results (e.g. *discover*, *recognize*), illocutions (e.g. *say*, *argue*) or feelings (e.g. *feel*, *afraid*), and many involve sub-technical words (e.g. *proof*, *conclude*). Using corpus evidence, Francis (1993) provides a preliminary classification of the hundreds of lexical items involved in such structures.

6.10.2   *World-creating predicates*

So, propositions about the world can be prefaced as, for example, accredited scientific fact or unaccredited possibility. Chafe (1986) compares evidentials in spoken and written corpora of dinner table conversations and academic articles. He finds that the two corpora have approximately the same percentage of evidential markers, but that they differ in the frequency of specific types of device. For example, speakers more frequently than writers signal that knowledge derives from personal opinion (e.g. *I think*, *I suppose*). And academic writing encodes hearsay evidence through reference citations. Chafe's examples include projecting clauses, though he does not draw specific attention to them.

Hunston (1993a) presents a comparable study. She starts from proposals by Halliday (1985a) and Stubbs (1986b), and compares projecting clauses in spoken political radio discussion and written academic articles. She finds significant differences in how these genres express modality, and shows that these differences in the use of projecting clauses provide evidence of how different value systems are expressed: whether personal opinion is valued, or whether an outside public source is given responsibility for the proposition, as in, respectively

> I think I'd probably argue that . . .

> Eisenberg concluded that . . .

None of these specific findings is surprising. For example, bibliographic references in academic articles are an elaborate convention for encoding hearsay evidence. However, the detailed statistics provided by Chafe and Hunston contribute to our understanding of how genres can be defined by the systematic variation in the occurrence of different selections from the language system.

Consider examples from texts G and E. Some projecting clauses attribute the following proposition to a source of judgement [+At]:

> the government has *recognized that* . . .

> farmers *discovered that* . . .

> several local people were *afraid that* . . .

> opponents of nuclear power *say that* . . .

When the source of the judgement is encoded, this is usually (as above) as the grammatical subject of the projecting clause. But other possibilities include

> it was clear *to BSC* that . . .

Others leave the source unattributed [−At]:

> it is *not surprising to learn that* . . .

> it has been *predicted that* . . .

> there are *fears that* . . .

> there is *no guarantee that* . . .

Frequent examples (as above) have impersonal constructions with *it* and *there*. But other possibilities include passives:

the *view* was taken *that* . . .

If the source of the judgement is attributed, then a further systemic choice is possible. Attributions can be personal [+P], by which I mean that the judgement is attributed either to an individual or to a group of people, however vaguely identified:

> *Dr Watson* explains that . . .
>
> *the people of Hull* hoped that . . .
>
> *some countries* felt that . . .

Or the attribution may be impersonal [−P]:

> *all three techniques* show us that . . .
>
> *their measurements* showed that . . .
>
> *the latest studies* seem to indicate that . . .
>
> *lack of investment* meant that . . .
>
> *a tabloid* reported that . . .

This coding is not without problems. Perhaps *a tabloid* implies a group of people, just as much as *some countries*. Nevertheless, the impersonal examples code sources of objective, public knowledge (in Popper's, 1972, 1994, sense). If most or all projecting clauses were of this type, the implication would be that studies, reports and the like generate their own truth without the reader being involved in interpretation (Hunston, 1993a). (See section 9.1.)

6.10.3   Comparison of texts G and E

These distinctions can be summarized in a small system network:

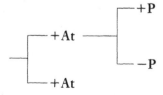

And tables 6.4, 6.5 and 6.6 give the occurrences in the two texts.

Table 6.4 Two books, projecting clauses

	+At		−At	n
	+P	−P		
Text G	18	26	33	77
Text E	48	21	17	86

χ^2 +P by −P = 9.08; d.f. = 1; $p < 0.01$.
χ^2 +At by −At = 10.19; d.f. = 1; $p < 0.01$.

Table 6.5 Two books, attributed and non-attributed projecting clauses

	+At	−At	n
Text G	44 (57%)	33 (43%)	77
Text E	69 (80%)	17 (20%)	86

χ^2 = 10.19; d.f. = 1; $p < 0.01$.

Table 6.6 Two books, personal and impersonal projecting clauses

	+P	−P	n
Text G	18 (41%)	26 (59%)	44
Text E	48 (70%)	21 (30%)	69

χ^2 = 9.08; d.f. = 1; $p < 0.01$.

6.10.4   Interpretation

First, relative to text length, text E has nearly three times as many projecting clauses as text G (2.9 versus 1 per 1,000 words of running text). Second, text E has significantly more ($p < 0.01$) propositions which are attributed to a source of knowledge: see table 6.5. And third, among the attributed propositions, text E also has significantly more ($p < 0.01$) personal attributions: see table 6.6. These findings all lie in the expected direction. The environmentalist book emphasizes more frequently and explicitly the status of the facts discussed. And it attributes responsibility for knowledge of those facts to individuals and groups. Again, the political stance is expressed in the syntax used.[3]

6.11   Some Principles For Text Analysis

There is a long way to go in developing descriptive methods for text analysis. In the past, it has often been difficult to find studies which build on previous work, and this is an indication that discourse studies have not always been on well defined problems in well defined areas. Bailey (1969, p. 218), in a historical survey of statistical stylistics from its inception in 1851(!), notes that 'the history of statistics and style shows few cases in which genuine expertise in language, literature and statistics have been combined in one investigator.'

I will conclude with a summary of some principles which outline a substantial cumulative research programme.

1   Comparative analysis. Interpretations of texts must compare differ-ent texts and text types: otherwise we cannot know what is typical or atypical, or whether features of texts are significant, linguistically or ideo-logically, or not.

2   Long texts. The analysis of short texts and text fragments must be complemented by the analysis of long texts, since some patterns of repetition and variation are only realised across long texts (such as complete books).

3   Text corpora. Similarly, some patterns of variation are realized only across text types, and categories of text can be studied only via samples of texts in a corpus.

4   Range of coverage of corpora. No corpus can represent the whole language: the language changes as new text types are constantly created. The concept of range of coverage may be more useful: corpora can be wider or narrower in their range of text types, and methods could be developed for assessing the range of text types represented by corpora.[4]

5   Textual homogeneity and heterogeneity. The present chapter has shown significant differences between two texts, which are on compara-ble topics within the same text type. On the other hand, I have assumed that texts G and E are internally homogeneous, though very few linguistic fea-tures are evenly distributed throughout a text. It has been claimed (e.g. Fairclough, 1992) that mixed genres are becoming increasingly common. But co-occurrence, homogeneity and heterogeneity (within texts, text types and authors) are not well understood.

6   Interpretation of frequency. Literary scholars take it for granted that meanings are conveyed by patterns of repetition and variation. (Burrows, 1992, is a useful discussion.) And register (text type, style, genre, etc.) is usually defined as systematic variation in the frequency of linguistic features across texts (Halliday, 1991; Biber, 1988). But there is no well developed

theory of how the frequency of linguistic features contributes to the meaning of individual texts. The comparison of my analysis with Gerbig's (1993) showed the need to combine the analysis of large-scale patterns across long texts with the detailed study of concordance lines.

7   Variables and variants. Many linguistic features are of potential stylistic interest, and several overlapping lists are proposed (e.g. by Fairclough, 1989, pp. 110–11; Fowler, 1991b, pp. 68ff; Myers, 1992; Biber, 1988, provides a list of lists). However, these lists summarize experience and intuition, as Fowler (1991b, p. 90) admits. Apart from Biber's, they are unformalized and only partly usable in computer-assisted studies. We lack a representative list of such variables and their variants. Since linguistic patterns are defined in different ways in different studies (and are often not explicitly defined), and since findings are often not quantified, it is often impossible to make precise comparisons across studies and work is not cumulative.

8   Comparative statistics. Such a representative list would facilitate the collection of normalized statistics for a range of linguistic features across a range of text types. This would make interpretations of individual texts much more reliable.

9   Statistical methods. Burrows (1992) and Woods et al., (1986, pp. 147, 181) warn that statistical tests generally assume that observed data are independent of each other. But linguistic features of texts are not independent variables: they normally occur in clusters. Sinclair (1991a, p. 3) admits that, in corpus linguistics, 'the numerical and statistical side has scarcely begun'.

10   Quantitative analysis. Perhaps the present chapter merely provides a little more detail on things which are already known from study of text fragments (for example, that transitivity choices have ideological implications). However, when quantitative analysis supports a familiar belief, the comment is often that everyone knows that. When it provides an unexpected finding, the comment is often that you can prove anything with statistics (Burrows, 1992, p. 183).

In summary, linguists should be developing methods to meet Frawley's (1987) objections that discourse analysis is either 'all program with no analysis, or simple analysis with no program' (p. 371): 'discourse analysis has no metamethod, no way of separating the correct and useful from the banal. One gets the impression that discourse analysis is an omnivorous field, where one thing is as good as another' (p. 363). The 'metamethod' must be based on explicit comparative description of substantial corpora of data, in which clearer relations are drawn between lexico–grammar and text, and which incorporates a theory of probabilistic grammar.

6.12　Conclusion: Computer-assisted Studies

Computer assistance does not bring pure objectivity to text analysis. It is evident that intuition is involved at several stages: which features to study, how delicately to code, how to interpret the findings. It has long been widely recognized that stylistic statistics merely provide quantitative evidence whose significance can be assessed only by experience and common sense (Posner, 1963; Thomson, 1989).

However, statistical stylistic studies show that concordances can identify syntactic features of texts which can then be semantically interpreted. Independent of intuitive judgement (within the limitations noted), a concordance program identifies every example in the data, and helps to ensure that analysts do not merely pick evidence to fit their preconceptions. It also helps to present quantitative evidence in ways which can be checked by readers.

It is currently fashionable to emphasize the interpretative aspects of such analysis, and to play down the inherent patterning in data (though Sinclair (1991a) provides a strong counter-argument). We select what to look for, on the basis of hunches or what others have found useful. But, as instruments of observation and memory, computers help considerably with the criterion of comprehensiveness of coverage. When correctly instructed, computers make it more difficult to overlook inconvenient instances, and are to that extent a move towards descriptive neutrality. We select what to look for, but should then accept as evidence what the computer finds (Sinclair, 1991a; Burrows, 1992).

(And note my use, for persuasive purposes, of four projecting *that*-clauses in the last three paragraphs!)

Appendix: Further Notes on Ergativity

The area of ergativity is in terminological confusion. For example, Trask (1993), in his *Dictionary of Grammatical Terms*, gives relevant entries under: causative, ergative, intransitive, labile verb, medio-passive, middle verb, pseudo-intransitive, pseudo-passive, transitive, unaccusative and unergative! Pullum (1991b) documents further confusion.

In work on universal grammar and linguistic typology, the term *ergative* is used to refer to morphological case marking in languages such as Dyirbal (Dixon, 1972). English is not ergative in this sense, and the very large comparative linguistic literature (see Comrie, 1981; Croft, 1990) on ergativity is not directly relevant. It is a useful reminder, however, that languages have different ways of grammaticalizing meanings such as agent–goal and giver–receiver, and that ergativity in various languages interacts with animacy (e.g. human versus non-human). It is because languages have different means for encoding the same semantic roles that causative constructions are a central topic in universal grammar. For example, Comrie (1981, pp. 158ff) studies semantic relations between events (which are often encoded in the verb) and participants (which are often encoded as subjects and objects).

So, ignoring squabbles about mere terms, the essential points are: (a) languages have different means of encoding causativity, and (b) observations about the verbs which I am calling ergative have been central to important theories of grammar, notably in work by Fillmore and Halliday.

Causative constructions were central in generative semantics (recall analyses of KILL as "cause to die"). And an indication of the theoretical importance of ergatives as a verb class is that Fillmore (e.g. 1969) uses them to motivate deep grammatical case in his proposals for case grammar. Fillmore's argument is that the traditional concepts of grammatical subject and object ignore important semantic facts. For example, 'there is a semantically relevant distinction between *the door* and *open* that is the same' (p. 363) in (invented) sentences such as:

the janitor will open the door

the door will open

the door will open with this key

this key will open the door

Fillmore gives a list of verbs which 'have a certain amount of freedom with respect to the syntactic environments into which they can be inserted' (p. 365). The list (although he does not use the term) consists of ergative verbs. And the behaviour of these verbs is then at the basis of his proposal for a case grammar which uses concepts including Agentive, Objective and Instrumental.

Halliday (1976) initially used the term *neutral* verbs, since it is not possible to decide which form is basic in (invented) examples such as

she poured the water out

the water poured out

Halliday also talks of *middle* and *non-middle* clauses. Lakoff (1970, pp. 33ff, 44ff) discusses relevant verbs as *inchoatives* and *causatives*. Palmer (1974, pp. 92ff) calls them *pseudo-passives*. (One of the most widely used grammars, Quirk et al. (1985), uses the terms *middle verb* and *pseudo-passive* differently from Halliday and Palmer respectively. Quirk et al. talk of transitive and intransitive verbs with reference to causality.) Fillmore uses *Objective* for the function which is the subject of an intransitive verb and the object of the corresponding transitive verb. This is what is called *Affected* by Halliday (1976) and *ergative* more recently by Halliday (1985a).

Fontenelle and Vanandroye (1989) define in detail ergatives in English, based on semantic, syntactic and morphological properties, and give a useful list of verbs. Fontenelle (1990) discusses the ergative verbs identified in the Cobuild dictionary.

7

Keywords, Collocations and Culture: the Analysis of Word Meanings across Corpora

Sociological linguistics is the great field for future research. . . . Loose linguistic sociology without formal accuracy is of little value. (Firth, 1935, pp. 65, 71)

7.1 Organization of the Chapter

Chapters 4 to 6 provided analyses of selected features of connected texts. This chapter does not analyse how linguistic features are distributed across individual texts. It analyses the collocations of individual words as they are distributed across a large corpus.

I present some introductory data in the form of statements by British public figures about language in education: these provide initial examples of recurrent key words and phrases which signal some central British cultural preoccupations. However, the main data analysed are from the Cobuild corpus (see notes on corpus data). I have used a sub-corpus of some 130 million words from exclusively British sources: 90 million words from various newspapers and magazines and from radio, and a further 40 million words from fiction and non-fiction books and conversation.

The chapter provides an analysis of some twenty words (lemmas and word forms) and associated phrases from semantic fields which are central to contemporary British culture. The predominant source of the data in various British mass media should therefore be borne in mind below when I give examples from the analyses. The main linguistic features analysed are the recurrent collocations in which these words occur.

One major aim of the analysis is to show how such attested corpus data can be used to study the cultural connotations of words, and the main findings are presented in the form of typical collocations of words which are central to British culture. A second aim is methodological. It is beyond the observational powers of a human analyst to scan such large corpora for significant collocational patterns. I therefore discuss how computer-assisted methods can be used to identify fixed and semi-fixed phrases in large corpora, and how such methods can document the characteristic use of words much more reliably and thoroughly than is possible from an intuitive reading of individual texts.

7.2   Text and Discourse: Different Senses of 'Discourse'

In previous chapters, I have used *text* and *discourse* to mean naturally occurring instances of language in use. However, *discourse* is also used in a very different sense to mean recurrent phrases and conventional ways of talking, which circulate in the social world, and which form a constellation of repeated meanings. I will illustrate this here initially with examples of the different ways in which education is talked about in contemporary Britain, and how this discourse uses key terms such as *(falling) standards*, *grammar*, *(back to) basics* and *discipline*.

This is *discourse* in the sense in which we refer to *academic discourse*, or *sexist* or *racist discourse*. Vocabulary and grammar provide us with the potential and resources to say different things. But often this potential is used in regular ways, in large numbers of texts, whose patterns therefore embody particular social values and views of the world. Such discourse patterns tell us which meanings are repeatedly expressed in a discourse community. (This is the sense of discourse, as it is developed by Foucault, 1972; see also Fairclough, 1992; Lemke, 1989.) Such recurrent ways of talking do not determine thought, but they provide familiar and conventional representations of people and events, by filtering and crystallizing ideas, and by providing pre-fabricated means by which ideas can be easily conveyed and grasped.

7.3   Introductory Example: Language and Nation

In chapters 4 to 6, I focused on linguistic features of texts, but paid relatively little attention to the wider discourse in which the texts appeared. This chapter discusses aspects of intertextual relations across texts.

The basic proposition of this book, that it is always possible to talk about the same thing in different ways, applies equally when the topic of discussion is language itself. Ideas from the social sciences circulate in and out of the social world (Giddens, 1984), and these include ideas about language diversity and social dialects, which have been imported into teacher education from sociolinguistics. But such ideas about linguistic tolerance have only a precarious foothold, given the deep-seated linguistic intolerance for which the British are well known.

Professional linguists have frequently formulated such matters in terms of an opposition between prescriptive and descriptive views of language. But there are many other ways of talking about language, used by politicians, purists, language planners and nationalists. Much of this discourse is characterized by debate around a relatively small set of key words which frequently recur, such as *standards, discipline, fundamentals, basics, common sense, literary heritage, nation, proper education.* (Raban (1989) provides an analysis of several key words in a speech by Mrs Thatcher, including *history, heritage, roots, proper, caring services.*) In Britain, particularly under the Conservative governments of the 1980s, particular phrases such as *British heritage, deteriorating standards* and *back to basics* were used to signal a cluster of related ideas, and were rallying calls within a broader discourse of conservative values and English (rather than British) nationalism. This discourse has features which are familiar across many countries and languages, and across hundreds of years of British commentary on language. These include: a high level of public interest, represented by extensive coverage in the mass media; a reverence for the past, represented by a narrow range of literature, often symbolized by Shakespeare and the King James Bible; fears that the national language is being threatened by internal diversity (dialects) and by external diversity (ethnic minority languages); an elitist condemnation of what is regarded as sub-standard language; and a strongly nationalist ethic with an emphasis on the unique and irreplaceable national culture.

Much of this discourse has a strongly irrational streak. It is very difficult, for example, to see how Standard English could possibly be under threat from other languages. But nationalist discourse is rarely rational. As Thomas (1991, pp. 135–6) documents, the many motivations for linguistic purism 'pale into insignificance beside nationalism as a determinant of puristic attitudes . . . nationalism and purism share many core features'.[1]

Consider the following quotes on language and nation, which are very similar in their wordings.

'In the future of its language there lies the future of a nation' (from a British Conservative government think-tank paper: Marenbon, 1987)

'... language above all else is the defining characteristic of an individual, a community, a nation' (from a British government report on English teaching: Kingman, 1988, p. 43)

'English ought to be the queen of the curriculum for any British child. It is one of the things that define his or her nationality' (from an editorial in *The Times*, 30 April 1988)

This claimed language–nationality relationship has very little basis in British law, but is constantly cited as a natural view. Rather, the view that a language embodies the genius of the people who speak it was developed within European Romanticism, especially by Herder and von Humboldt in Germany in the 1700s and 1800s. Crowley (1991, p. 245) points out what Marenbon actually means, and rewrites the Marenbon quote more accurately to: 'In the *past* of our language there lies the *future* of our nation.'

7.3.1   Different discourses

By the mid-1980s in the UK, the post-war consensus of optimistic liberalism was at an end. The 1980s were a time of rapid social change and enormous social uncertainty. At such times, language becomes a focus of debate, because of the ways in which it symbolizes social and personal identity (Crowley, 1989). And I have discussed elsewhere (Stubbs, 1989) some of the differences between professional and lay discourse on language, with reference to a British government report on English teaching in schools, and the way in which this report was mediated by newspapers, radio and television, and interpreted very differently by prominent politicians and other public figures, and by professional teachers.

There is a very wide gap between the way in which linguists discuss such issues and much of the discussion in the mass media. For example, speaking on Radio 4 in November 1985, Norman Tebbit (ex-chairman and influential member of the right wing of the Conservative party) claimed a causal connection between the decline in grammar teaching and the rise in football hooliganism (cited by Graddol and Swann, 1988):

> we've allowed so many standards to slip ... teachers weren't bothering to teach kids to spell and to punctuate properly. ... If you allow standards to slip to the stage where good English is no better than bad English, where people turn up filthy ... at school ... all those things tend to cause people to have no standards at all, and once you lose standards then there's no imperative to stay out of crime

This is a claim about linked events: standards of language are indicative of standards in general, and if standards slip, then people slip into crime. Tebbit is here weaving a seamless web of associations: 'all those things' are evidence of a breakdown of respect for authority. Grammar, discipline, authority, hierarchy: they are all related. He is not wrong about the symbolic meaning of 'all those things'. Grammar was dropped from many school English syllabuses as one part of a child-centred movement in teaching, which also had the explicit aim of changing teacher–pupil relations in schools. Tebbit's interpretation makes perfect sense within a particular discourse. But he offers only a very partial interpretation, as though it was comprehensive. The absurd logic of the spelling–crime link is not spelled out.

Such statements show that the debate over Standard English and grammar is part of a much larger ideological debate: a battle over ideas which are very deeply entrenched in British society. There is a general assumption, central to the background ideology, that anyone who speaks English knows what is meant by good English, and knows how to teach it: no special expertise is required, and supposed educational experts are charlatans. The key ideological move is to endorse a common sense position which requires no analysis, because everyone knows what the truth is.

One major intervention in the media debate was made by Prince Charles. As *The Daily Telegraph* put it, he 'launched a scathing attack on standards of English teaching'. The Prince made his comments, apparently off the cuff, at a seminar with business people, and they were reported verbatim in most papers the following day (29 June 1989). It is not possible to reconstruct exactly what he said, but reports in several papers give this:

We've got to produce people who can write proper English. It's a fundamental problem. All the people I have in my office, they can't speak English properly, they can't write English properly. All the letters sent from my office I have to correct myself, and that is because English is taught so bloody badly. That is the problem. If we want people who write good English and write plays for the future, it cannot be done with the present system, and all the nonsense academics come up with. It is a fundamental problem. We must educate for character. That's the trouble with schools. They don't educate for character. This matters a great deal. The whole way schools are operating is not right. I do not believe English is being taught properly. You cannot educate people properly unless you do it on a basic framework and drilling system

Some of the papers had fun reporting counter-attacks on the Prince's swearing, and the fact that most of his secretarial staff went to public (that is, non-state, private) schools. But more serious are the unanalysed clichés in his statements: that there is an unproblematic good, 'proper' English; that English is taught badly; that strength of character is related to good English; and that 'proper' education requires drilling.

If regarded rationally, the statements are a sequence of non-sequiturs. It does not make sense to think that everyone who speaks good (that is, Standard?) English has a strong character. But the statements do not operate at this level. (Remember Tebbit on dialect and crime.) They are part of a discourse which calls up a set of linked key words, symbols and beliefs about schools, language and the nation. They depend on a set of premises, which are unstated and probably unconscious. The utterances generate a 'recognition effect' (Hall, 1982, p. 74). Readers know what sort of thing is being said, what position is being adopted. It is a confirmation of the obvious. An explicit and rational argument would draw attention to the premises, and therefore admit that other premises are possible.

Ideas gain stability when they fit into a schema. Many everyday ideas about language fit very firmly into a schema which contains terms such as *standard, standards, accurate, correct, grammar, proper, precise*. For linguists, the same terms mean something quite different because they fit into an entirely different schema, which contains terms such as *dialect, language planning, high prestige language, social variation*.

These schemas are systems of meaning, which use particular vocabulary, take particular things for granted, appeal to different states of knowledge (for example, lay and professional), and therefore allow only particular argumentative moves. Much of the public debate is a struggle over competing definitions. *Grammar* has a wide range of connotations: discipline, rules, authority. *Bilingual* is often a euphemism for "black", "immigrant", or "poor working class". *Dialect* has quite different connotations in everyday and academic discussion. In everyday discourse, *dialect* means "distortion, deviation from Standard English, sub-standard English". *Equality* (as in *all languages are potentially equal*) is often read as a slogan of the political left: and linguists are classed along with trendy teachers. *Trendy* is a code term for "left wing" (Graddol and Swann, 1988; Cameron and Bourne, 1989).

Using methods described in detail below, I checked the common collocates of *trendy* in a large corpus of British and American English. They were: *fashion, left, lessons, methods, new, teachers, theories, yuppies*. The word occurs in sentences such as

> Prince Charles is furious at *trendy teaching* which has axed Shakespeare from many schools [A] (British tabloid newspaper)

today's *trendy teaching methods* are not getting the three R's through [A] (British tabloid newspaper)

the *left wing canker of trendy theories*, low expectations and poor achievement [A] (American newspaper)

On 2 July 1989, three days after Prince Charles's statement on 'proper education', Kenneth Baker (then Secretary of State for Education) published a long article in the *Sunday Express*, which contains many examples of the background ideology. Here are some brief extracts.

> When the Prince of Wales said that English is taught badly . . . he was echoing the concerns of parents and employers. . . . It has been fashionable to use 'socio-economic' factors to excuse poor standards. The bleaters were always looking for excuses. . . . [This was] the argument trotted out for so long by the glib fashion designers of education. . . . [The National Curriculum] means clear standards for reading, writing, spelling, punctuation, grammar and hand-writing. . . . Common sense is winning out. Common sense is back in fashion. Standards of English must improve. . . . We must not let our children down for they are the future of our nation

Common sense is contrasted with expertise. Expertise is identified with fashion (compare *trendy*). And *ad hominem* remarks replace rational argument. Despite a great deal of talk about *the basics*, it is in the interests of some groups to keep the discussion trivial, and to deny the complexity of the issues. The frequent accusations of complexity, jargon and education-speak are a central aspect of the public debate. (See, for example, explicitly right-wing government supported publications such as Lawlor (1988) and Letwin (1988).)

In the theory of educational success expressed in the article, only two factors count: a good school and individual motivation. It is unusual that the victim is here not blamed for his or her own failure (unless, of course, he or she is lazy or unmotivated). 'Bad schools' are squarely blamed, though there is no discussion of what makes good schools. Many of the other key words in the discourse occur in the article: the *basics, grammar, new standards, common sense*, 'our children . . . are the future of our nation'. But they are unanalysed. It is often said that Thatcherism had no theory of the public or social world, only of individuals.

Not explicitly mentioned at all are other assumptions of cultural heritage and assimilationism (Phillipson and Skutnabb-Kangas, 1989): 'monolingual policies must be all right because they got us where we are'; 'many languages divide a nation'; and 'overt class conflict and discrimination have almost disappeared'. Such views are widely held, although they are either questionable or untrue.

On 19 December 1989, Prince Charles delivered a long speech on the English language, based mainly on the view that the King James Bible and the Book of Common Prayer represent the high point of English and that things have been declining ever since. The speech falls squarely within the complaints tradition (Milroy and Milroy, 1985), and Prince Charles himself admits that complaints about falling standards of English stretch back into the last century. No evidence of decline is presented, beyond a few examples of earlier and more recent Bible translations, and a stated preference for the King James version. There is merely a claim that a consensus about such decline exists, and an artificially constructed comparison between Hamlet's 'To be, or not to be' soliloquy in the original, and Prince Charles's own parody of it in what is said to be modern English. The whole speech is based on the confusion that the English language as such has become 'impoverished, sloppy and limited', rather than some uses of it (that is, some users of it) having become sloppy. Otherwise, the speech is based on familiar key symbols: learning poetry by heart, grammar, the need for higher standards in a competitive world, the Bible and Shakespeare, and the British heritage (with no distinction made between British and English). Every daily newspaper reported the speech, sometimes at length.

On 22 April 1991, Prince Charles delivered a further lecture on Shakespeare, arguing that his neglect in schools is 'symptomatic of a general flight from our great literary heritage'. This lecture also contains many of the key words and phrases in such educational debates: *cultural inheritance, cultural roots, national identities, so-called experts, fashionable trends*. It is evident that we are involved here with something deeply symbolic and important for national identity, when the heir to the British throne chooses to make several substantial public statements on the link between English teaching and national (English? British?) language, heritage and literature. In 1994 Prime Minister John Major widened the debate over basics in education into a much more general 'back to basics' campaign, though this move caused considerable confusion about what such a phrase might actually mean.

The late 1980s represented a considerable upheaval in British educational politics, but in a longer-term perspective, they were the continuation of a centuries old debate between vocational training and a liberal education (Williams, 1961). The ideological debates behind the National Curriculum are just a small part of the long struggle over the authority of different sources of knowledge. These broad questions of knowledge and control are well beyond the scope of this book. They include: the conflict between professional and lay knowledge; the politicization of the school curriculum; media simplification and control of complex knowledge; and a culture which encourages disdain for professionals and the view that common sense is always the best guide, even in complex areas.

Such topics are frequently discussed within cultural and media analysis. Here I will show how corpus analysis could provide more systematic data on the mechanisms of such public debates. So far, I have not provided any methods for finding such recurrent phrases, beyond reading key texts and identifying them intuitively. The main aim of this chapter is now to discuss how linguists can help to analyse some of the rhetoric involved in such issues, when words such as *standards* and *basics* are given incompatible meanings within incompatible discourses. I will show how the analysis of large corpora can provide detailed documentation on how key words are used, present findings on some of the key words above and outline a broader project for documenting key words in British culture.

7.4   Firth on Focal Words

In chapters 2 and 3, I referred to Firth's (1935) famous paper, 'The technique of semantics', in which he outlines a project in text analysis with both a formal and a sociological component. These two components are very explicit in his proposals for

> research into the detailed contextual distribution of sociologically important words, what one might call *focal* or *pivotal* words . . . a systematic study of the use of all sorts of words in their actual contexts in the heart of everyday life. (pp. 40, 51)

He gives examples of such focal words in areas such as work and leisure. In chapter 3, I quoted his proposal to study such words as *work*, *labour*, *trade* and *leisure*, in all their variants in sociologically significant contexts.

In this chapter, I will illustrate how Firth's project could be carried out, given the computer-assisted methods of analysis which, sixty years later, are now available. I will describe a technique for studying such *focal* words across large corpora, and will outline how these examples could be developed into a more substantial project: a dictionary of keywords in British culture.

7.5   Williams on Keywords

Firth used the terms *focal* and *pivotal* words. Williams (1976) had in mind something very similar in his concept of *keywords*. Although Williams discusses linguistics elsewhere (e.g. 1977), he seems not to have been familiar with Firth's work. Williams characterizes his work in various ways: as historical semantics, the history of ideas and social criticism (1976, p. 11). Cameron (1992, p. 117) refers to it as a project in 'politicized lexicography' (see also Hodge and Kress, 1988, pp. 186ff).

Keywords: a Vocabulary of Culture and Society consists of 110 short essays, one to five pages in length, on 'a critical area of the vocabulary' (Williams, 1976, p. 23). The keywords fall mainly into sets which have to do with society and how it is conceived. Many entries concern social organization: individual, family, education, employment, society and nation. Other terms fit fairly easily into a few other main semantic fields, including high culture (e.g. *aesthetic, art, fiction, literature*), politics (including partly Marxist terms, e.g. *alienation, bourgeois, capitalism, democracy, dialectic, hegemony, revolution*) and some terms in the history of ideas (e.g. *philosophy, science, unconscious*).

This categorization is rough, though it is clear what Williams's essential interest is, and what sets of assumptions, ideas and values he is pointing to. In fact, there is no easy categorization: one of Williams's main points is that he has to make constant cross-references between entries in *Keywords*, since words in such semantic fields are by their very nature ambiguous. For example, the words *culture* and *cultivated* have meanings in farming (*agriculture*) as well as in the arts:

> the *cultivated* area was under irrigation [A]
>
> he is a *cultivated* man with a soft, rich voice [A]

Similarly, a *class* can be a unit in a school or in a society (e.g. *middle class*). And when one is talking about how nature and society are *classified*, then one expects such ambiguities. Therefore, the essays contain cross-references to other head words, but also discuss further semantically related words: for example, *educated* has cross-references to *culture* and *intellectual*, and mentions also *un-educated*.

Williams took his data from the 20-volume *Oxford English Dictionary*, and this allowed him to carry out a diachronic study of changes in meaning over time. The *OED* is a dictionary designed on historical principles, and contains attested data in the form of citations from a range of written sources from the 1100s on. Williams was interested in the synchronic complexity and variation in the meanings of words, which are a result of diachronic change.

He does not discuss Labov's (1970) work on the ultimate inseparability of the Saussurian concepts of synchronic and diachronic. But the structure of Williams's argument is exactly the same as Labov's. Labov observes that synchronic variation, in the phonology or syntax of a language, is the observable result of unobservable historical change. Williams presents the same argument for words which have related, multiple meanings. For example (1976, pp. 76–82), he shows that *culture* has nowadays such a variety of distinct meanings because of semantic extensions at various times in the past, leaving, as it were, layers of meanings, which have been deposited over time. From its earliest meaning concerning "tending crops or animals", the word was extended to human development (from the early 1500s). It was then further extended to the abstract general process (from the late 1700s) and acquired social class connotations. The development of the word in English was also influenced by cognate words in French and German. As a result, we now have, alongside each other, the different meanings evident in uses such as *sugar-beet culture*, *germ culture* and culture in the sense of "music, literature and the arts".

Williams was, at the time, able to use the *OED* only in the form of a multivolume book. He did not have at his disposal the *OED* on CD-ROM, which would nowadays allow many ways of developing his study. Jucker (1994) discusses some of the research projects possible with the CD-ROM version. Traditional printed dictionaries allow access to words only via the alphabetically ordered head words. But in the CD-ROM version, words can be accessed in several other ways: for example, it is possible to find all words first recorded in a particular year, or recorded in citations from particular authors. It is also possible to access words via their appearance in the definition texts. For example, one might search for all occurrences of the word form *work* in the definitions of other words. Since *work* is a frequent word in the basic vocabulary, and is a general superordinate term for other related words, there is a high chance that such a search will unearth a whole series of more specialized hyponyms, such as *duty* ("work one has to do"), *labour* ("hard, often unskilled work"), *toil* ("physically tiring work") and so on.

Although Williams was working with a conventional dictionary, and could study predominantly only single head words, he nevertheless gives many examples of fixed and semi-fixed phrases. The entry for CLASS discusses examples such as *lower classes, working classes, lower orders, privileged class, class consciousness, class war*, where the phrase means more than the sum of its parts. But he can provide no data on the relative frequency of such phrases, and he has no way of searching for other phrases, or of knowing whether he has identified the most typical and significant units. For example, the following were among the most frequent collocates (in descending frequency) of *class* in the Cobuild corpus (n = number of collocations in 130 million words).

middle, working, first ($n > 2,500$)

upper, second, top, world ($n > 500$)

high, ruling, lower, social, school, third ($n > 200$)

Even from such simple frequencies, one can see that several different overlapping meanings are common: in talking about society (*social class*, *ruling class*), about education (*school class*, *top of the class*), and in passing judgements, often in sports (*top class*, *world class*).

7.6   Other Studies of Cultural Keywords

Two of the most famous and thorough analyses of keywords are Williams (1973) on *The Country and the City* and Said (1978) on *Orientalism*. Said (1978, pp. 5, 54) points out, along with Vico and Marx, that human beings make their own history, but also that they make their own geography (see chapter 6). Both Williams and Said talk about the geographical and cultural divisions which are represented in literature, and which come to be accepted as conceptual grids for thinking about societies.

Williams studies the meanings, associations, images and connotations of two 'very powerful words'. COUNTRY is ambiguous: both a "nation/state" and "nature" (*countryside*). The word connotes rural England's *green and pleasant land* (he notes a rather different history for Scotland and Wales). It connotes the recurrent myth of a happier and more natural past, nostalgia for *the good old days*, the pastoral view of a simple, organic, innocent, Eden-like, rural community (often conveniently forgetting the property relations on which city–country relations are based); but it also connotes the stereotype of backwardness and of the boorish peasant clown. TOWN and CITY connote progress and modernity, but also noise, dirt, worldliness and ambition. Williams's main source is British literature, including the representations in authors such as Jane Austen, Thomas Hardy, George Gissing, Charles Dickens and D. H. Lawrence. And there are new ways of talking about such relations: not only *country* and *city*, but also *suburbs*, and the *environment*. *Ecology* is one of the words added in Williams (1983) (see also

Giddens, 1991, on environment). Williams (1985) is a study of the keywords *economic*, *management*, *law and order* and *community* as used in media coverage of the coal miners' strike in Britain in 1984–5.

Said's source is the European representations of the Orient in poets, essayists, administrators, philologists and cartoonists. These representations construct a view of the *mysterious East*. Orientalism is a style of thought, a regular constellation of ideas, a system of knowledge, a set of stereotypes and myths, which provide recurrent images of the Other. Said bases his argument explicitly on Foucault's concept of discourse. By discourse, Said means 'the vocabulary employed whenever the Orient is spoken or written about' (p. 71), 'that collection of . . . images and vocabularies available to anyone who has tried to talk about what lies east of the dividing line' (p. 73), 'certain types of statement . . . a manner of regularized writing, vision and study' (p. 202): the knowledge created by texts (p. 94). One example of these ways of talking is recurring collocations, such as (pp. 32, 203) *Oriental atmosphere*, *Oriental despotism*, *Oriental sensuality*, *Oriental tale*.

A check on my corpus data produced the following examples, which corroborate several such stereotypes:

a soft oriental rhythm came through entrancingly

an oriental orgy of monumental proportions

spices and other oriental exports

one could never be quite sure when dealing with an Oriental

that orientalized, barbarized population

all hours of the twenty-four are alike to Orientals

Such examples illustrate a clear general argument: fixed and semi-fixed expressions (collocations, catch phrases, clichés and idioms) encode cultural information. Such recurrent phrases, which derive partly from works of literature and cultural history, are one of the ways in which experience is represented and transmitted. The study of recurrent wordings is therefore of central importance in the study of language and ideology, and can provide empirical evidence of how the culture is expressed in lexical patterns. The cultural assumptions connoted by such patterns, especially when they are repeated and become habits, are an important component of socialization. However, the methods used by Williams and Said are entirely intuitive. They have recorded and categorized examples, largely from literary sources, but they have no method of identifying collocations which occur with significant frequencies.

Fairclough (1990, 1992, pp. 187–90) studies how the meanings of the word *enterprise* have been changed by political circumstances. The word was used by the British Conservative government in the 1980s in expressions such as *enterprise culture*. This was in turn a key phrase for core political aims. Fairclough's main data are a corpus of speeches given by Lord Young between 1985 and 1988, when he was Secretary of State in the Department of Trade and Industry (later renamed the Department of Enterprise).

With reference to Williams (1976) and Foucault (1972), Fairclough studies the new meanings which this word acquired in the 1980s as a result of deliberate semantic engineering by government ministers. He argues that the vocabularies of enterprise, skills and consumption were strategically manipulated and restructured, in order to exploit different meanings of the non-count noun *enterprise* as "engagement in a bold undertaking" and (in collocation with *free* or *private*) as "private business". He points out that the word often remains ambiguous, even in context, but that characteristic collocations, such as *enterprise and employment, self-reliance and enterprise* and *professionalism and enterprise*, exploit this ambiguity to give the word positive connotations.

I have checked the predominant contemporary meanings of *enterprise* (using the methods described below) in contemporary British data. Its collocates show how earlier meanings of the count noun *an enterprise* as "something one undertakes" or as "a business", and the meaning of *enterprising* as "adventurous", have been developed into the concept of *the enterprise culture*. In the Cobuild corpus, apart from the collocation with *Starship*(!), the most frequent collocates for singular (and non-count) and plural, respectively, are

> agency, business, capitalist, centre, councils, culture, development, flourishing, free, initiative, local, profitable, scheme, spirit, training, zones

> business, capitalist, commercial, economic, industrial, large, private, privatized, profitable, shares, small

Fairclough (1990, 1992) also argues that such shifts in the meaning of this individual word are part of a more general extension of the discourses of consumerism, marketing, management and counselling into educational discourses (where students are represented as *customers* or *clients*).

However, Fairclough's corpus was not computer readable, and he did not search it systematically for all examples and collocations. Nor were other corpora (for example, of newspaper texts) searched to check how far such uses had spread. The identification of culturally significant words will always involve personal intuition (as with Firth's and Williams's selection of the field of "work"). But having identified such words, we require a method for systematically searching for fixed phrases in corpora.

In a short article in *The Independent* newspaper, Hartston (1995) uses computer methods to compare the frequency of articles in this newspaper in which selected words occurred in 1993 and 1994. Mentions of *recession* went down (from 2,765 to 1,540). Mentions of *sleaze* went up (from 47 to 293): owing to increasing discussion of alleged corruption among politicians. Some figures require local knowledge for interpretation. The mention of *floorboards* went up (from 39 to 57): owing to stories about a mass murderer who disposed of his victims under the floorboards of his house. Such counts are now easy to carry out, given the availability of newspapers on CD-ROM, and can provide indications of how the media help to construct social trends.

Moon (1994) is one of the few studies of the frequency and distribution of fixed expressions both in a specific text (the editorial in a British news-paper) and across large corpora. She discusses the textual functions of such fixed phrases: to represent socio-cultural schemata and appeal to shared cultural values, by making allusions, exploiting quotations and using meta-phors and proverbs. Fixed expressions present familiar ideas in pre-packaged and stereotyped forms and thereby encourage their acceptance by leaving less room for meaning to be negotiated.

A major methodological advance in such study is made by Campanelli and Channell (1994), who study 'how ordinary people understand and use the term *training*'. This is a word which is at the centre of national debates about vocational education and workforce planning. (The analysis was car-ried out for the Department of Employment.) In the Cobuild corpus, they identified over 5,000 relevant examples of the word forms *training*, *train*, *trains*, *trained*, *trainee*, *trainees*. (Irrelevant meanings were excluded, such as "railway trains", and meanings with non-animate things, such as *to train a gun on* or *to train a rose bush*.) A few major points, from their detailed analysis of patterns of occurrence, are as follows. Main fields of activity are animals, sports and occupations. Uses differed significantly in different text types. For example, among newspapers, the "occupations" meaning occurred in 42 per cent of uses in *The Times*, but in only 24 per cent of uses in the tabloid *Today* (where the commonest use was the "sports" meaning). In spoken data, 67 per cent of uses were in the "occupations" meaning. Use with occupations was limited to those requiring defined and delimited training periods, e.g. military, medical, teaching, police. Fixed phrases included teacher training, management training, youth training, staff training, military training; trainee architects, trainee bus conductors, trainee car mechanic, trainee doctor

The frame *train as a* also collocates with occupations (e.g. *train as a cook, lawyer, nurse*). The frames *train to* and *train in* collocate with skills and occupation names (e.g. *train to manage libraries, be discrete, resuscitate heart attack victims; train in counselling techniques, home economics, first aid*).

One of Williams's (1976) keywords is *educated*. But he does not discuss the related *trained*, and his analysis could be greatly developed by such methods (see further below).

7.7   The Formal Component: Collocations

I will now show how quantitative techniques of corpus analysis can be used to analyse the meaning and use of cultural keywords, The main concept is that words occur in characteristic *collocations*, which show the associations and connotations they have, and therefore the assumptions which they embody. These collocations are open to introspection only in a very rough and ready way: often native speakers' intuitions about collocations are very inaccurate, and intuitions certainly cannot document such collocations thoroughly. We therefore require techniques for studying the characteristic associations of words across large corpora.

Two necessary concepts have occurred frequently in earlier chapters: lemma and word form. An apparently simple example of the distinction is the lemma CLASS, which can be realized by various word forms *class, classes, classed, classing*. The distinction is often treated as a rather trivial linguistic problem, but lemmatization hides difficult issues. For example, does this lemma include *classify* and *classification*? In traditional linguistic uses of the concept lemma, these word forms would not be included, although they are semantically related to some meanings of CLASS, and these relations are culturally important.

Corpus analysis shows that one form of a lemma is usually much more common than others (Sinclair, 1991a, pp. 68–9). In addition, different word forms can have quite different collocates. A striking example is provided by EDUCATE. In 130 million words, frequencies were: *education* 27,705, *educated* 3,450, *educate* 858, *educating* 463, *educates* 29. The form *education* collocates primarily with terms denoting institutions (e.g. *further, higher, secondary, university*). The form *educate* collocates with approximate synonyms such as *enlighten, entertain, help, inform, train*.

EDUCATE is one of Williams's (1976) keywords. But his methods were not fine-grained enough to document the different meanings of different word forms. In fact, although he gives this keyword in the form *educated*, he misses a pattern which can be seen in corpus data. The form *educated* frequently collocates with *at* (often in the phrase *he was educated at*), and then with a range of prestigious institutional names, including *Cambridge*, *Charterhouse*, *college*, *Eton*, *Harrow*, *Harvard*, *Oxford*, *school*, *university*, *Yale*. The collocates of the form *educated* therefore provide a little list of ways in which men (much less frequently women) are classified and talked about.

The concept of collocation, which I have used in earlier chapters, now needs a more explicit and detailed definition. Firth (1935) proposes formal methods for studying the distribution of words, including their tendency to co-occur with other words. Collocations constitute one of the many levels to which meaning is 'dispersed'. His famous definition of collocation is 'the company a word keeps': 'The habitual collocations in which words under study appear are quite simply the mere word accompaniment. . . . Collocations are actual words in habitual company' (Firth, 1957b, pp. 11, 14).

It is standard to talk of a node word, and of the collocates which occur within a certain span of this node, say within four words to left and right. This is the span used in the data cited below.

One of Firth's examples is that part of the meaning of *ass* is its habitual collocation with words such as *silly* (1935, p. 11). The example *silly ass* was chosen in the 1930s, and nowadays sounds rather old-fashioned or quaint, and this in itself illustrates a feature of language change that is not often discussed, since collocations can only be established in attested texts. (For further discussion of fixed expressions, clichés, recurring collocations, idioms, fixed syntactic structures, etc., see Sinclair, 1991a, pp. 109ff; Miller, 1993).

A particular collocational phenomenon has been identified by Sinclair (1991a) and Louw (1993): what they call a semantic prosody. This is prosody in its Firthian sense of a feature which extends over more than one unit (see section 2.6): here over a span of words. For example, Sinclair (1991a, p. 112) points out that HAPPEN is 'associated with unpleasant things, accidents and the like'; and that the main vocabulary which collocates with SET IN refers to unpleasant states of affairs, such as rot, decay, disillusion, infection and so on. Note that this a statement about probabilities: these are the most common uses of the word as attested in large corpora.

I demonstrate in detail in other work (Stubbs, 1995a,b) that the lemma CAUSE has a strongly negative semantic prosody. Based on an analysis of some 40,000 examples across 120 million words from the Cobuild corpus, I show that its typical collocates are overwhelmingly unpleasant. The most characteristic include

> accident, concern, damage, death, trouble

It only rarely occurs with 'positive' collocates: *cause for concern* is very much more common than *cause for confidence*. Although many words seem to have such negative prosodies, some words, such as PROVIDE, have positive prosodies.[2] For example, *causing work* usually means bad news, whereas *providing work* is usually a good thing. Typical collocates of PROVIDE are from the semantic fields of care, food, help, money and shelter. The most frequent object nouns are

> aid, assistance, care, employment, facilities, food, funds, housing, jobs, money, opportunities, protection, relief, security, services, support, training

This provides a further detailed example of the co-selection of lexis: once either CAUSE or PROVIDE has been selected, one can predict semantic features of accompanying words (see section 2.6).

7.7.1   Quantitative methods

The formal, systematic and contextual component of Firth's project involves distributional analysis. Semantic analysis would regard meaning 'chiefly as situational relations in a context of situation . . . the inter-relations of the terms of the actual observable context itself' (1935, p. 53). Firth is here proposing empirical, text-based methods of semantic analysis. Meaning is not regarded as a purely mental phenomenon, but is analysed distributionally on the basis of observable, objective textual evidence. Firth was clear about both sociological purpose and formal distributional method, but he lacked the computational resources to carry out such an analysis. Such methods involve compiling a concordance for the lemma from a corpus of data, and inspecting this in a traditional way (that is, by eye!), but also using quantitative methods to analyse such concordance data further. As Sinclair (1991a, p. 17) points out, 'One of the principle uses of a corpus is to identify what is central and typical in the language.'

An important fact to be extracted from corpora is simply the absolute frequency of each collocation, since what we are looking for is recurrent phrases which encode culturally important concepts. However, for two reasons, we also have to know how often node and collocate occur independently. First, if node and/or collocate are themselves very frequent, then they might occur in collocation just by chance. Second, a word might itself be infrequent: but, when it does occur, then it often occurs in collocation with one other word.

An example is the word *quintessentially*: it occurs only 170 times in 130 million words of British English (from the Cobuild corpus), but on 55 occasions it occurs in the collocation *quintessentially English*. A further 54 occurrences are with other nationality adjectives. Many of the remaining occurrences are other geographical terms, mainly names of towns, or names of famous people. Examples are

> the quintessentially English game of cricket
>
> quintessentially English porcelain
>
> baseball, the quintessentially American game
>
> the quintessentially French provincial French hotel
>
> the music is quintessentially Rod Stewart
>
> a quintessentially Thatcherite figure

Thus, *quintessentially* is itself not very common: about one occurrence per million words of running text. There are therefore only 100 examples of collocations with nationality adjectives. But these account for nearly 60 per cent of the occurrences of the node word. We must therefore look at both absolute frequency of collocations, and the frequency of collocations relative to the frequency of node and collocate.

One way of identifying recurrent collocations is just to look at concordance lines, especially when they have been alphabetically sorted. This procedure works well for short texts (and is what I did in chapter 4, when I studied collocations of *happy*). It is easy to inspect even a few hundred concordance lines in such a manner. However, to study larger corpora and to compare words, we require a method of summarizing concordance data and of calculating the frequency and the likelihood of association between words. Such a method requires software which can carry out the following tasks:

- identify in a corpus all occurrences of a node word (word form or lemma) and its frequency;
- keep a record of collocates of this node which occur in a window of defined size (e.g. four words to left and right);

- count the frequency of joint occurrence of node and each collocate, i.e. the frequency of each collocation;
- count the absolute frequency of each collocate in the whole corpus.[3]

7.8   Other Examples of Collocations and Semantic Prosodies

We now have two main concepts. *Collocation* means the habitual co-occurrence of two (or more) words. And *semantic prosody* is a particular collocational phenomenon: some words (e.g. CAUSE) have a predominantly negative prosody, a few (e.g. PROVIDE) have a positive prosody, many words are neutral in this respect, but all words are restricted in the collocates with which they occur. In addition, we have a computational method of identifying fixed and semi-fixed phrases in corpora. This technique can now be used to study words which have, intuitively, cultural significance.

In earlier chapters, I gave brief examples of the connotations which words have, and I have constantly emphasized the need to analyse texts comparatively, especially against the background of what is expected in the language as represented by general corpora. I discussed the collocations and connotations of the lemmas HAPPY (section 4.5), REEL, HIT, SMASH, etc. (sections 5.4, 5.6.2) and TRENDY (this chapter). In section 6.3, I discussed the metaphorical uses of LOSE in formulations such as: *the area lost population* and *many jobs were lost*. We now have concepts and a method of investigating such connotations more systematically.

7.9   The Sociological Component: Encoding Culture in Lexis

Now that I have presented the formal component, I can illustrate how one might carry out Firth's proposal to investigate lemmas such as WORK and EMPLOY. This semantic field is also one of the most important discussed by Williams (1976). Many points in his analyses (based on the citation data in the *OED*) are corroborated by the quantitative analysis of contemporary corpus data. But a corpus study allows a much more fine-grained analysis of the most frequent and characteristic collocations of a lemma and its different word forms. I will draw attention to features of Williams's (1976) analysis, and to the meanings provided in the Cobuild dictionary (first edition, Sinclair, 1987a) since this is based on attested corpus data.

Williams's (1976) main observation about WORK and several related lemmas is that they have developed historically from more general meanings of "doing something", to more restricted and specialized meanings concerning the social and economic relationships of paid employment. WORK retains very general meanings: one can *work* in the garden. But, historically, there has been a shift to the predominant meaning of a paid social relationship, so that a *woman who works* or a *working woman* is a woman with a paid job, not a woman who does *housework*. Thus, to be *in work* or *out of work* refer to having a paid job. Similarly, JOB also still has general senses, which can apply to limited and occasional pieces of work, as in *doing some jobs around the house*, or *the price for the job*. But it has become the normal term for paid employment of whatever kind, and has been extended (at least in spoken language) to cover what were previously *appointments, positions, posts* and *situations*: one can talk about the job of a coalminer or of the prime minister. LABOUR still shows its earlier general sense in *laborious*, but, again, has been specialized to the economic abstraction evident in phrases such as *supply of labour*. The social class implications are evident in phrases such as *labour movement*. EMPLOYMENT and UNEMPLOYMENT show similar shifts. Thus *unemployed* can still be used in its earlier meanings of "not used" or "idle". But out of the earlier meanings, which concerned individual and personal conditions, has developed a more modern sense of "in" or "out of paid work", particularly with reference to the social conditions of a country. And again, INDUSTRY has developed from a meaning of "personal diligent effort" (cf. *industrious*) to the meaning of "institutions which produce something".

WORK. These points are confirmed by the first sense of WORK (out of nearly forty) identified by the Cobuild dictionary: "People who work have a job which they are paid to do", e.g. *He was working in a bank*. Two features of the word, which Williams does not record, but which are very evident in alphabetically sorted concordance lines, are that different forms of the lemma have very different collocates, and that they contribute to a very large number of compound words and fixed phrases. It is evident that the word form *working* occurs in fixed phrases such as *working class, working conditions* and *working mother*, whereas the word forms *work, works* and *worked* have quite different collocates. For example, *work* occurs in a large number of compound nouns, such as

> workaholic, workforce, workload, workplace, workroom, worksheet, workshop, workstation, worktop, workwear

Some of these forms (e.g. *workforce*) are very frequent, and others (e.g. *workstation*) are relatively recent, and show that this compounding is productive. *Worker* also occurs in a large number of fixed noun–noun phrases. Very frequent are

> aid worker, factory worker, office worker, social worker

But attested examples of nouns immediately preceding *worker* include, among many others,

> airport, bakery, bank, brewery, building, care, charity, coalface, community, construction, defence, farm, forestry, government, health, hospital, hotel, housing, kitchen, maintenance, morgue, sex, steel, welfare, youth

Such constructions are also productive and are replacing other terms (e.g. *bank worker* = *bank clerk, coalface worker* = *miner, farm worker* = *agricultural labourer*). Corpus data show the very broad extension of the word *worker*, across both *blue-collar* and *white-collar jobs*. The identification of people as workers, and the changing identity of the *working* and *middle classes*, has been a central theme in cultural studies, from Hoggart (1957) onwards. And the long struggle over the meaning of the word is also visible in the key media term in the 1950s, *the affluent worker*. This phrase was also the title of a famous sociological study published in the 1960s.

JOB. The Cobuild dictionary's first definition (out of many) is "the work that a person does regularly to earn money", e.g. *a good job as a secretary*. This central meaning is confirmed by collocates such as

> full-time, office, permanent, promotion, proper

JOB occurs frequently in fixed phrases such as *to do a good job*. Jobs can be *cushy, easy* and *workmanlike*, and can *give satisfaction*. But, in both senses of "piece of work" and "paid employment", JOB often has negative collocates (see section 6.3 on jobs being *axed, lost*, etc.). Other collocates include

> botched, crummy, difficult, hard, hatchet (i.e. hatchet job), menial, shitty, stressful, thankless, unenviable, unglamorous, unskilled, wangled

The negative features of JOB were recorded by Johnson in his dictionary of 1755: 'A low word now much in use, of which I cannot tell the etymology. 1. A low mean lucrative busy affair. 2. Petty, piddling work; a piece of chance work. 3. A sudden stab with a sharp instrument.'

CAREER. Williams (1976, p. 44) notes two essential points which are borne out by the corpus data: career has been extended to "any favourable or desired or flattered occupation", and a career is a job in which there is "some implicit promise of progress". The Cobuild dictionary emphasizes the progression; but not the predominantly high prestige nature of the work. CAREER has a strong positive prosody. It is used predominantly of high-prestige public professions, and collocates with

> acting, director, film, international, journalistic, literary, managerial, opera, political, professional, public

> brilliant, distinguished, glittering, illustrious, meteoric, promising, successful

A career has a structure and goals. This is seen from collocates such as

> advancement, begin, development, embark, establish, goals, highlights, launch, life, pinnacle, promotion, prospects, pursue, relaunch, spell, stages, start, structure, varied, year, years

However, against the expectation of success and progress, careers can also *take a nosedive* and can be

> blighted, chequered, flagging, inauspicious, ruined, undistinguished, wrecked

LABOUR. The Cobuild dictionary gives as the first meaning "very hard work, often work that does not need a lot of skill" (e.g. *manual labour*). LABOUR can be *productive* and *skilled*, but the word also has many negative collocates (do the British Labour Party know this?), such as

> casual, cheap, deskilling, manual, semi-skilled, unemployed, unproductive, unskilled

Labourer collocates with low-prestige or low-paid professions:

> agricultural, building, casual, clerk, farm, manual, poor, shop, unemployed, unskilled

Collocates also include *black* and *Irish*. (See below on stereotypes of national groups.)

APPRENTICE. The Cobuild dictionary gives a definition which

expresses no value judgements: a young person working "in order that they can learn a skill". Cobuild notes that it can have an old fashioned ring: its commonest collocates in the corpus are *sorcerer* (presumably a reference to Goethe's – or Walt Disney's! – story) and *journeyman*. It collocates with terms for occupations which are largely manual:

> *in* engineering; *as a* carpenter, chef, electrician, jockey, painter, plumber

A striking feature of concordance data on *apprentice* and *apprenticeship* is that the word forms frequently occur in longer semi-fixed phrases: lexis and grammar are co-selected (see section 2.6). Note the characteristic verbs and references to times, dates and ages. These are selected from dozens of such parallel examples:

> started an apprenticeship as a carpenter
>
> begin an apprenticeship as a heating engineer
>
> served a brief apprenticeship as a draughtsman
>
> completed a 5-year apprenticeship at the station hotel
>
> started work at the age of 14 as an apprentice pastry cook
>
> began his artistic career as an apprentice glass painter
>
> joined the RAF as a boy apprentice in 1923

UNEMPLOYMENT. The Cobuild dictionary notes as the first meaning "the number of people in a country or area who do not have jobs although they want one". As a second meaning, it gives "the situation of someone not having a job when they want one". As examples, Cobuild gives *the level of unemployment in Scotland* and *the miseries of unemployment*. It is the statistical concept which is predominant in the corpus data. *Unemployment* applies to areas and populations, rather than to the people who are unemployed. It collocates not with references to individual people, but with references to groups and categories of people and to areas, and with quantitative expressions:

> adults, men, pensioners, students, workers, young
>
> blackspot, structural
>
> average, fall, grow, increase, level, numbers, per cent, rate, reduce, rise, rocket, seasonally, soar

It occurs in many fixed phrases such as

high(er) unemployment, mass unemployment, massive unemploy-
ment, rising unemployment, soaring unemployment; fear of unem-
ployment, growth in unemployment, rise in unemployment, level of
unemployment, problems of unemployment, rate of unemployment;
unemployment benefits, unemployment figures, unemployment
rates

In data from BBC radio, the word *unemployment* is much more frequent
(over five times) than the word *unemployed*. That is, the topic is talked about
mainly as a general structural economic phenomenon, not as something
affecting individual unemployed people.

EMPLOYMENT. The Cobuild dictionary gives: 1. "work that you do in
order to earn money"; 2. "the fact or condition of employing people"; 3. "the
availability of jobs for the population of a town, area or country". These
definitions do not quite capture some of the implications of the collocations
in the corpus data. Again, *employment* is not used primarily in connection
with individuals. It collocates with *persons* (e.g. *persons seeking employment*)
rather than with *people*. It has many collocates which indicate a legal use,
often concerning different categories of employment. And again it occurs, to
some extent, in collocations with statistical expressions:

commission, conditions, contract, disabled, discrimination, law(s),
legislation, opportunities, protection, provisions, rights, services,
terminate

alternative, figures, fluctuations, full, gainful, growth, industrial, self,
status, sources, temporary

There are many other words in the semantic field of work and employment, and, as I note above, a thorough search for such words could be done
by checking the definitions in a machine readable dictionary.

In retrospect, such lists of collocates can often seem very obvious to
the native speaker: they seem intuitively right. But this is the wisdom of
hindsight: native speakers are quite unable to document such collocates
thoroughly from intuition alone.

7.10 Designing a Dictionary of Keywords in British Culture

If such preliminary examples are to be turned into a complete dictionary,
then detailed questions of design arise. In particular, how could a list of
keywords be established?

One starting point is the 110 head words in Williams's (1976) original book. One might document their most typical collocates in contemporary English. However, while Williams's list contains many items which might be widely agreed as essential for such a dictionary (e.g. *bureaucracy, educated, work*), the list is in some respects a personal one. It was constructed in the 1960s and 1970s by a white male Marxist (as one of my colleagues put it), and reveals some of his personal biases towards predominantly literary and Marxist terms, which have limited general cultural interest (e.g. *dialectic, formalist, hegemony*). Some such words might easily be excluded by imposing a lower frequency limit for occurrence in corpus data. Furthermore, Williams's list is in some ways already out of date: indeed, it was up-dated by Williams (1983) himself in a revised second edition of the book, in which he added a further 20 head words including *ecology, expert* and *western.*

In cultural domains, words can move rapidly in and out of fashion. A list of head words for a dictionary would have to be sensitive to current cultural and political trends and debates (for example, in Britain, on nationhood, on a 'proper' education, etc.), but avoid shorter-lived political slogans and buzz words. Some ways of talking relate to passing party political concerns and catch phrases, but are manipulated by politicians precisely because they are trying to exploit major concerns which have a long history. One example is COMMUNITY. In the early 1990s, both right- and left-wing political parties in Britain were emphasizing *community values.* The British Conservative government's proposal of a *community charge* in the late 1980s was definitively rejected – not only the tax, but also the term itself: the population renamed it *poll tax.* (See below on *community care.*) But there is also a much longer history and debate around this word: see Williams (1973). Similarly, *back to basics* may represent a relatively local and short-lived political slogan, with which, again, the British government attempted to tap popular anxieties in the early 1990s. But such concerns with literacy and a 'proper' education are also part of a much longer debate over vocational versus liberal education: see Williams (1961).

Many key concepts and associated expressions are explicit in interpretations of modern society and culture, and there is often a considerable overlap in the key concepts identified independently in various sources. For example, Firth's original examples of WORK occur as a central theme in both Williams (1976) and Foucault (1980).

7.10.1   Lifestyle and professionalization

Two major themes in studies of contemporary society are: the changing life cycle of the individual, and personal identity; and the professionalization of modern life. And these themes provide two major underlying dimensions for a dictionary of cultural keywords. The life cycle of the individual could be regarded as: birth, health, sickness, death. From the point of view of place and identity, it could be seen as widening circles, from private to public life: family, home, education, employment; or individual, family and friends, community, town and country, society and culture, country and nation.

Many theorists of contemporary society (Foucault, 1980; Bernstein, 1990; Giddens, 1991, pp. 31, 173; Fairclough, 1992) discuss the changing relations between private and public life, and point out that areas of life which were traditionally private and beyond public control (except perhaps by the priest) are more and more invaded by experts, professionals and specialists, and by people in *the professions*, such as scientists, technicians, technologists, managers, administrators, counsellors, therapists and social workers. Sampson's (1992) study of contemporary British society is organized largely around categories of people: *politicians, bureaucrats, judges* and *lawyers, students, scientists* and *engineers, bankers, industrialists, journalists* and other *workers*. Bernstein's (1990) account of the 'new professions which regulate the mind' identifies the professions of symbolic control, including *counsellors, journalists, social workers* and *teachers* (see section 1.6). Giddens's (1991) study of modernity and self-identity and Foucault's (1980) study of technologies of power and control similarly identify the increasing power of experts. *Expert* is one of the head words which Williams (1983) added in his second edition.

7.10.2 Example analyses

Such dimensions generate many important clusters of words and phrases. For example, consider the huge amount of discourse around health. The phrase *National Health Service* alone contains three keywords. Common phrases with SERVICE identify other important social institutions:

> BBC World Service, civil service, diplomatic service, health service, medical services, postal service, public service, social services, welfare service

Frequent collocating verbs are: NEED, PROVIDE (see above), SUPPLY. Other frequent phrases include

> conditions of service, financial services, goods and services, years of service

Health and other social services are often now talked about in terms of CARE. This lemma is perhaps not an obviously political word, but it signals important ways of talking about society as an economic and national unit. *Caring* has collocates such as *genuine*, *loving*, *sharing* and *sincere*, and is frequent in personal columns of newspapers:

> seeks caring male, for sincere honest relationship
>
> seeks a caring honest unattached lady 20–36

But CARE also has collocates which indicate more recent political concerns. A key phrase is *caring society*, and other significant collocates include

> association, community, costs, professional, professions, services, social, system

Concordance lines reveal a cluster of fixed phrases, in medical and social work areas, such as

> child care, children in care, child care workers, community care, care in the community, day care, health care, intensive care, maternity care, medical care, pastoral care, residential care, skin care, specialist care, health(-care) workers (See above on *worker*.)

Many phrases, such as *care and resettlement* (*of offenders*), signal considerable shifts in the discourse around how society deals with its deviant members. A more thorough analysis here would investigate a whole set of ways of talking about health and illness in terms of market forces, cost effectiveness and performance indicators, and in terms of professionalization (Hall, 1991), and also ways in which the discourse of counselling has been extended to many areas of public life (Fairclough, 1992). (See below on PROFESSIONAL in phrases such as *health professionals*. And see Kress (1994, pp. 39–45) for an analysis of the representation of *care* in British newspaper texts.)[4]

FAMILY (one of Williams's headwords) also occurs in collocations which signal important changes in social structures: the *extended family* gives way to *single-parent families* and *unmarried mothers*, terms which have caused trouble for the British Conservative government. *Parenting* is a new term which helps to constitute what it describes (Giddens, 1991, p. 33). The word *generation* has acquired new uses, and become detached from its sense relative to an individual family (grandparents, parents and self). One now talks of generations in relation to absolute time: *the generation of 1968* or *of the 1960s* (Giddens, 1991, p. 146).

An entry missing from Williams (1976, 1983) is that quin
British word HOME. It is often difficult to translate into other l;
one could predict from its use to name a complex cultural unit wniu.
implications for how we regard prototypical cultural organizations: as in
homesick, homeless person, broken home, she left home at sixteen. Fillmore
(1992) provides a thorough corpus-based analysis, both of its unique grammar, sometimes adverb, sometimes noun, and of its complex semantics. It
enters into different semantic oppositions, of very different scale: home
versus school, or home versus work, and home versus abroad (as in *Home
Office, Home Secretary, home affairs*). Corpus data show its most frequent
uses and collocations in fixed phrases, without an article, such as *at home,
bring home, come home, get home, go home*, and in a wide range of further fixed
phrases such as *convalescent home, nursing home, old people's home* (see above
on CARE), *stately home* (see below on HERITAGE), plus *holiday home,
mobile home*, etc.

As I pointed out in my introductory examples from British public figures,
there is much debate around national identity, and an important semantic
area is therefore one around country and nation, and around words for
different countries. There are many fixed phrases, from the rather quaint
(e.g. *nation of shopkeepers*) to the hotly disputed (e.g. *in the national interest*).
In one sense, lists of collocates for different countries provide no news. The
stereotypes for different countries and nations are often highly visible, for
example in newspaper cartoons. In his novel *Kettle of Roses*, Nash (1982)
parodies many fixed expressions which refer to different countries and
nationalities:

> your average b. foreigner; your decent British lad; England's green
> pastures; rolling English countryside; very dark and Welsh; sunny
> Spain; Viennese waltz; Blue Danube

So it is not surprising that British corpus data confirm that France is
constantly mentioned 'in the same breath as' cycling, restaurants, rugby and
wine; that Germany is associated with banks, Daimler Benz, Hitler and
Nazis; and Japan with banks, emperor, exports, industrial, scandal, shame
and trade. But a corpus-based study can document the recurrent phrases
which are one mechanism which constructs such national stereotypes. Nam-
ing and labelling are powerful ideological tools, and corpus analysis allows us
to study directly the labels which are repeatedly applied to groups of people
and the selective perceptions which this represents. (See Clark (1992); also
section 1.7.2 on Jucker's (1992) study of noun phrases in British newspapers,
and this chapter above on Said (1978) on Orientalism.)

Collocates of NATION show the classifications in which nations are talked about:

> biggest, European, favoured, industrialized, largest, trading, wealthiest

NATIONALIST has a predominantly negative prosody. It collocates with

> demagogue, disrupt, extreme, extremists, fanaticism, fascists, fervour, hardline, ideologue, militant, rabid, radical, rightwing

But *nationalist* is also used in connection with various nationalisms – Arab, Catalan, Hindu, Scottish, Tibetan, Welsh or whatever – which presumably acquire guilt by association with the negative collocates of the general term (see my comments below on *Jewish* and *Marxist*).

BRITISH is largely neutral. Many of its collocates are due to fixed phrases for organizations:

> Airways, Aerospace, Empire, Government, Rail, Telecom
>
> army, champion, companies, economy, forces, industry, troops

But ENGLISH collocates with words which reveal stereotypes:

> eccentrics, language, football, literature, heritage (see below), Channel, clubs, cricket, history, national, quintessentially, traditional, Oxford

IRISH has some collocates and fixed phrases which concern current politics (e.g. *Anglo-Irish agreement*), but others signal stereotypes, through words which are not especially frequent, but, when they do occur, have a tendency to occur with *Irish*:

> Anglo, army, border, liberation, Republic, republican
>
> accent, brogue, Catholic, fairylore, folk, folktale(s), handcrafts, navvies, peasantry, tinkers

SCOTTISH shows a similar pattern:

> devolution, national, Labour, Office, Royal, Nationalists

baronial, highlands, lairds, Munros (= "mountains over 3,000 feet"), pipers, salmon

WELSH (like IRISH) has collocates which provide an almost pure list of stereotypes, not all positive:

border, coalminers, clubs, cup, Eisteddfod, language, mountain, national, pony(ies), rarebit, rugby, sheepdog, team, windbags

In the contemporary politics of representation, HERITAGE signals shifting concepts of national identity and unity (see the statements above from Prince Charles). This word also acquired new meanings in British government discourse in the 1980s. The British government set up a Department of National Heritage, and other political parties have *national heritage spokesmen*. It is a different term for *history*. Its collocates show both the positive prosody and also the state intervention now involved in its construction:

ancestral, architectural, artistic, cultural, musical, priceless, rich

centre, department, English, foundation, fund, guarding, Minister, national, preserving, save, state

Words in the semantic field of professionalization differ considerably in their connotations. Corpus data show that EXPERTS are typically found in financial, legal, medical, military or other technical areas. They are often *baffled* or *confounded*, and sometimes talk *balderdash*! PROFESSION-ALISM has a strong positive prosody (Fairclough (1990) notes the collocation *professionalism and enterprise*: see section 7.6 above). It collocates with

admire, competence, consummate, dedication, efficiency, enthusiasm, highest, integrity, praised, pride, quality, respected, sheer, skill, standards, utter

A PROFESSIONAL is generally found in sport or in medicine. The phrase *health professionals* is increasingly common (see above). Williams (1976, p. 141) points out that *intellectuals* indicates "a category of persons, often unfavourably". As an adjective, INTELLECTUAL collocates with both strongly positive and strongly negative words, such as

accomplishments, brilliance, honesty, superiority, vigour

dishonesty, fads, ferment, gigolo, laziness, pretension, pseudo, snob(bery)

Many collocations for the word form *intellectuals* (the plural noun) show a strong negative prosody. That is, collocates such as the following would be interpreted negatively in many circles:

activists, contempt, dissident, hippie, ideology, leftist, leftwing, liberal, students, young

Note then how difficult it is to reject the assumptions underlying collocations such as *Jewish intellectuals* and *Marxist intellectuals*. There is nothing explicitly negative in such collocations: and their negative force can easily be denied. But the word *intellectuals* acquires negative connotations due to its collocations with explicitly negative words such as *contempt*. And the semantic prosody spreads to other collocates which occur in the same lexical frame.

7.10.3   Ambiguity of keywords

One rule of thumb for recognizing keywords (as both Williams and Foucault emphasize in their different ways) is their extreme ambiguity across different social domains and major institutions: education, the law, medicine, religion, the army. (See above on CLASS, COUNTRY and CULTURE.)

For example, AUTHORITY can mean both knowledge (*an authority on x*) and power (*respect for authority*). But in addition it can mean a social institution itself: *the authorities* (= "government, the police"), a *Local Authority*. CONFESS: one confesses sins (in religion), crimes (in the law), thoughts (in psychotherapy); in a phrase such as *Confessions of a Taxi Driver* (Sinclair, 1987a), the implication is sensationalism and scandal in the public media. CHARITY (one of Williams's keywords) can mean both an attitude which you show towards someone, and an organization or institution with a legal status, which raises money for good causes (*local charities, charity workers*). DISCIPLINE can mean both a branch of knowledge (*academic discipline*) and a system of control and punishment (*harsh discipline*); therefore both an educational and a military term. EXAMINATION can be a procedure both in education (*university examination*) and in medicine (*medical examination*); examinations are therefore at the heart of discipline, used to observe, judge, normalize and possibly punish. EXERCISE has an educational meaning of "a piece of school work" (*exercise book*), a physical training meaning of "energetic movement" (*take lots of exercise*) and a military meaning of "manoeuvres" (*peacetime exercises*); one can also *exercise power*. INDUSTRY (one of Williams's keywords) can mean "personal diligence", and also the people and processes involved in manufacturing something (*the oil industry*). INSTRUCT can mean knowledge (*read the instructions*), and has the educational meaning of "teach" (*instruction in French*), but can also mean an order. ORDER has to do with things being in their correct place (*in alphabetical order*), but also with power (*public order; law and order, to be given an order* – by someone *in authority*); and again, it can mean an institution itself (*monastic order, new world order*). PUBLIC: the anomalous use of *public school* to refer to a "private school" is well known. But its semantics are very complex: consider *public figure, public house, public order, public relations, public works, in public, the public,* as well as *publish, publication,* etc. SERVICE has a wide range of meanings. It can be the activity of serving someone, for example in a shop or restaurant (*service is not included in the bill*); or it can mean a religious ceremony (*church service*); or it can refer to an organization which provides something for the public (*train service, postal service*). In the plural, it usually means "the armed services".

Foucault, in many works, provides detailed discussions of the complex relations around confession, control, discipline, examination, knowledge, order and power.

7.11 Sample Dictionary Entries: Culture and Cultural

Any such list of keywords is open-ended and will always reveal the interests of the compiler, but some of the underlying principles are not difficult to make explicit. There are also practical constraints on the number of words which could be accommodated in any such book: one way of limiting the entries would be by frequency of occurrence in a given corpus.

Other details of the design of such a dictionary would depend on its purposes, as a reference book (possibly in appearance much like a traditional dictionary) or perhaps as a teaching book, with a series of short essays for use in cultural studies courses. Since such a book would provide detailed information on how fixed phrases tend to make certain ways of talking seem natural, it would inevitably have a critical function. But the social and cultural criticism could be more or less explicit. There are therefore many forms which the entries in a such a dictionary might take. However, as a concrete example of the kind of information they might contain, here are two sample entries.

CULTURE

As Williams (1976, p. 76) points out, '*culture* is one of the two or three most complicated words in the English language'. It has shifted from early meanings concerned with the tending of crops or animals (cf. *agriculture, horticulture*), to the range of meanings which are current today. The Cobuild dictionary distinguishes several main meanings, including 1. A whole society or civilization (*There are deep divisions over science in our culture*). 2. The ideas and customs of a society (*Roman and Greek culture*). 3. The intellectual and artistic aspects of a society, or the arts considered together (*high culture*; *dance, music, poetry and popular culture*). 4. The quality of being well-mannered, etc. (*a person of culture*). 5. The development of your body (*physical culture*). 6. The practice of keeping animals, etc. (*bee culture*). 7. A group of bacteria, etc., grown in a laboratory (*a culture of cholera germs*).

All these meanings are evident in the corpus data: 1, 2 and 3 are particularly relevant here.

Culture seldom (<20 per cent) occurs on its own, as the only content word in a noun phrase. It has a strong tendency to co-occur with other abstract nouns, or with a preceding adjective, or with a following qualifying phrase (often introduced by *of*). Despite (or because of?) its complex meanings, the word *culture* often has little definite content of its own, and requires to be semantically supported by other words. *Culture* often co-occurs with other abstract nouns, such as

art(s), education, history, language, politics, religion, society

in phrases with *and*, such as

art and culture; belief and culture; economy and culture; language and culture; culture and history; culture and politics; culture and religion; race, language, religion and culture

Culture is frequently preceded by an adjective which classifies it according to area, country or social group:

American culture, Black culture, Chinese culture, European culture, French culture, Indian culture, Japanese culture, Jewish culture, Western culture

Classifying adjectives in *-al* are especially common, and other frequent phrases include classical culture, commercial culture, institutional culture, intellectual culture, local culture, material culture, oral culture, political culture, social culture, theatrical culture, traditional culture

Some of these phrases show a meaning not recorded in most dictionaries: "a set of attitudes, beliefs and practices, which are shared by members of an institution or social group". This meaning has only recently become frequent, as evidenced by its absence from most dictionaries, and is often particularly clear in the collocation *a/the culture of* . . . :

a culture of official lying; a culture of mediocrity; a culture of dissent; the culture of the Labour Party

But this meaning is also apparent in phrases such as

an academic culture, business culture, a cafe culture, canteen culture, enterprise culture, gay culture, macho culture, market culture, masculine culture, science culture, youth culture

The "shared attitudes" meaning is more evident in longer contexts. Some such uses are positive:

a common *culture of* liberty and responsibility

But the majority have strongly negative connotations:

the almost inescapable pathology of the surrounding research *culture*

the stereotypes and myths of the *corporate culture*

the seamier side of *pub culture*, fights, rows, bad language and the temptation of fruit machines

an all-pervading, initiative-stifling, mind-numbing *culture of* mediocrity dedicated to preserving inefficiency

they may reproduce a *culture of* stultification, oppression and inequality

a war produces its own *culture* and it's usually a *culture of* muffled dissent

Other important fixed phrases are

ancient culture, contemporary culture, modern culture

mass culture, popular culture, pop culture, working-class culture

culture clash, culture shock, culture vulture

counter-culture, sub-culture

The plural *cultures* occurs in sense 1 above, as in

different nations and cultures

there have been cultures in which obesity in women was considered the ideal

An important phrase with the "shared attitudes" meaning is *the two cultures*. This is a reference to a famous lecture by C. P. Snow in 1959, entitled *The Two Cultures and the Scientific Revolution*, in which he distinguished between opposing, and possibly incompatible, views of the world, humanistic/artistic and scientific/technological:

the atmospheres of the two cultures are even less easily mixed than oil and water

CULTURAL

Cultural is used more narrowly than *culture*: 1. relating to a society and its ideas, customs and art; 2. involving music, literature and the other arts. With reference to these meanings, *cultural* shows some of the same characteristics as *culture*.

The commonest collocates are other adjectives, such as

economic, educational, ethnic, historical, linguistic, racial, religious, social

Cultural often has little definite content of its own, and requires to be semantically supported by other words. It often occurs in phrases with *and* or *or*, such as

commercial and cultural interests; political, economic and cultural sovereignty; literary and cultural tradition; cultural or ethic differences; sport or cultural activities

Other common phrases are:

cultural anthropology, cultural background, cultural differences, cultural diversity, cultural elite, cultural events, cultural heritage, cultural identity, cultural imperialism, cultural relativism, cultural studies, cultural traditions, cultural values

the Cultural Revolution (referring to events in the People's Republic of China from 1966)

the cultural life of [name of city or country]

cultural backwater(s), cultural desert

cross-cultural, multi-cultural

7.12   Conclusion

If you re-read the Baden-Powell texts, in the appendix to chapter 4, you will discover that they use several of the keywords which I have discussed, around the topics of work (for the girls), career (with its strongly positive semantic prosody, for the boys), home, family, training, life and death.

And many other empirical analyses of keywords are available. For example, several articles in Corfield (1991) provide detailed analyses of the key term *social class*, of related terms such as *social rank* and of different terms within such classifications; for example, *labouring classes* and *industrious classes*. Corfield (p. 27) poses the recurring puzzle very clearly:

> Does *class* exist before it is named? If so, why is it not identified from the start, but later discovered? If, on the contrary, *class* has no existence before it is named, how does naming create it, especially when some people refer to it while others do not? Can *class* be made to go away if it is never mentioned at all?

In their very different ways, Firth, Williams and Foucault isolate a stratum of analysis at which discursive regularities can be discovered. Foucault conceives discourse to be thought as social practice. Discourse comprises perceptual codes and structures, ways of ordering things, unconscious conceptual grids and principles of classification. It is governed by rules which no one knows or is responsible for: this is anonymous discourse with a life of its own. We reproduce it, but piecemeal, and unintentionally. No one has designed the whole.

Phrased in Foucault's style, this all sounds very abstract: pure discourse without the knowing subject. And although Foucault uses documentary evidence, he provides no methods for analysing discourse in this sense: as Merquior (1985, p. 12) puts it, his methods belong to a 'litero-philosophical' tradition which is 'wantonly free of analytic discipline'. Often such ideas can therefore seem vague and mystical: other writers talk of 'structures of feeling' and 'patterns in the mind' (Williams, 1961), the 'deep semantic structures of a culture' (Hall, 1974), or 'socially shared mental representations' and 'social cognitions' (van Dijk, 1993).

In this chapter, I have illustrated one concrete mechanism of representation which reinforces cultural stereotypes. I have presented an empirical method for studying culturally important keywords and fixed phrases, the kinds of things that are repeatedly said, in discourse which is jointly constructed, but which is known consciously by no one. To talk repeatedly of education in terms of *falling standards* or *trendy teachers*, or to talk of employment in terms of *job losses*, *cheap labour* or *unemployment blackspots*, is to maintain familiar and limited sets of categories and metaphors for talking and thinking about the social world. Since such repeated collocations are simply used, as part of our habitual ways of talking, their connotations are not made explicit, are difficult to question and can seem merely natural. Hall (1982) discusses ideology, not as intentional bias, but as the reproduction of a dominant discourse, in which particular definitions and classifications acquire, by repetition, an aura of common sense, and come to seem natural and comprehensive rather than partial and selective.

A large corpus is a collection of texts, which can be analysed regardless of who has spoken or written them. Usages can be picked out by concordance or collocation software, without regard to authors and their intentions. The computer picks out only the recurrent patterns: pure discourse without the knowing subject. Unconstrained by conventional units such as books or authors, such collocational software can provide empirical data for studying how objects of discourse are formed.

As I am arguing throughout, all texts encode representations of the world. Speakers and writers choose (often unconsciously) particular ways of speaking and writing about things, people and events, and their choices embody categories. When fixed or semi-fixed phrases are used, then more than one choice (often unconsciously) is made at once. In this chapter, I have presented data on collocations which occur across many texts and authors (largely from mainstream published language and/or mainstream radio and newspapers). By searching out frequent collocations, we can glimpse the recurrent wordings which circulate in the social world, and glimpse how linguistic categories become social categories. We have one way of studying the 'interconnection of the mundane nature of day-to-day life with institutional forms stretching over immense spans of time and space' (Giddens, 1984, pp. 362–3).

Two points have important implications for linguistic theory. First, connotation is just as important as referential meaning, and often more so: this is shown in many studies of language and ideology. It's not what we say, but the way that we say it. Second, the creativity of language use is often emphasized, and the importance of the routine is therefore often underemphasized. The balance between creativity and routine is being reinstated as a result of text and corpus studies (Halliday, 1993; Miller, 1993; Sinclair, 1991a, pp. 109ff).

I should, however, also emphasize limitations on the kind of study I have presented here. First, it is not possible to study everything at once, and I have discussed language forms of only one kind. Linguistic representations of the social world can take many other forms. I have not discussed how familiar schemas and scripts can be used by the media to encode events in familiar ways. Nor have I discussed the kind of metaphors (Lakoff and Johnson, 1980; Lakoff, 1992) which can also form repeated associations between words, and can therefore mediate and reproduce taken for granted ideas. Second, I have not presented any evidence on how repeated collocations are interpreted by newspaper readers or radio listeners. There is always a category shift when one moves from discussing forms of language to forms of thought. I have assumed that if collocations and fixed phrases are repeatedly used as unanalysed units in media discussion and elsewhere, then it is very plausible that people will come to think about things in such terms. Third, I have emphasized that many of the data I have used are from the mainstream press. Such language inevitably encodes the interpretations which are made by the political elite. I have not discussed whether such codings differ significantly in other uses of language, and I have given no examples of oppositional representations and encodings. However, we have to understand the mainstream wordings in order to understand the force of oppositional codings.

Bernstein (1990, p. 170) demands of a theory of cultural reproduction that it must 'translate micro into macro, and macro into micro'. We must be able to specify not only the message but also 'the structure that allows . . . it to be carried . . . that structure which makes the message possible' (p. 169). In this chapter, I have provided many examples of one such structure, which helps to convey meanings, systematically and regularly, around the core areas of social life: home, family, education, work, class and nation. I have tried to show how evidence from 'corpus, concordance and collocation' (Sinclair, 1991a) can help to explain 'class, codes and control' (Bernstein, 1990).

8

Towards a Modal Grammar of English: a Matter of Prolonged Fieldwork

What I shall have to say here is neither difficult nor contentious; the only merit I should like to claim for it is that of being true, at least in parts. *The phenomenon to be discussed is very widespread and obvious, and it cannot fail to have been already noticed,* at least here and there, *by others. Yet I have not found attention paid to it* specifically. (Austin, 1962, p. 1, emphasis added (or subtracted?))

8.1 Organization of the Chapter

This chapter is the last in a series of chapters which analyse text and corpus material. It is placed at the end of the sequence, since it is different from the earlier chapters in two ways. Chapters 4 to 7 proceed from form to function: for example, they use concordance lines to help identify in texts lexical and syntactic patterns, whose meanings can then be discussed. Moreover, chapters 4 to 7 present analyses of the distribution of patterns across individual texts or across corpora.

In this chapter, this direction is reversed. First, I proceed from function to form. I start from an area of meaning (modality) and discuss the different ways in which it can be expressed in English. Second, I therefore cannot restrict my analysis to linguistic features which happen to occur in individual texts: I have to search for them where they occur, and therefore cite inevitably isolated examples from various corpus data.

The main data analysed in this chapter are examples identified in the various corpora described in the notes on corpus data used. Linguistic features which express modality in English occur at different levels of language: individual lexical items, illocutionary forces and propositions. I give detailed examples to show how such meanings are encoded in lexis, in noun and adjective morphology, in the verbal group, in modal verbs and in logical and pragmatic connectors. The main findings concern the wide range of ways available in English for encoding point of view and stance.

One purpose of the analysis is methodological: to show that a corpus is necessary for the analysis of such meanings. The second purpose is to show that the encoding of such meanings is a central organizing principle in language.

8.2   Introductory Example: Propositional Information

In previous chapters, I have illustrated in detail that there are always different ways of saying the same thing. Because one way is selected (often unconsciously), it follows that utterances always encode a point of view. I have given examples of how speakers and writers express their stance towards the information which they are conveying; for example, how much reliability or authority they mean it to have. I have analysed examples such as how different versions of truth are represented in a courtroom and how authoritative facts are conveyed in school textbooks. These analyses included examples of modality, such as modal verbs in a judge's summing-up and projecting clauses in a school textbook.

A summary of these points is that utterances express two things: propositional information, and also the speaker/writer's attitude towards this information. This is a rather simplistic formulation, since one cannot always make a clear separation between these two components. However, it will do as a start, and this chapter will discuss some of the resources which English has for encoding such attitudes.

Here is an example of how commitment and detachment to propositional information can be expressed. A BBC radio newsreader reported an explosion in a water-processing plant which had killed sixteen people:

1   A spokesman from the Water Board refused to speculate on whether methane gas could have caused the explosion [A]

In 1, the BBC are declining to commit themselves to the proposition, let's call it p1, that:

2   p1: "Methane gas caused the explosion"

The BBC mention this proposition but remain detached from it. First, p1 is modalized. Methane gas *could* have caused the explosion: "it is possible that" p1. The source of this view is not stated, though someone must have formulated it. It is presented as a rumour from an unidentified origin: someone has said that (it is possible that?) p1. The BBC do not comment directly on even this. They cite a spokesperson refusing to speculate, and saying, in effect: no comment. The logical structure is something like:

> 3   The BBC say that (a spokesperson says nothing about (the rumour that (it is possible that (p1))))

This is a very guarded statement, although when the institutional source of a proposition is the BBC, then this can already give it some authority. We can infer that a BBC reporter thought p1 plausible enough to put it to the spokesperson. One of the most general interpretative principles is no smoke without fire. That is, there is a general assumption that there is method even in apparent madness and that speakers expend the minimum effort: propositions are therefore not even mentioned (in the technical sense) without reason. Remarks in conversation are not understood as stating the obvious, but as drawing attention to some unusual feature of the situation: the features must be literally remarkable. And speakers do not make their contribution more informative than required: they do not say what is already familiar (Garfinkel and Sacks, 1970; Grice, 1975).

The following day, the BBC news reported:

> 4   According to a Water Board official, there had been a sizeable build-up of methane in the pipe [A]

The commitment to p1 is still far from total. The cause of the explosion is still not made explicit, but left to real-world knowledge or to an inference (that methane in enclosed spaces causes explosions) and the implication that this could have been the cause in this case. This view is attributed to an official: it is presented as an utterance report.

Several months later, the BBC reported the outcome of the inquest on the incident, a verdict of accidental death:

> 5   An engineering inspector told the inquest that the explosion was caused by methane, but that it had not been possible to discover what had ignited the gas [A]

Other statements were also introduced with prefaces which attributed propositions to various sources, named or not [all A]:

the court was told how . . .

a Water Authority official told how . . .

one expert told the inquest it could have been . . .

In section 6.10 I gave examples of propositions being attributed to different sources, using projecting clauses such as

scientists have discovered that . . .

the latest studies seem to indicate that . . .

and I showed that two school textbooks differed significantly in whether they attributed propositions to identifiable sources. One discourse strategy used by the BBC is to attribute views to someone else. This does not in itself convey either commitment or detachment. It depends what credence is given to the source. We would probably interpret an example such as

the noted educationalist A H Halsey has claimed that "p" [A]

not as an utterance report, but as an indirect assertion. That is, we would interpret it not as objectively reporting an external event (Halsey's claim), but as subjectively expressing the speaker's belief. Some people's words are reported as such, and it can be news when some people say *No comment*. But some people are quoted in order to add credence and commitment to what the speaker says.

Beliefs and commitments to propositions can be attributed to different sources. Torode (1976) gives these three examples [all A] from classroom discourse:

shut up, Alan, you're a distracting member of the class, you know that, don't you?

somebody talking, you know what will happen, no five minute break

Here, propositions are presented as shared knowledge, known to an individual child or to the class as a whole. The Gricean maxim of quantity is contravened, in order to generate an implicature. Alternatively a proposition may be presented as part of some enduring legitimate order:

right now, I think we know the order of events, you've got to get on by yourselves today, and I don't want to see anybody off their seats

8.3   The (Limited) Relevance of Speech Act Theory

Speech act theory would appear to be a good starting point for investigating speakers' expression of stance, because it has a lot to say both about explicit illocutionary verbs (such as *claim*, *speculate* and *tell* in the examples above) as markers of commitment, and about indirect and inexplicit speech acts.

However, despite its origins in ordinary language philosophy, speech act theory is very ambivalent in its attitude to attested data (see section 2.5). Austin (1962, p. 148) suggested that a main task was to collect a list of explicit performative verbs as a guide to illocutionary forces, and that this was a 'matter of prolonged fieldwork': hence the sub-title of my chapter. However, what he had in mind by fieldwork was looking through a diction-ary: 'a concise one should do', he says. Austin had an odd view of fieldwork, but his theory is urbane and unrigid, based to some extent on observations of everyday language. Searle's (1969, 1979) systematization of Austin is much more rigid, and moves even further away from actual behaviour, leaving speech act theory in the odd position of demanding a study of language as social action within a theory of social institutions (see section 3.1), but studying almost nothing but invented data.[1]

I propose to return to Austin's suggestion of prolonged fieldwork: but by studying attested instances of illocutionary verbs, not by looking for them in a dictionary; and also by studying them within a more general theory of commitment and detachment to words, propositions and illocutions. This will avoid two main problems with speech act theory: a lack of attested data, and the fact that illocutionary verbs are seen as a special category.

8.4   Evidentiality, Factivity, Modality

Several overlapping terms are used for speakers' or writers' expression of attitude towards propositional information: evidentiality, factivity, modality. The term *evidentiality* emphasizes how speakers encode the kind of evidence they have for making a factual claim. The term *factivity* emphasizes how propositions are encoded: as fact or as mere opinion. The term *modality* (probably the most widely used) is most familiar via the term *modal verbs* (such as *must*, *might*, *would*), but has much wider applicability. Modal meanings are also encoded elsewhere in the language system.

In many languages, it is obligatory for speakers to encode in the verb morphology the source of evidence for their statements. For example, in the Papuan language Fasu (Trask, 1993, p. 95), a speaker must signal in the verb form for a sentence such as *It's coming* the source of evidence for the proposition: "I see it", "I hear it", "I infer it", "somebody says so, but I don't know who", "somebody says so, and I know who" or "I suppose so". Palmer (1986) and Chafe and Nichols (1986) give many other examples of languages which have obligatory encoding of meanings such as personal sensory experience, hearsay, circumstantial inference, expectation, confirmation and surprise.

German encodes hearsay and other aspects of evidentiality in modal verbs and in the form of auxiliary verbs, as in these (invented) examples:

> er hat es getan ("he has done it")
>
> er habe es getan ("he is said to have done it")
>
> sie ist sehr klug ("she is very clever")
>
> sie soll sehr klug sein ("she is said to be very clever")
>
> er ist zu Hause ("he is at home")
>
> er wird (wohl) zu Hause sein ("he'll probably be at home")
>
> sie hat ihn gesehen ("she has seen him")
>
> sie will ihn gesehen haben ("she claims to have seen him")

For English, Lyons (1981) discusses cases where auxiliary verbs encode inference and degrees of certainty:

> that *will be* the postman [I]
>
> the postman *must have* come by now [I]

A characteristic of many of the invented data used in pragmatics and speech act theory is that they are grossly simplified. Pragmatics therefore has a tendency to overemphasize the inferences performed by hearers, and to underemphasize the surface indicators of modal meanings which are available to hearers (and findable by computers: see Channell, 1993). In real data, several markers of evidentiality or modality often co-occur, italicized in this example:

> *evidently* she *must have* talked to her mother about them *you see because* on one occasion . . . [continues with reason for inference] [A]

I will use the term *modality* to mean the ways in which language is used to encode meanings such as degrees of certainty and commitment, or alternatively vagueness and lack of commitment, personal beliefs versus generally accepted or taken for granted knowledge. Such language functions to express group membership, as speakers adopt positions, express agreement and disagreement with others, make personal and social allegiances and contracts.

8.5   Summary

In ordinary life, a certain laxness in procedures is admitted – otherwise no university business would ever get done. (Austin, 1962, p. 37)

Corpus evidence shows that such expressions of modality are pervasive in English. For example, Coates (1982) shows that epistemic modals are more frequent in a corpus of informal spoken and personal written language than in formal impersonal language. And Holmes (1983), using a small corpus of 50,000 words, has estimated that lexical items expressing degree of certainty make up on average 3.5 per cent of any text, but are twice as frequent in speech as in writing. Chafe and Nichols (1986) and Hunston (1993a) also provide corpus studies: see section 6.10.2.

When we speak or write, we are often vague, indirect and unclear about just what we are committed to. This might appear, superficially, to be an inadequacy of human language: but only to those who hold a rather crude view of the purposes of communication. Vagueness and indirection have many uses. Politeness is one obvious reason for deviating from superficially clear or rational behaviour, and claiming precision is done appropriately only in certain situations. However, we often signal that our utterances are vague. So, whenever speakers or writers say anything, they encode their point of view towards it: whether they think it is a reasonable thing to say, or might be found to be obvious, questionable, tentative, provisional, controversial, contradictory, irrelevant, impolite or whatever. The expression of such speakers' attitudes is pervasive in all uses of language. All utterances encode such a point of view, and the description of the markers of such points of view and their meanings is a central topic for linguistics.

8.6   Lexical, Propositional and Illocutionary Commitment

The BBC example in section 8.2 concerned the guarded expression of a proposition. In general, it is possible to modalize just three kinds of linguistic unit: individual lexical items (words or phrases), illocutionary forces and propositions. This is most visible for illustrative purposes in utterances where speakers shift in their commitment. For example, in these examples, speakers commit themselves to a lexical item, an illocutionary force and a proposition, but then partially withdraw the commitment:

> consumer durables – as the Economist calls them, whatever that means [A]

> we'll be offering the course – subject to the availability of staff and facilities [A]

> we move in on Thursday – all being well [A, from a telephone conversation about moving house]

Such examples motivate two layers of meaning: the content of an utterance and the speaker's attitude to this content. Charles M. Schultz points to this commitment and withdrawal pattern in a Snoopy cartoon. Snoopy is writing a story: '"Our love will last forever," he said. "Oh, yes, yes, yes!" she cried. "*Forever* being a relative term, however," he said. She hit him with a ski pole.'

8.7   Degree and Manner of Commitment

We need more precise definitions of commitment and detachment. There is a continuum of commitment, whose end points are complete commitment and complete detachment. In the case of propositional information, full commitment can be made by a categorical assertion that "p" is the case. By complete detachment from "p", I do not mean a categorical assertion that "not-p": this would involve full commitment to "not-p". Complete detachment involves, rather, some kinds of quotation or mention, as in

> suppose, just *for the sake of argument* that . . . [A]

It is not possible to specify the number of points on the degree scale, since many utterances are indeterminate and could not be placed at a definite point on the scale. In addition, it may be possible, in principle, just to mention a proposition, *for the sake of argument*. But in practice, a general interpretative principle will search for the reason for the mention: see the BBC example above. The extreme end point of the detachment scale is elusive.

Utterances such as *It could be that p* are ambiguous. But they are likely to leave the speaker partially committed to "p", rather than fully committed to "possibly p". This is the difference between subjective and objective epistemic modality (Lyons, 1977, 1981). In natural language use, subjective modality is much commoner.

Degree of commitment is distinct from manner of commitment. For example, a speaker is committed to the same degree to a proposition "p", whether "p" is asserted or presupposed:

(I assert that) p. I realize that p

Both convey full commitment to "p": the test is that the speaker could not, without logical contradiction, deny "p". But "p" can be presented within the illocutionary act of assertion, or presupposed by being embedded under a factive verb (such as *realize*). Other manners of commitment include the many different lexical or syntactic markers illustrated below, and assertions versus implicatures (that is, propositions which are not asserted, but inferred and therefore deniable: Grice, 1975). Some manners of commitment are always deniable and therefore less than full. A great deal of work in pragmatics has been concerned with establishing the difference between propositions which are logically entailed by what is said and those which are defeasible in context (Levinson, 1983, gives a thorough review).

It might be objected that just asserting "p" does not involve full commitment, since a speaker might say:

I'm *absolutely sure* it's just around that corner [A]

I *honestly believe* he loved her but was afraid to show it [A]

However, such forms cannot increase commitment beyond a logical maximum. What they do is perform the discourse function of responding to another speaker's uncertainties.

So, commitment concerns whether a proposition is presented as true, false, self-evident, a matter of objective fact or of subjective opinion, shared knowledge, taken for granted or debatable, controversial, precise or vague, contradictory to what others have said and so on. This is what Lyons (1981, p. 240) refers to as self-expression, in the literal sense of the speaker's expression of him or herself: the subjectivity of utterances – how speakers report their own beliefs, attitudes and so on. Lyons claims that relatively few utterances make unqualified assertions (certainly this one does not). And, as we have seen above, in some languages it is not even possible to do so. But to discover just how many utterances are qualified, and to what degree and in what manner in different contexts, is a matter of prolonged fieldwork.

The above points apply *pari passu* to illocutionary commitment. For example, if an illocutionary force is indirect or off the record to some degree, it will be possible to claim, if challenged, that it was never issued. And similarly with lexical commitment.

The concepts of commitment and explicitness are closely related. Explicitness implies commitment, since if you state something explicitly, you go on record; whereas inexplicit statements remain vague and therefore deniable. There have been two related themes in speech act theory: the indirection argument, that the surface lexical, syntactic form of an utterance often does not make explicit the illocutionary intent of the speaker; and the expressibility principle, that the illocutionary force of an utterance can always be made explicit. Thus, a common starting point in speech act theory is the formula $F(p)$, where F is the illocutionary force which may be marked by an illocutionary force indicating device, (for example, an explicit illocutionary preface), and p is a proposition. Austin (1962, pp. 61–2) talks of a performative being expanded into a form with a first-person singular present-tense verb, and of such expansions making explicit both that an utterance is performative and also which act is being performed; see his p. 103. And Searle (1969, p. 68; 1979, p. ix) argues that 'wherever the illocutionary force of an utterance is not explicit it can always be made explicit. . . . Whatever can be meant can be said.'

However, first, not all speech acts can be made explicit; for example, there cannot be explicit hints. In general, explicit utterances are not deniable. Second, explicitness is not a mere stylistic preference, but something which is done in only some social settings; for example, it is more characteristic of written than spoken English. Third, it is impossible ever to say in so many words exactly what is meant (Garfinkel, 1967). I do not mean to adopt a mystical position that there are things of which one cannot speak, but only to point out that being explicit changes the meaning.

Explicitness does not mean saying all that can be said (which is impossible), but finding the right balance between what is said and what can be assumed, and therefore not giving more information than is needed or wanted (see Grice (1975) on the maxim of quantity). The distinction between what has to be made explicit and what can be assumed therefore has implications for what is conveyed about group membership. It follows that explicitness, clarity and ambiguity are not inherent properties of texts, but are a function of texts in contexts. And some contexts (for example, academic textbooks, the law) are less tolerant of ambiguity than others.

8.8   Modality and Lexis

I will now look in more detail at examples of lexical, illocutionary and propositional commitment and detachment.

8.8.1   Morphology and pragmatic information

It is widely recognized that many languages encode modality, especially in their verb morphology. It is less commonly noted that English can also encode interpersonal, pragmatic meanings in noun morphology. Levinson (1983, pp. 8–9) points to pairs such as *rabbit* and *bunny*, where information about speakers and hearers is encoded in the lexical distinction. Both words have the same logical meaning of "furry animal which eats lettuce, gets kept as a pet, gets put in stews" and so on. But *bunny* has additional connotations of childishness and cuteness. This meaning is lexicalized and does not depend on context. More generally, the morphological ending -*y* (or -*ie*) often encodes a range of related pragmatic meanings. The clearest cases involve pairs of words, such as

> aunt, auntie; cat, pussy; child, kiddy; comfortable, comfy; dog, doggie; pup, puppy; nightgown, nightie; sweets, sweeties; stomach, tummy; underwear, undies
>
> Charles, Charlie; Deborah, Debbie; Fred, Freddy; Jennifer, Jenny

The -*y* variant encodes meanings such as informality, intimacy, childishness and femininity. (The sexist implications of the intimate–childish–feminine relation, and of phrases such as *bunny girl*, are obvious.) There are many other examples:

> baby, cookies, nanny, nappies, teddy (as baby talk)
>
> buddy, dearie, duckie (as informal terms of address)

barmy, dotty, loopy, loony, potty (in the sense of "mad")

argy-bargy, itsy-bitsy, shilly-shally, tenny-weeny

There is a tendency for -*y* forms to refer to males, and for -*ie* forms to refer to females. For example, *Bobby* (male), *Bobbie* (female), or *Fergie* (as in the name used in British tabloids for Sarah Ferguson, Duchess of York), *Georgie* (from *Georgina*, as in the film *Georgie Girl*), versus *Harry* (from *Harold*). But this is only a tendency: cf. *Jenny, Sally*. There is also a tendency for the -*y* member of a formal–informal pair to use the basic spelling system: contrast *crumb, crummy, dumb, dummy, lunatic, loony* (Carney, 1994, pp. 96, 140, 245, 431, 456).

Such formations are productive, and occur in language addressed to children [both A]:

did you have a nice sleepy last night?

hey what you chewing those fisties for?

But they also occur much more widely. The following examples are from adult usage, mainly spoken [all A]:

we're Labour and lefty

sort of research studenty kind of people

English is a very teachy subject

Another Charles M. Schultz cartoon has Snoopy say: 'If she's a creepy-crawly icky-fuzzy worm I'll probably scream.' Often, two or more *y*-forms co-occur [all A]:

the print's all *weeny* and *scribbly*

it's a very big *hustly bustly* city

if you were a *trendy lefty* Islingtonite

veggie cafes in the *studenty* North Laine market area

this *marshy laky landspitty* sort of area

snotty and *cliquey*

you can have *ginny* things or martini type things or *squashy* type things

Frannie giggled, feeling sort of *comfy-groggy*; this is such a *sleepy* town

chosen life styles, *comfy* not *snazzy*

in patched trousers and *comfy woolly* he stood in front of his two bar electric heater

In these example, the form encodes informality and vagueness, and therefore less than full commitment. Several are mildly insulting, e.g. *trendy lefty*, *loony lefty*, *tedious lefty* [A]: see section 7.3. Such productive uses could, by definition, be documented only from attested corpus data.

8.8.2   Lexical commitment

Speakers and writers do not always identify with the words and phrases which they use. Lakoff (1972, pp. 197ff; 1987, pp. 122ff) discusses expressions which can suspend part of the meaning of words. For example, *strictly speaking* points to meanings which are inherent in the word. And *technically* points to meanings which are stipulated by experts: that is, meanings of words can be related to expert institutionalized knowledge held by groups such as lawyers and scientists.

Paul's a friend of mine, well *strictly speaking* my sister's friend [A]

he was *technically* in breach of contract [A]

Fairclough (1992, pp. 30ff, 120ff) takes an intertextual view of such examples. For example, if someone talks of a *so-called democracy*, he or she is assuming that a country has been referred to in this way in other discourse, which is possibly very nebulously conceived as general opinion. Preconstructed phrases and fixed collocations circulate in discourse, in the more general sense of discourse as the way in which people regularly talk about things (see section 7.2).

Items such as *so-called, as I would call it, so to speak* and *quote unquote* provide examples of surface markers of detachment. Consider examples [all A] such as:

one of the *so-called* binary star systems

this *so-called* improvement in the standard of living

hospital of tropical diseases or *whatever it's called*

the old idea of a certain code of behaviour, *what I would call* being a gentleman

what they call musicology

I was prepared to push the others under the carpet *so to speak* in order to make the marriage work

we came to Minsk and there we dug in *so to speak* for the winter

not the person who needs to be *quotes* treated

people who were in *inverted commas* distress

These various cases are related. Such markers of detachment signal that a lexical item is being mentioned as well as used, and that the meaning of a word or phrase is problematic: its meaning lacks general acceptance, or is technical, or is unknown to the hearer, or differs among different speakers. The speaker may be disassociating him or herself from some group, or not assuming that the hearer is a member of some group. Such items are among the innumerable ways of conveying in-group membership.

Forms such as

loosely called, often called, so-called, traditionally called; what might be called; as x calls them

and similar phrases with *describe, refer*, etc. are very common in both the Lund and LOB corpora, relative to the frequency of lexical items in corpora of this size. Such phrases are by far the most common use (well over 90 per cent) of the lemma CALL in LOB.

Speakers have many ways of referring to the same referent, and can therefore achieve reference without being committed to the truth of the referring expression. It follows that different forms can be used to convey other information; for example, to pick out some feature of the referent, to convey an attitude towards it, to convey group membership by choosing a description that the hearer does not know and so on. Since reference is utterance-dependent, the referring expressions which speakers use can be studied only by textual and corpus analysis and by ethnographic observation (Schegloff, 1972).

Consider the following more complex examples (from Andrew Gilling, personal communication):

today's *so-called teachers* are themselves frequently uneducated [A]

the anti-social behaviour of these *so-called women* [A]

The words *teachers* and *women* are not being used purely descriptively. The referents *are* teachers and women. But some of the normal commitments to these words are suspended, in order to convey a moral point of view. The strategy has been called the no–true–Scotsman move (Flew, 1975, p. 47). Imagine a Scot who reads in his newspaper about the dastardly exploits of a fiendish English criminal. He might say to himself: *No Scotsman would ever do such a thing*. But then suppose he reads, the next week, of Angus McSporran, who has committed even more dastardly deeds in Aberdeen. He might then argue: *No true Scotsman would ever do such a thing* – thus converting his initial statement to one which is irrefutable, since it is now true by arbitrary definition.

8.8.3   Vague lexis

Other cases of extreme denotational vagueness are provided by these examples [all A]:

I'm going to be in and out of libraries *and things* today

don't get yourself worked up into a state and run into lampposts *and things*

discussions of world food problems *and things like that*

a great horsehair sofa *and that kind of thing*

the boys aren't left to do the washing up *and that kind of thing*

Channell (1980, 1994) discusses what would be a suitable semantics for vague expressions. She points out that such examples pose problems for truth conditional semantics, since it is impossible to specify when such utterances cease to be true. The vagueness does not disappear even in context: it is an inherent property of language. Since the denotational range of all lexical items is inherently vague, the same point could be made of all utterances: it is simply more striking in cases containing markers of lexical detachment (vague category identifiers, in Channell's term). Channell's observations are also based on a prototype theory of lexical meaning in which category membership is a matter of degree from typical to marginal (see Lakoff, 1972; Rosch, 1975).

Austin (1958, p. 12) pointed out that truth depends on the use and purpose of utterances. For example

Italy is shaped like a boot and France is hexagonal [I]

is accurate enough as a mnemonic for school children, but not for geographers and tour operators. Channell also points out that the interpretation of vague utterances depends on the discourse context: an informal discourse context is likely to demand less absolute accuracy in denotation, although a discussion of, say, the performance of motorcycles may demand precision even in informal contexts. That is, sociolinguistic conventions affect semantic representations. (Channell (1994) provides detailed discussion and many examples from the Cobuild corpus.)

Such examples appear to argue for degrees of truth, and therefore a many-valued logic, which is dependent on different sociolinguistic conventions. But speakers can themselves specify the standards against which they wish the truth of their utterances to be judged. Markers of commitment and detachment are instructions to interpret utterances in more or less rigorous ways.

8.9 Modality and Illocutionary Force

Illocutionary forces can also be modalized.

8.9.1 Explicit illocutionary prefaces

Explicit performative verbs are much more common in some contexts than others. I have studied a small corpus of business correspondence, which is one context which produces a large number of explicit illocutionary prefaces. These include forms [all A] such as:

> further to my letter of . . . , I would advise you that . . .
>
> with reference to my letter of . . . , I am authorized to inform you that . . .
>
> I was merely seeking to point out that . . .
>
> I would however draw your attention now to the following regulation
>
> may I wish you a successful and interesting conference
>
> I emphasize that . . .
>
> let me say again how sorry I was that . . .
>
> X, I'm sorry to say, died several months ago

a quick note to tell you that . . .

I would suggest that . . .

you have my consent for . . .

The invented data in the speech act literature consist mainly of examples which combine first-person singular with a simple present tense form (e.g. *I promise*, *I warn*). But a striking feature of real data is that such forms are rare, and are restricted to certain verbs and/or to very formal contexts. *I apologize* is the only such form which is common. *I thank you* co-occurs with *Dear Sir* in a letter from a bureaucracy. *I hereby certify* occurs on a legal form. *We announce formally* (not singular, of course) occurs in a letter about a company merger. Such first-person simple verb forms therefore have stylistic implications. They are not a 'paradigm device', as Searle (1969) calls them.

In my corpus data, the commonest surface form is modal plus lexical illocutionary verb, often referred to as a hedged performative:

I *would* advise you that p

I think we *should* decline your offer

X and I *would* like to extend to you our thanks.

But there are very many others, and another striking feature of the data is the surface variation, what Brown and Levinson (1978) call a 'baroque ensemble' of forms for performing indirect speech acts. This also makes the use of intuitive data very dubious, since intuitions about linguistic variation are notoriously unreliable. This variation involves not only illocutionary verbs, but also illocutionary nouns and other parts of speech. All [A]:

this is our suggestion . . .

I'm only putting it forward as a suggestion

well, look, honestly Mrs X, my suggestion to you would be that if . . .

in answer to your second question . . .

congratulations!

In many such cases, the use of modal verbs and other surface forms is almost entirely conventionalized. It is difficult to see much difference in meaning at all between *I wish you* and *May I wish you*. However, speakers also explicitly distinguish between different degrees and sources of commitment:

> I would like to thank you, officially for the Association and personally for me
>
> this is very much a preliminary letter . . .

And they speak and write on behalf of other people:

> I am writing at the request of the Board to invite you to . . .
>
> I am writing on behalf of X to thank you very much for . . .

And illocutionary forces do not have to be conveyed directly to the addressee. They can be passed around. The following examples are from spoken business settings:

> perhaps you would pass on my apologies
>
> could you give Professor X's apologies for the mathematical society meeting on Friday

That is, A asks B to pass C's apologies to D. When exactly do such illocutionary forces come into operation? Perhaps not till months later, when they appear in writing in the formal minutes.

The question of who is committed to what is also unclear, because of different degrees of commitment. One might get the impression from reading Searle that a promise is a promise is a promise. However, illocutionary forces are not categorical, but scalar and often indeterminate (Leech, 1983, discusses this in detail). For example, it is possible to refer to less than fully committed acts, such as half-promises:

> having more or less promised [A]
>
> he'd sort of had half promises [A]

A tentative promise might be made by uttering:

> so is it possible to say provisionally yes and that I will confirm as soon as I can . . . I'll ring again to definitely confirm it [A]

Are the following utterances offers or not?

I would be interested to offer a course of lectures next session [A]

the cheapest I can offer you at the moment is [product name], which is priced at forty-nine fifty [A]

Are the following invitations?

if you are ever in this part of the world, I'd be delighted to invite you to give a lecture [A]

I hope you will be able to attend this weekend, for which you will be receiving an official invitation soon [A]

I do not think that these questions are answerable, since the meaning of many utterances is negotiable, deniable, indeterminate. Speech act theory has ignored such examples, due to its reliance on introspective data which do not reflect such indeterminacy.

The practical importance of such matters is evident in courses in business English (possibly in EFL), and in campaigns for plain English. Gowers's (1954) influential book *The Complete Plain Words* contains what is in effect an analysis of hedged performatives. He criticizes such forms as *I would inform you that* or *I have to inform you that* as being 'crushingly stiff', and (central to my topic here) as obscuring the source of the commitment, and giving the impression of a remote bureaucracy staffed by robots. Gowers recognizes that illocutionary verbs occur in particular settings, that they can be used both to put things on record and to obscure commitment.

8.9.2   *Two types of speech act*

However, it is not possible to prevaricate or give less than full commitment to all types of speech acts. Consider these examples [all I]:

1　He almost excommunicated me

2　He almost promised to come

3　He did sort of christen the child

4　He did sort of promise to come

Example 1 means that he did not excommunicate me: perhaps he changed his mind at the last minute. Example 2 is ambiguous: perhaps he changed his mind at the last minute, or perhaps he entered into some kind of commitment. Example 3 seems to imply an unconventional ceremony. Example 4 again could mean that he entered into some commitment.

These (invented) examples motivate a distinction between two types of act. Type 1 acts can be performed by anyone whose English is good enough to convey his or her intention: anyone can make promises, requests or complaints. But type 2 acts are institutional and conventional, and therefore not illocutionary at all: because they cannot not be performed by any speaker of the language, but only by someone by virtue of occupying some social role. For example, one must be specially authorized in order to christen or excommunicate people, appoint them to or fire them from jobs, name ships, sentence offenders, declare war and so on. These are all declarations in Searle's (1976) sense, in which saying really does make it so. They bring about a correspondence between words and the world, owing to consciously formulated (and therefore not linguistic) conventions.

Although Searle (1969. p. 71) claims to be setting up an institutional theory of communication, and distinguishes between brute and institutional facts (see section 3.1), he does not make this distinction between two types of act (and therefore misclassifies declarations as a type of illocutionary act).

8.10 Modality and the Truth Value of Propositions

So, all utterances express both content and the speaker's attitude towards that content. This claim may seem so general that it is self-evident or true by definition. So far, I have shown only in a very general way that commitment and detachment are expressed in various ways in syntactic and morphological form. A stronger type of argument would, in addition, provide a pragmatic or functional motivation for many otherwise disparate features of surface syntax. I would then be able to provide an explanation for previously unexplained syntactic phenomena.

8.10.1 Simple forms versus ing-*forms of verbs*

The following is a case where matters of truth and certainty interact with syntactic and morphological form. Probably the most semantically complex area of English syntax is the verbal group, and one long-standing puzzle is the difference in meaning between pairs such as:

I go, I am going; I warn, I am warning.

I will use the terms simple form and *ing*-form to refer to the surface morphology and syntax. We must make a clear distinction between surface forms and meanings, since these forms can be used to convey tense, aspect and modality. It would thus be prejudging the issue to use a term such as 'simple present-tense form'.

Many descriptions of English provide detailed discussion of the basic facts about different classes of verbs which are 'typically' or 'normally' used in one form or the other, and about the range of meanings of the two forms with different verb classes.[2] It is often argued that performative verbs differ from other verbs in the relation between the two forms (Austin, 1962, p. 64). With many verbs, reference to the moment of utterance is made using the *ing*-form (*I'm working, go away*), but performative verbs use the simple form (*I promise*): a common view is that performative verbs are odd in this respect. It is also well known that stative verbs (e.g. *contain, own*) often do not admit the *ing*-form: but they are also regarded as an exception among verbs (e.g. Quirk and Greenbaum, 1973, pp. 15, 21). However, these observations leave unexplained the relation between performative and stative verbs, and also disguise the fact that many types of verbs take simple forms, either exclusively or regularly.

The following are main categories of verbs often said to be regularly or normally used in the simple form. If such claims refer merely to frequency of use, then they are true. But a mere frequency statement cannot explain what the less frequent form means when it does occur. The essential difference is:

- the simple form encodes certainty and permanence;
- the *ing*-form encodes uncertainty and change.

8.10.2   *Verb classes and uses*

1   Psychological verbs and verbs of cognition (e.g. *believe, like, love, realize, suspect, think, understand*).

I know/*am knowing he's right

I love/?am loving it

An *ing*-form can, however, occur, to indicate change of state. Note the co-occurring words which indicate change in these examples:

we *are understanding more and more* how the earthquakes are produced [A] *more* of our passengers *are realizing* the benefits of travelling by coach [A]

and *for the first time* people *are suspecting* that he might not win [A]

he *is loving his second chance* at fatherhood [A]

Botham *is loving* his *new* lease of life too much [A]

2   Verbs of perception (*feel, look, smell, sound, taste*).

that tastes/*is tasting funny

But, again, *ing*-forms can imply recent change:

former hostage Terry Anderson *is tasting* his first full day of freedom *today* [A]

after three lean years, Wall Street *is tasting* fat *again* [A]

3   Verbs of conveying and receiving information (e.g. *hear, see*), especially with reference to the recent past:

I hear you were at the bungalow the other day [A]

I see what you mean now [A]

The simple form is also used when the information is given (authoritatively?) in a book:

as Foucault puts it [A]

Again, *ing*-forms imply recent or current change:

medical personnel *are hearing more and more* about this technique [A]

we *are seeing* the *beginnings* of a revolution [A]

I *am seeing* the spotlight turned *increasingly* on so-called unproductive partners [A]

Verbs such as *see, hear, feel* often occur in the simple form when they are used non-literally. When used literally, to refer to physical sensations, they usually co-occur with *can*: see below (Sinclair, 1990, p. viii).

4   Relational verbs and verbs of permanent state (e.g. *belong*, *consist*, *depend*, *deserve*, *matter*, *possess*). Such verbs are normally used in the simple form:

I own/*am owning six cars

it contains/*is containing arsenic

Here a mere statement of frequency avoids an explanation of the semantics. Again, with at least some such verbs, an *ing*-form can be used to indicate change:

more and more people *are owning* their own houses and perhaps inheriting parents' houses [A]

5   Performatives.

I promise/*am promising to come

It is often claimed that *ing*-forms can only used for repetitions of speech acts, but forms such as *I'm warning you* are common (see the large literature on performative *ing*-forms, e.g. Edmondson, 1981).

Certain uses also require either the simple or *ing*-form.

6   Definitions, eternal truths, habitual states, permanent and timeless states.

a normal curve by definition describes an infinite number of cases [A]

the region where frontal depressions form is where the polar and tropical air masses are adjacent to each other [A]

Harry smokes/*is smoking after dinner [I]

7   Permanent states versus impermanent or recently changed states. A simple form implies a permanent or at least settled state of affairs, whereas an *ing*-form implies a temporary state:

you're unreasonable [I]

you're being unreasonable [A]

my dad works in Saudi Arabia [A] (Sinclair, 1990, p. 247)

I'm working as a British Council officer [A] (ibid., p. 248)

8   Future states of affairs which are predictable, possibly because they are part of some official scheme. Several grammars of English give examples such as

> the exams start/?are starting on Thursday [I]

Corpus data show, however, that both forms are used to refer to events which are timetabled and therefore certain:

> the first of ten flights *leaves* tomorrow [A]

> we're *leaving* tomorrow morning on the 7.30 ferry [A]

However, *ing*-forms are used to indicate a hypothetical statement about a future event:

> looking into 1994, [name of organization] *should be seeing* profits start-ing to flow [A]

And, in a case which explicitly signals indeterminacy and uncertainty, the simple form seems impossible:

> it *is* always *starting* tomorrow and tomorrow never seems to come [A]

A case where a simple form seems quite impossible is where it refers to a future event which is inherently undecidable, such as a sports event. Hence the oddity of:

> *Scotland beat France tomorrow

But the oddity of even such cases disappears if the context makes it clear that a fixed schema is involved:

> I've fixed everything, bribed the referee and the linesmen: Scotland beat France tomorrow and lose to Germany next week [I]

9   Demonstrations and commentaries.

> I take/?am taking six eggs . . . [I]

> I place/?am placing the rabbit in the hat [I]

> Gray takes the ball upfield, passes to McInally [A] (Sinclair, 1990, p. 247)

10　Headlines, captions below pictures, etc. The following are from captions in a reference book:

> Gromyko lies in state in Moscow [A]
>
> Students march into Tiananmen Square [A]
>
> UN forces move a wounded Swapo guerrilla [A]

11　Directions of various kinds, e.g. stage directions:

> The doorbell rings. The young man enters. Grandma looks him over [A]

Or instructions:

> you test an air-leak by . . . [I] (from Leech, 1971, p. 13)
>
> you take the first turning on the left past the roundabout, then you cross a bridge . . . [I] (from Leech, 1971, p. 13)

Leech (1971, p. 13) finds such examples 'hard to classify'. However, they fit easily into a view which sees the simple form as an expression of authoritative knowledge.

12　Summaries of stories, narratives in 'historic present'.

> he sits down at his desk chair, reaches for the telephone and dials a number [A] (Sinclair, 1990, p. 257)

Elsewhere (Stubbs, 1983a, pp. 197ff), I provide several examples of the simple present forms characteristically used when people summarize stories. Lakoff (1987, p. 473) also points to structures such as *Here comes Susan* and *There goes my bus*, where reference is to the moment of utterance.

8.10.3　*Other parallels:* can *plus verb*

There are other parallels between performatives and some of the above categories. For example, universal truths are also formulated with *can*:

> ice can float on water [I]

And other categories above also take non-literal *can* or *could*. In all the following cases [all A], *I can/could hear*, etc., means "I do/did hear", not "I am/was able to hear".

I *could hear* the murmur of voices

I *could see* a firefly winking to and fro in the bushes

they *can smell* another major spy scandal

as I opened the door, I *could smell* her perfume

I *can understand* she doesn't want to rake up the past

he won't report you, I *can promise* you that

Sinclair (1990, pp. viii–ix) points out that such verbs are used with *can* when they refer to physical sensations, but occur without *can* in broader psychological meanings. Contrast the examples above with these [also A]:

Jenny *could feel* her hands trembling

he *could* feel the warmth of her breath against his mouth

I did feel a little sorry for him

I feel kind of responsible for her

My conclusion is as follows. The uses of the simple form illustrated above have the following in common. They all report events which are habitually or eternally or necessarily true, which are certain or predictable or presupposed to be true, or which are authoritative or unchallengeable in some way. This includes events to which the speaker has privileged access (what Labov and Fanshel (1977) call A-events). If I claim that *I feel ill*, you may accuse me of lying, but you have no way of checking on the truth of my claim. For this reason, the terms *private verbs* or *mistake-proof sentences* (Ljung, 1980, pp. 50ff) are sometimes used. Other events are unchallengeable because the speaker has some special expertise: in a radio commentary, the hearers cannot see the original events. This is essentially Palmer's (1974, pp. 60ff) argument, that the simple form is used for reports in those special cases where we need to report present activity: normally we do not have to, since present activities are normally observable.

The simple form in all these cases conveys that speakers have special reasons to be confident of the truth of the proposition. In some cases, they could not, logically speaking, be wrong. In all cases, their confidence derives from more than publicly accessible observations. It follows that performatives can be analysed naturally as reporting propositions which are true by virtue of being uttered. If I say that *I promise*, then it is true that I have promised, even if I have promised in bad faith and have no intention of keeping my promise. The commitment has been made. And it follows that performatives are not a special class of verbs. They are especially difficult to distinguish from private verbs and reporting verbs.

In summary, performatives and stative verbs are not clearly distinct from other verb classes. They are not odd.[3]

8.10.4   Other verbal forms

It is well documented that other verbal forms also encode modal meanings. A present perfect form with *have* signals the speaker's evaluation that a past event is still relevant:

> it has been provisionally arranged for next Thursday [A]

> the Minister of Defence has been working on the plan for some months [A]

Past tense forms signal unreal or hypothetical states of affairs; for example, in counter-factual conditionals which commit the speaker to the falsity of a proposition (*If only he was here . . .*). *If she was still here,* . . . implies that she isn't. *If she is still here,* . . . leaves open the possibility that she is. Past tense forms are also used to signal politeness:

> I wondered if we might take the car [A]

> I was wondering if you've a book on birds I could borrow [A]

Such uses signal remoteness. A past tense form shifts the speaker back in time, thus distancing speaker from hearer, and putting a hedge on illocutionary force.

In general, what are traditionally known as past, present and future tenses have more to do with expressing modality than with time reference (Lyons, 1981, p. 239). And as Lyons (1977, p. 817) also points out, it is no accident that the so-called future tense in English uses *will*, which also expresses inference (cf. *That will be the postman*). References to future time are necessarily hypothetical and predictive. (See also Levinson (1983) for a detailed argument that almost every utterance encodes the speaker's point of view in the sense of deixis, and that the pervasiveness of deixis has also been greatly underestimated in linguistic description.)

8.10.5   *Private verbs*

Another case of a relation between pragmatics and syntax is the use of private verbs (e.g. *believe, expect, suspect, think*) as markers of tentativeness. Such verbs are often ambiguous between objective and subjective interpretations. Utterances such as

> I *think* my mother had visions of my swimming the Channel [A]
>
> I *don't think* there's a fracture, just a bad sprain [A]

are unlikely to be fully committed statements about the speaker's personal beliefs (objective modality), and more likely to be tentative assertions that "x is probably the case" (subjective modality). Similarly,

> it looks like dried blood [A]

could be a dogmatic assertion about an appearance (objective), but could also be a qualified assertion that "it is probably dried blood" (subjective). Thus private verbs can be used to make statements about internal psychological states. But they also have modal uses which release speakers from total commitment to propositions. It can be difficult to recognize which use is intended, and this can depend on the content of the proposition. An example such as

> which brings me to what *I think* is the clue, the common factor [A]

could be taken either way: an expression of tentativeness or of firmly held personal conviction. In examples such as

> I believe the situation in South Africa is now in a state of ferment [A]
>
> I believe that murderers should be hanged – provided they're sane, of course [A]

the deletion of *I believe* alters the meaning very little, if at all. And it is natural to interpret them as assertions about personal beliefs (objective interpretation), though there is nothing in the surface syntax which signals this. One rule of interpretation is that if the proposition is not empirically verifiable, then the utterance will be given a personal belief interpretation.

However, on other occasions, the syntactic behaviour of these verbs does reflect these different interpretations. For example, the structure *believe in NP* can only be used as a psychological report, either meaning "be sure something exists":

believe in God/fairies/Father Christmas/hell [A]

he never believed in the possibility of a general peace settlement [A]

or meaning "be in favour of":

countries that believe in freedom [A]

both directors believed in the closest personal contact with their customers [A]

The subjective modal use is signalled by the use of *so* or *not* as a dummy clause in structures such as: *I believe so, I think not*. Similar constructions are possible with

believe, expect, guess, hope, imagine, suppose, it seems

8.10.6   Logical and pragmatic connectors

A third case of the interaction of pragmatic and syntactic matters is provided by the so-called logical connectors (e.g. *and, but, or, if, because*). Their uses in everyday English are not reducible to their logical functions in the propositional calculus, but have to do with speakers justifying their confidence in the truth of assertions, or justifying other speech acts. There is a large literature on connectives: Johnson-Laird (1983) summarizes much psycholinguistic material; and see Davison (1975), van Dijk (1979), Morreal (1979), McTear (1980) and Stubbs (1983a) for many further examples and discussion.

The main notions are evident in the behaviour of *because*, which has two uses, logical and pragmatic, as in these examples:

he was drowned because he fell off the pier [I]

he was drunk, because he fell off the pier [I]

The first has the structure: effect plus cause. The second: assertion plus justification. In the second, pragmatic, use an inference is often signalled by epistemic *must*:

he *must have been* drunk, *because* he fell off the pier [I]

Attested data contain a large number of such examples:

the sky *must have been* clouded over, *because* the stars had disappeared [A]

The disappearance of the stars does not cause the sky to cloud over. Their disappearance is cited to justify the inference. The same statement–justification structure is seen in

his anaesthetic *must have been* as old as he was, *because* I needed five injections to numb my molar [A]

evidently the Cessna was too slow *because* he had the strip enlarged and bought a small Lear [A]

Such uses are common in casual conversation:

but wait till you have a baby *cos* you'll find sort of dirty nappies in every corner and sort of banana skins [A]

There are several syntactic tests which distinguish between these two uses of *because*. The pragmatic use does not allow reversal of the clause sequence, clefting of the *because*-clause, or *yes–no* interrogation of the whole sentence.

*because he fell off the pier he was drunk

*it is because he fell off the pier that he was drunk

*was he drunk because he fell off the pier?

(Assuming that the last example is spoken as a single tone group.)

Similar points hold for pragmatic *if, or, but* and *and*. Consider these examples:

there's some food in the fridge, if you're hungry [I]

there's some food in the fridge, or aren't you hungry? [I]

where the *if-* and *or*-clauses provide reasons for making the statement: that is, they turn the statement into an offer. Or:

A. Let's eat. B. But I'm not hungry [I]

where the *but*-clause questions the justification of the preceding utterance.

Channell (1994) points to the non-logical use of *or* in vague expressions, such as *Could you get some apples or oranges or something*. The items linked by *or* must be recognizable as members of the same set, as in

> sort of safari trips taking . . . Australian girls round Europe or something [A]

> not wanting to live in Derby or Bootle or something [A]

8.11   Modal Grammar

Ideally, grammars should be organized in such a way as to reflect the communicative functions of language. In earlier chapters, I gave some functional explanations of surface syntactic phenomena. Passivization (see section 4.10) allows the deletion of the agent, and therefore avoidance of commitment to certain propositional information. Nominalization can turn actions into static things (see section 4.5) and therefore attribute objective reality to states of affairs. And ergative verbs can present things from the point of view of the actor or the action (see section 6.8).

It is possible to show that many features of surface syntax have the function of presenting speakers' attitudes to words, propositions and illocutions, and individual cases are widely discussed. However, these have yet to be brought together into a unified description, in what could be called a modal grammar of English. A case of items which function to express speakers' attitudes to the truth of what is said is sentence adverbs such as *frankly* and *obviously* (on attitudinal and style disjuncts, see Greenbaum, 1969; Biber and Finegan, 1989). But many other syntactic features have this function. For example, a large number of syntactic structures can trigger presuppositions: including factive verbs, cleft sentences and non-restrictive relative clauses (Levinson, 1983, pp. 181–4). And transferred negation (e.g. *I don't think that "p"* versus *I think that not "p"*) can signal the speaker's attitude towards propositions and interlocutors, including degree of certainty, politeness and speaker involvement: Bublitz (1992) shows this in detail using data from the London-Lund corpus.

The uses of *some* and *any* (Lakoff, 1969) can signal speaker expectations.

In questions, *some* signals the expectation of a positive answer (*has someone come?*), whereas *any* remains neutral or signals the expectation of a negative answer (*has anyone come?*). The form of tag questions is similarly explicable only with reference to discourse. They allow statements to be presented as obvious, dubious or open to challenge. Tags with the same polarity as the main clause (*he is, is he?*) refer to propositions whose source is the addressee. Tags with reversed polarity (*he is, isn't he?, he isn't, is he?*) refer to the speaker's own beliefs. One major function is to implicate: "I am certain/not certain that p"; "I want to check if you believe that p" (see Bublitz, 1978, pp. 140–61).

Lyons (1981, p. 241) argues that there is much in the structure of languages that cannot be explained without reference to the notion of subjectivity of utterance; and (pp. 235–6) that much work in semantics and pragmatics is seriously flawed, because it has not given sufficient prominence to the concepts of modality, subjectivity and locutionary agency. I have tried in this chapter to provide some data to illustrate these claims, and to begin to show what data a modal grammar of English has to explain.

8.12   Applied Linguistics

The kind of modal grammar which I have proposed has various applications. I have briefly mentioned teaching business English. More generally, the sociolinguistic competence to make tentative or tactful statements, about controversial subjects about which one has reservations, is a problem for foreign learners. It is difficult to translate modal particles from one language to another (Bublitz, 1978). And it is well known that non-native speakers of English can sound rude, brusque or tactless if they make mistakes in this area. Often mistakes are not recognized as linguistic, but as social ineptitude. It is also widely recognized that foreign learners have comprehension problems with indirect forms (Holmes, 1983).

Gumperz (1982a,b) shows that in modern bureaucratic industrial societies, with their unprecedented cultural diversity, an increasing amount of communication is not in small familiar face-to-face groups, but between strangers who are interacting not as individuals but as members of social roles. But the interpretation of indirect utterances depends on shared, taken-for-granted knowledge, and there are cultural differences in the expression and use of indirectness. Gumperz has carried out detailed ethnographic work on cross-cultural differences in the expression and perception of credibility and trustworthiness, and documents legal cases where prosecutions hinged on whether defendants were perceived as being convincing or trust-worthy, and argues that, owing to linguistic problems, they were not (see chapter 5 appendix).

Bell (1984) has studied how news stories arrive in New Zealand via agencies such as Reuters, in a form designed essentially for printed trans-mission in newspapers, and are then abbreviated for transmission on radio news. He shows that the radical shortening can lead editors to reduce details, round figures, delete hedges, omit attributions to spokespersons and so on. And he shows how the degree and manner of commitment can be altered between the original text and the broadcast version.

Slembrouk (1992) has studied how the spoken language of parliamentary debate is represented in a written form in Hansard. He shows that, although Hansard is often regarded as a verbatim record of what is actually said in Parliament, considerable changes are made to the words spoken. There is 'a general tendency to under-represent interpersonal meanings, especially modal constructions, hedges, expressions of degrees of commitment to-wards what speakers say, etc.' He finds that expressions such as *I hasten to stress*, *I think*, *I can only say* and *actually* are deleted in an attempt to reduce the record to ideational claims. There is a 'systematic removal of interper-sonal and textual dimensions of utterances' (p. 110) from the written record. (A knowledge of such features of language is also of great practical use to linguists working on other written representations of spoken language, such as when spoken interview evidence is recorded by police: see chapter 5 appendix.)

8.13   Conclusion

There are many other aspects of vague and indirect language. I have not discussed so-called metaphorical language, or the many non-literal or non-serious uses of language in lying, irony, exaggeration, teasing and joking. Such aspects of language, which have previously been swept under the carpet, are now being taken on board, so to speak, by some linguists. Often the pendulum has swung full circle and upset the apple cart. Aspects of language which often seemed to linguists to be far from the bread-and-butter side of language study are now being seen as the backbone of the enterprise. Fieldwork can be an uphill grind. But if you can feel which way the wind is blowing and swim with the tide, then it is possible to grasp the nettle, by taking the bull by the horns, instead of clutching at straws or planting primroses in a gale. We are not necessarily on the horns of a dilemma, between theory and data: one linguist's Scylla is another's

Charybdis. Opening a can of worms does not mean throwing caution to the winds. If we can get our foot in the door, then the little acorn may grow into a mighty oak as it snowballs downhill with the theoretical wind in its sails.

9

The Classic Questions

The ultimate test of any set of ideas in linguistics is whether they make a contribution, however modest, to answering some of the classic questions in the human and social sciences. These questions, as they are continually posed by otherwise very diverse thinkers, revolve around the critical analysis of what we normally take for granted, and especially around language as an often taken-for-granted background for everyday thought and action.

Many questions about the relations between language and the world have been posed at a time either when they were unfashionable, or when systematic empirical methods for studying them could not be explicitly formulated or carried out in practice. The questions themselves were then sometimes abandoned and derided as being unscientific. Two clear examples are questions about the value of corpora as data for linguistics, and about the relations between language and thought.

9.1　Language and Corpora

Much of the twentieth-century debate in linguistics around *langue* and *parole* has been a continuation of the centuries long debate over mind–body dualism. In its modern form, this debate derives from work in the 1600s by Descartes, who argued for a sharp distinction between mental activities (including language abilities) and physical or bodily states. On the face of it, Saussure (working in a French-language rhetorical tradition) and Chomsky (author of a book on Cartesian linguistics) are dualists. They both emphasize that language is not only behaviour (*parole*, performance), but also social knowledge (*langue*) or individual knowledge (competence). But they both then argue that the concrete behavioural aspects are idiosyncratic and uninteresting, and attempt to base a systematic linguistics exclusively on the other term of the opposition.

Several leading twentieth-century linguists have been even more uneasy about such dualisms, and have adopted explicitly monist positions. A monist position was adopted by Bloomfield (1933, p. vii) in his famous abandonment of psychology in favour of mechanism. He argued that language involves observable behaviour, that science has to be based on observable facts and that the admission of mental facts would therefore be an unnecessary complication. Quine takes a similar view: 'The bodily states exist anyway: why add the others?' (quoted by Popper, 1994, p. 8). The Firth–Halliday–Sinclair approach has also been explicitly monist (see section 2.8). Here, the rejection of dualism proceeded by arguing that apparent dualisms are merely the result of looking at the same phenomenon from different points of view. This variant of reductionism is a favourite Hallidayan rhetorical move. He similarly argues (e.g. 1994, p. xii) that lexis and grammar are complementary perspectives on the same phenomenon. And he supports this type of argument with reference to the analogy between instance–system and (local–global) weather–climate (see section 2.8).

The computer-assisted study of large corpora provides a glimpse of a way out of such paradoxes of dualism, by providing a method of observing patterns of a type which have long been sensed by literary critics, but which it has not been possible to identify in empirical detail.

Corpus linguistics has as yet only very preliminary outlines of a theory which can relate individual texts to text corpora, which can use what is frequent in corpora to identify what is typical in the language, and which can use findings about frequently recurring patterns to construct a theory of the relation between routine and creative language use. It is not surprising that the nature of corpora and the methods used to study them have hardly been theorized. Smallish corpora (of a few million words) have been easily available for use on individual PCs only since the late 1980s, and very large corpora (of hundreds of millions of words) were only becoming available for major lexicographic and grammatical projects in the early 1990s.

Within a very short period of time, linguists have acquired new techniques of observation. The situation is similar to the period immediately following the invention of the microscope and the telescope, which suddenly allowed scientists to observe things that had never been seen before. The combination of computers, software and large corpora has already allowed linguists to see phenomena and discover patterns which were not previously suspected. To that extent, the heuristic power of corpus methods is no longer in doubt.

To say that corpus linguistics is at only a preliminary stage is not a very strong defence. However, even preliminary investigation and description are useful. When computer methods are used to study large corpora, they may confirm what was suspected or known all along: but even such confirmation will usually provide vastly more detailed information than would otherwise be possible (for examples, see section 7.9). The kind of computer programs which I have used in this book are simple tools to do simple jobs (searching, displaying and counting) and provide simple results.

The jobs would be impossible to carry out without computer assistance. But the real power of such simple methods and results is that one thing leads to the next. When new quantitative methods are applied to very large amounts of data, they always do more than provide a mere summary. By transforming the data, they can generate insight.[1] And substantial findings have already emerged at different levels of interest. A second characteristic of corpus linguistics is that it produces not only new facts, but facts of previously unsuspected kinds. For example, Hudson (1994) discovers, much to his surprise, that in corpora of written text 'about 37 per cent of word tokens are nouns'. He carefully documents this finding, and its small but predictable variation, across different text types and different languages, but admits, with commendable candour, that he has no explanation for his finding. However, third, the new facts have led to far-reaching new hypotheses about language, for example about the co-selection of lexis and syntax (see section 2.6), and about previously undocumented types of relation between lexical, syntactic and semantic categories (see section 7.8, and Louw (1993) and Stubbs (1995a) on semantic prosodies, and see Sinclair (1990) for many lexis–syntax relations).

However, despite rapidly accumulating and very substantial findings, we still have a long way to go in understanding the nature of corpus data. Often the only question asked of corpora is whether they are representative of the language. Even this question is not always accepted as valid. Some corpus linguists argue simply that it is not possible to have a representative sample of 'a language', since the population being sampled is infinite in extent and constantly changing. Rather than agonize about such questions, they argue, it is more important to proceed, and see what we can discover. (The word *representative* does not even occur in the index of Sinclair (1991a).) A more modest position would be to admit that corpora may be narrower or broader in the samples they contain (see section 3.9). There is a wide range of text types which are unrepresented in most corpora.

During the rapid expansion of linguistics in the 1950s and 1960s, it could not have been foreseen what such data and methods would make possible. This means that some of the well known objections to corpus study (e.g. by Chomsky, 1957, pp. 50ff) are no longer applicable. At some point, quantitative increases, in amount of data and speed of calculation, become so great that they are experienced as a qualitative shift. They mean not just more data, but new types of data. New methods and data make it possible to study patterns which are not limited to what an individual can perceive (compare telescopes and microscopes) or remember, and provide new ways of studying the material base of many of society's activities. Nor are worries about the nature of performance data justified. The classic objection to performance data (Chomsky, 1965, p. 3) is that they are affected by 'memory limitations, distractions, shifts of attention and interest, and errors'. However, the main topic of analysis for corpus study is recurrent collocations and repeated co-selection of lexis and syntax. It is inconceivable that such repeated co-occurrences could be the result of performance errors. Quantitative work with large corpora automatically excludes single and possibly idiosyncratic instances, in favour of what is central and typical.

It is often said that a corpus is (mere) 'performance data'. But this is a shorthand formulation which disguises important points. Utterances are actual behaviour, spoken or written. A corpus is a collection of utterances and therefore a sample of actual behaviour. However, a corpus is not itself the behaviour, but a record of this behaviour. This distinction may seem pedantic, but it has crucial consequences. Consider a record of changes in temperature, as might be collected by meteorologists. The temperatures are physical states in the world. But the record has been arranged, for some purpose, by human beings. The sequence of temperatures cannot be directly studied for the patterns it displays: but the record can be. Through the intermediary of human intention and design, the physical states in the world can be converted into a form of public knowledge. (This example is from Popper, 1994, p. 7.) And, developing Halliday's analogy (see section 2.8), such temperature records can be used to study not only local variations in the weather, which might be directly observable in a rough and ready way, but also longer-term variations in the climate, which are certainly not directly observable.

A corpus (such as LOB), which is designed to sample different text types, is one stage further away again from a record of performance. First, it is a sample of the language use of many speakers, not of one individual's performance. Second, it embodies a theory: corpora are constructed according to theories of language variation. This design may be better or worse and is open to discussion and criticism. And third, the corpus can exist in many copies, on paper and in computer-readable form. This leads directly to one of the most important implications of corpus study, that the data of linguistics become publicly accessible. There is an alternative to the ultimately private data of intuitions. And studies done on the corpus are therefore also open to criticism. (For example, Biber's (1988) detailed findings from the LOB corpus are carefully criticized by Ball (1994).)

Hudson's (1994) generalization (37 per cent of word tokens in running texts consist of nouns) is a feature of his corpora: 'it turns out to be true (with some systematic variations) of any reasonably large body of written English'. That is, it is a public fact which exists independently of the linguist and which can be checked by other linguists. It is also a fact which exists independently of users of the language. At the level of utterances and texts, individual human agency is clearly involved: people produce language acts with the intention of getting things to happen. And such intentions are constantly inferred as we try to make sense of each other's language. When writers write they intend to communicate messages. But they do not intend to produce texts which contain particular percentages of given word classes. Yet such percentages are an unintended consequence of their behaviour, which can be discovered with quantitative methods.

An alternative to both monism and dualism is an explicitly pluralist position. Language, depending on how we look at it, is utterances (unique events, realized by actual physical behaviour), subjective knowledge (individual, personal competence) or the patterns observable across the usage of many speakers, when their behaviour is recorded and made publicly accessible in corpora.[2]

9.2   Language and Thought

Questions about the relation between language, thought and the world are often traced back to 1757, when the Berlin Academy of Sciences asked: 'What is the influence of people's opinions on the language, and of the language on the opinions of the people?' The prize winning essay is thought to have influenced Herder and von Humboldt, who viewed a language as the spirit of the people who speak it. Another major source of such questions is Saussurian structuralism, which leads almost inevitably to the view that the language system itself creates meaning. Meanings are not external to language: language does not passively reflect external reality. On the contrary, meanings are internal to language: they depend on the oppositions and contrasts in the language itself, and language actively constructs a social reality. The most explicit source of such questions is Whorf's articles, written mainly in the 1930s (and published posthumously as Whorf, 1956).

This work is often taken as the definitive formulation of the view that the grammatical categories of language construct implicit theories of the world: that 'the linguistic system fashions the ideas, it is the programme and guide of individual mental activity' (p. 12), and that there is 'an agreement that holds throughout our speech community and is codified in the patterns of our language' (p. 215).

Many aspects of the questions posed in 1757 are open and unresolved. And it is particularly difficult to escape from the circularity of arguments where language is both cause and evidence. However, as I have tried to demonstrate throughout this book (and in Stubbs, 1996), we now know how Whorf's question can be reformulated to apply to the choices available within a language. It is not (only?) a language which influences thought, but the process whereby repeated codings constitute 'semantic habits' (this is the Hallidayan reformulation of Whorf's question: Halliday and Martin, 1993, pp. 9ff). And it is becoming clearer how methods of lexical and syntactic analysis can be used to study such codings in texts and corpora.

There is no convincing evidence that language determines or constrains thought in any absolute way. On the contrary, all languages provide resources which always allow things to be expressed in different ways. However, it is highly plausible that if these resources are constantly exploited in recurrent codings, then such 'semantic orientations' (Halliday, 1978, p. 111) become salient, and habits of language can mediate and support thought. This may be negative, if it leads to stereotyped thinking, but such codings also have positive functions; for example, in the development of scientific language.

It is difficult to find scholars these days who argue that there is an ideal realm of thought which exists entirely independent of its expression in texts. There is a widespread consensus that language is never neutral and texts are never innocent. Things can always be formulated differently, any linguistic expression of the facts chooses some aspects of reality and downplays others, and all choices are political (Martin, 1985). Representations are always from a point of view, and express group interests. Such points of view are not usually explicit, are often denied and may not be directly observable, because they are often a matter not of individual words, but of patterns of distribution and frequency. This is why we may need quantitative methods to study them.

One of the strengths of Firth's work is that he proposed concrete, empirical methods for studying such apparently intangible questions. The outlines of a project for studying 'language in the heart of social life' (Firth, 1935, p. 51) were set out explicitly between the 1930s and the 1950s in work by Firth and others, although some of the necessary methods of study have been available only since the 1980s and 1990s. Firth never lost sight of the need to relate language use and language system, individual human agency and institutional structure. And his articles are full of statements such as: 'We are in the world and the world is in us' (Firth, 1957b, p. 29).

The neo-Firthian vision has been data-driven, bottom-up, experientialist and materialist, unlike much other linguistics in recent years, which has been developed independently of descriptions of attested language data. The problem for linguistics, and for structuralism more widely, has always been to relate texts back to the external world (Giddens, 1987, pp. 93–4). Linguistics, even broadly conceived as including speech act theory and pragmatics, has no theory of human agency. The problem for text and corpus analysis is to reconcile analyses of the details of individual texts, their context of production and reception, and intertextual patterns across large corpora.

9.3   Conclusion

Language is debated widely outside linguistics, and concepts developed in linguistics circulate in and out of the social world which they analyse (Giddens, 1984, pp. 351–4), especially in education. Given the central importance of language in the world – in education, in the law, in the mass media and so on – it would be absurd to think that language is not worthy of systematic study. To that extent, linguistics needs no special defence. As is regularly argued in introductory textbooks, human society is inconceivable without language.

However, linguistics hardly holds a central position in intellectual debates. And linguists are often unable to demonstrate, to students and others, that detailed analysis of language structure and function is a significant social pursuit. Linguists have never solved the question of how their sometimes very technical knowledge about language can be simplified and mediated, without distortion, to those who need it. Particularly sharp forms of the question arise in the law (where legal professionals, language professionals and lay people may have quite different views about language and interpretation) and in education (where teachers, politicians, journalists and linguists may all have different views about prescriptivism and descriptivism).

The essential defence of linguistics is that all knowledge is language based, and depends both on the clear formulation of arguments and theories, and on the relation between language and the world. The British philosopher Warnock (1989) has put forward a general defence of an arts education.

She argues for the usefulness of the humanities, which are language based and provide training in interpretative, hermeneutic, textual analysis.

> A study of the humanities is of the most crucial importance in education at all levels, simply because it is language based, and offers the chance of practice in clear expression and logical analysis. . . . It is essential that there should be those . . . who are trained to think critically about the relation between language and the world. (Warnock, 1989)

An important general aim of a degree in the arts or social sciences is to train students to analyse complex information in areas where there are usually no single correct answers. Students should learn much more explicitly about the relations between writers, texts and readers. As the production and transmission of knowledge becomes increasingly complex, it is increasingly important to understand the principles underlying the selection, storage, retrieval and reproduction of knowledge. Such topics are an essential part of cultural analysis and of a critical and rational understanding of society.

There will be no doubt about the value of linguistics – although it may not be popular in some circles – if linguists can continue to provide concrete textual analyses of the relations between language, knowledge and social institutions, and if they will take more seriously again the classic problems of how language relates to the world.

This book is part of a project to construct a humanist and social linguistics which can empirically analyse some of the relations between individuals and society. I have certainly not solved some of the exceedingly difficult problems of dualism, which continually arise in discussions of language, mind and society. However, texts, spoken and written, are one of the empirical, material bases of society, and computer-assisted text analysis reveals some of the everyday routines which reproduce social institutions.

Notes

Chapter 2

1 Sinclair submitted important evidence to the Bullock Committee (1975) on English mother tongue teaching. And several British linguists, notably Quirk, are involved in the public debate over Standard English. Chapter 7 gives brief examples of the political and educational debate around English teaching. Sinclair has also developed materials which relate language and literature teaching at university level (Sinclair, 1971), materials for schools which help children to develop communicative and cognitive strategies (Sinclair, 1973; Wight and Norris, 1970) and EFL materials based on discourse principles for people studying at university level in a foreign language (Morais, 1980–1). And from work for the Cobuild dictionary (Sinclair, 1987a) has come an EFL lexical syllabus (Willis, 1990).

2 Bloomfield (1933) makes irritated references to the ways in which linguistics could help in education, both in mother tongue and foreign language teaching, if only educationalists were willing to listen, and he helped to prepare language teaching materials for the American military. But his line of thought seems to have gone from theory to practice: behaviourism is the way to view things; therefore one should use drills and repetition in language teaching. In famous statements, Chomsky (1970) actually denies the educational relevance of linguistic ideas.

Chapter 3

1 There are other tests which distinguish these two major classes. One is that lexical and grammatical words are treated differently by English spelling: with very rare exceptions, only grammatical words are spelled with less than three letters (e.g. *bee*, *be*; *buy*, *by*; *inn*, *in*; *two*, *to*).

The lexical–grammatical distinction is not absolute. For example, certain words have little independent meaning in common uses. The verbs in phrases such as *have a drink, take a bath, give a smile* are semantically empty. And pro-forms, such as DO (e.g. *she studies linguistics – she does, does she?, he's done the lawn, he's done the car*) also show that some words can be both lexical and grammatical in their functions. Some words are changing in their form and functions: for example, *going to* and its uses as an auxiliary verb as *gonna*. And the cline from independent lexical words to dependent grammatical forms is evident in these examples [A] from the Cobuild dictionary:

the car-parks are absolutely full

a garden full of pear and apple trees

a cupful of rice; every mouthful of food

a hundred hopefuls stood in a queue

Presumably forms in *-ful* are productive. See Hopper and Traugott (1993, p. 7).

But these additional details do not disturb the very broad distinction between the two categories, and as long as the definition is kept consistent across the analysis of different text samples, then they do not affect the analysis.

Chapter 4

1 The original documents are undated, but it is known from his wife, Lady Baden-Powell, that he wrote them many years before his death, and it is known from internal textual evidence (the form of his name in the signature on the Scouts text) that he wrote these messages some time before 1929. He then carried them on his travels, along with other papers, in an envelope marked *In the event of my death*. Details about the publication of the texts were provided to me by the archivists at the two Associations (see acknowledgements), and I am most grateful to them for providing me with much information, including photocopies of the original letters and of their original published versions.

Chapter 5

1 My report was considered in the Court of Appeal, where it failed as a ground for appeal. The Lord Chief Justice ruled that 'what the meaning is of the language used by a learned Judge in the course of his directions to the jury is a matter for this Court to determine and is not a matter for any linguistic expert'.

2 Given the importance of such analyses as one factor in deciding guilt and innocence, such methods of authorship attribution also have to be tested through blind trials. Some methods of stylistic analysis have been accepted by the British courts, but have been severely disputed (for example, by Canter, 1992).

Chapter 6

1 Syntactic coding was usually straightforward, but it is important to record
   carefully how it was done: text is always messier than grammars imply. Passive
   included constructions with BECOME and whiz-deletions (both infrequent).
   Further, any form with BE plus -*ed* (plus other endings on irregular verbs, and
   plus phrases with words intervening between BE and past participle) was coded
   passive, with no distinction between stative and dynamic passives. For example,
   both of the following were coded passive:

   during World War 2, aircraft factories were *dispersed*

   the clothing industry is more *dispersed*

2 In projecting clauses, *that* may be omitted, or verbs may be followed by *how* or
   by an *it*-construction, as in text G:

   census statistics *show* people here may not have an inside toilet

   most people *realize* how . . .

   figure C *shows how* . . .

   we don't *expect it to* . . .

In other words, the computer did not find every relevant example. However, a
reverse check on relevant verbs showed that examples without *that* are infrequent in texts G and E. I have no reason to suspect that the occurrences with *that*
are unrepresentative of projecting clauses in the two texts. See Ball (1994) on
problems of recall and precision in computer-assisted work.

3 In his major study of the LOB and Lund corpora, Biber (1988, pp. 114, 159)
   discusses *that*-complements, as I do here, as an indication of the stance of the
   speaker towards information. But he finds the co-occurrence patterns 'surprising' (p. 154) and 'counter to previous theoretical expectations' (p. 113). The
   point relevant to my analysis is that such *that*-complements are not found to be
   characteristic of academic prose. Indeed, it is questionable whether academic
   articles constitute a well defined genre. In this case, therefore, it makes little
   sense to average across the samples in LOB to study whether attributed or non-
   attributed clauses are typical or not. The LOB samples from the category of
   academic writing simply differ on this feature.

4 Lexical density could be used for such a purpose. The LOB corpus is unrepresentative in many ways: for example, it contains no samples of either textbooks
   or business correspondence, both massive written genres. However, it does
   represent a range in lexical density from under 40 to over 60 per cent (see section
   3.9). So, we know that if other corpora do not show *at least* this range, then some
   text types are missing.

Chapter 7

1   The recurring themes in this discourse are thoroughly documented in work on
    language purism and standardization. Thomas (1991) documents widely observ-
    able patterns with reference to many different languages. Milroy and Milroy
    (1985) give many details of how speakers of English have been complaining for
    hundreds of years about how other people speak. Crowley (1989, 1991) docu-
    ments relations between language, history and cultural identity, with particular
    reference to the standard language question in British cultural debates. He
    presents and comments on famous examples from John Locke (1690), Jonathan
    Swift (1712), Samuel Johnson (1747), Noah Webster (1789) and others, up to
    recent examples from a British Conservative government think-tank which pro-
    duced several papers in connection with the establishment of the National
    Curriculum in England and Wales in the late 1980s. More generally, the social
    history of English and the relation between Standard English and the British
    education system are well documented by Williams (1961) and by Leith (1983).
    And one of the longest and most important essays in Williams (1976) is on the
    multiple meanings of STANDARD.
2   I am grateful to Susan Hunston for pointing out to me examples of positive
    semantic prosodies, e.g. on PROVIDE.
3   Such software has been written for corpus work at the University of Trier by
    Oliver Jakobs. Software in use at Cobuild is described by Clear (1993). Other
    related work is by Church and Hanks (1990) and Church et al. (1991). In Stubbs
    (1995a,b), I discuss in detail these methods for identifying the central and typical
    collocates of a word. The essential formulae involve the observed raw frequency
    of a collocation in a corpus of a given size, and also the ratio between this
    observed frequency and its expected frequency, that is, the number of times it
    might be expected to occur merely by chance, given the frequency of node and
    collocate in the corpus.
        The findings reported in this chapter use both absolute and relative fre-
    quencies. I occasionally use phrases such as *frequent* or *relatively infrequent*,
    though I only occasionally attribute precise figures to such phrases. In Stubbs
    (1995a), I discuss in detail the inadvisability of attributing levels of statistical
    significance to such figures. First, the frequency of individual words in different
    corpora is highly sensitive to the content of the texts which make up the corpus.
    Second, normal statistical procedures are inapplicable to such linguistic data,
    since normal statistical assumptions of random occurrence do not apply to textual
    data. Third, although there may be only a few observed instances of a given node–
    collocate pair, what is significant is the occurrence of many such collocates from
    what is obviously (to the human being, if not the computer) a semantic set (for
    example, of 'unpleasant' collocates). The occurrence of such sets is linguistically
    highly significant, even if conventional statistical tests do not apply.
        However, all the lists of collocates which I cite here are significant in the sense
    that they are taken from the top 50 collocates of a given node across a corpus of
    130 million words. These lists are either of the most frequent collocates of the

node (corrected to give less weight to word forms which are themselves highly frequent); or of collocates which are frequent relative to the frequency of the collocate. The reader can decide whether the lists of collocates are, with the benefit of the hindsight provided by such lists, (a) intuitively significant, but (b) impossible to document by intuition alone.

4   I am grateful to Joanna Channell for pointing out to me the importance of recent changes in uses of CARE.

Chapter 8

1   Austin's theory has an interactional emphasis which is lost in Searle's work. Lyons (1981, p. 172) argues that the term *language act* is better than *speech act*, and thus draws attention to Searle's abstract, decontextualized view of language. Speech act theory applies to written language as well as spoken, but has no theory of speech-writing differences. It appears to be based on the dubious view that language can be studied independently of its medium of transmission. (Chomskyan linguistics is at least explicit about this: speech act theory is not.) But speech and writing have different possibilities for commitment: consider requests to *let someone have it in writing*, or the type of commitment made possible by a signature, for which writing is a prerequisite (Stubbs, 1983b).

   There is a large literature on hedges and disclaimers: Lakoff (1972) is a classic paper. And much speech act theory (from Searle, 1975, on) discusses indirection in language use. Brown and Levinson (1978) and Leech (1983) propose theories of politeness and tact. Lyons (1981) argues that more attention should be paid to the subjective attitudes which speakers convey towards the propositions they express: see section 8.11. And Goffman (1981) deconstructs the concept of speaker, distinguishing between the animator (who produces the sounds), the author (who selects and encodes the message) and the principal (who is committed to the beliefs expressed).

2   See practical grammars for teaching English as a foreign language such as Thomson and Martinet (1969, pp. 92ff), or scientific grammars such as Quirk et al. (1985, pp. 175ff). Leech (1971) and Palmer (1974) give thorough accounts, although both are based on introspective, invented examples (Leech, 1971, p. viii; Palmer, 1974, pp. 7–8). The relation of the examples in Quirk et al. (1985) to attested corpus data is unclear: see section 2.5. The Cobuild grammar (Sinclair, 1990) is unique in being based on corpus data. It provides many attested examples (pp. 246ff) to show that such forms express modality, and not mere time reference. The simple forms express states of affairs which are settled or generally true, whereas *ing*-forms encode states of affairs which are changing or temporary. And they give (pp. 458–9) a list of about 70 verbs 'which are not usually used' in the *ing*-form, including: *love, own, see, sound, smell, understand*. However, as I illustrate, these verbs can take the *ing*-form under certain circumstances.

3   I do not think that the *hereby* test for performatives is reliable. The word *hereby* is almost entirely restricted to written legal settings: it does not occur once in the Lund corpus of half a million words of spoken British English, and fewer than 100 times in a 120 million word sample of the Cobuild corpus. This throws doubt on its traditional use as a test for performative verbs, since its use will therefore disturb intuitive judgements (unreliable at the best of times). The only test I know which distinguishes performatives from other verbs is that they take optional *you*: *I promise (you) I'll come*; **I deplore you what he's done*.

Chapter 9

1   I am grateful to Mike Scott for discussion of these points.
2   It is often pointed out that Saussurian *parole* is equivalent to Chomskyan performance: both are personal, idiosyncratic behaviour. However, whereas Chomskyan competence is individual and psychological, Saussurian *langue* is interpersonal and social: a social fact. (Though Saussure is notoriously vague on the ontological status of such social knowledge.) If we put Bloomfield, Saussure and Chomsky together, we have a three-fold solution to traditional paradoxes of dualism.

Precisely such a pluralist position is developed in detail by Popper (1972, 1994), who proposes an interactionist theory of knowledge and the body–mind problem. He proposes three spheres of experience. World 1 is the objective world of physical bodies with their physical states and processes. World 2 is subjective knowledge: that is, the subjective, private, mental states and processes (thoughts, beliefs, feelings, intentions, etc.) of individual human minds. World 3 is objective knowledge: that is, the public products of human minds, including the contents of books, arguments, theories, problems, critical discussions. World 3 is closely dependent on written language, since it is when arguments are written down and formulated clearly that they become most easily available for criticism. On this account, utterances are physical World 1 phenomena. Competence is a mental World 2 phenomenon. And corpora are World 3 phenomena. Popper also argues that languages are themselves World 3 objects.

I have discussed some aspects of the relation of written language and World 3 knowledge elsewhere (Stubbs, 1980, pp. 104–7). And I have implied such a pluralist position at several points in this book. In section 1.3, I discussed the view that meaning is partly in texts (World 3), but that the meaning of texts results from the interaction of texts and readers' interpretations (World 2). In section 1.7.3, I discussed Swales's (1990) view of the documentary world of science, an institutional variant of the World 3 view of knowledge. In section 3.5, I referred to Giddens's (1984, pp. 8–12) views on the importance of the unintended consequences of intentional actions for a theory of the social world. Some of the details of Giddens's argument are very close to Popper's. In section 8.10.5, I discussed private psychological verbs which indicate subjective knowledge, and in section 6.10, I discussed projecting clauses which mark objective knowledge. Popper (1994, p. 3) points out that when we say *He knew he was exceeding the speed limit*, then we are talking of subjective World 2 knowledge. But when we say *It is well known that water consists of hydrogen and oxygen*, then we are talking of objective World 3 knowledge.

References

Aijmer, K. and Altenberg, B. (eds) (1991) *English Corpus Linguistics*. London: Longman.

Andreski, S. (1974) *Social Sciences as Sorcery*. Harmondsworth: Penguin.

Atkinson, D. (1992) The evolution of medical research writing from 1735 to 1985. *Applied Linguistic*, 13(4), 337–74.

Atkinson, M. and Drew, P. (1979) *Order in Court*. London: Macmillan.

Austin, J. L. (1958) Performative-constative. In J. R. Searle (ed., 1971), *The Philosophy of Language*. London: Oxford University Press, 13–22.

Austin, J. L. (1962) *How to Do Things with Words*. Oxford: Clarendon Press.

Bailey, R. W. (1969) Statistics and style: a historical survey. In L. Dolezel and R. W. Bailey (eds), *Statistics and Style*. New York: Elsevier, 217–36.

Baker, C. and Freebody, P. (1989) *Children's First School Books*. Oxford: Blackwell.

Baker, M. (1992) *In Other Words*. London: Routledge.

Baker, M., Francis, G. and Tognini-Bonelli, E. (eds) (1993) *Text and Technology*. Amsterdam: Benjamins.

Bakhtin, M. (1981) *The Dialogical Imagination*, trans. C. Emerson and M. Holmquist. Austin: University of Texas Press.

Ball, C. N. (1994) Automated text analysis: cautionary tales. *Literary and Linguistic Computing*, 9(4), 295–302.

Beard, R. (1972) *Teaching and Learning in Higher Education*, 2nd edn. Harmondsworth: Penguin.

Bell, A. (1984) Good news – bad copy: the syntax and semantics of news editing. In P. Trudgill (ed.), *Applied Sociolinguistics*. London: Academic Press, 73–116.

Bell, A. (1991) *The Language of News Media*. Oxford: Blackwell.

Berk-Seligson, S. (1990) *The Bilingual Courtroom*. Chicago and London: University of Chicago Press.

Berlins, M. and Dyer, C. (1989) *The Law Machine*, 3rd edn. Harmondsworth: Penguin.

Bernstein, B. B. (1973, 1975, 1990) *Class, Codes and Control*, Volumes 1, 3, 4. London: Routledge & Kegan Paul.

Biber, D. (1988) *Variation across Speech and Writing*. Cambridge: Cambridge University Press.

Biber, D. (1990) Methodological issues regarding corpus-based analyses of linguistic variation. *Literary and Linguistic Computing*, 5(4), 257–69.

Biber, D. and Finegan, E. (1989) Styles of stance in English: lexical and grammatical marking of evidentiality and affect. *Text*, 9, 93–124.

Bligh, D. A. (1972) *What's the Use of Lectures*, 3rd edn. Harmondsworth: Penguin.

Bloomfield, L. (1933) *Language*. Chicago: Chicago University Press.

Bodine, A. (1975) Androcentrism in prescriptive grammar: singular 'they', sex-indefinite 'he', and 'he or she'. *Language in Society*, 4, 129–46.

Brown, E. K. and Miller, J. (1980) *The Syntax of Scottish English*. Report to Social Science Research Council.

Brown, P. and Levinson, S. (1978) Universals in language usage. In E. N. Goody (ed.), *Questions and Politeness*. London: Cambridge University Press, 56–311.

Bublitz, W. (1978) *Ausdrucksweisen der Sprechereinstellung im Deutschen und im Englischen*. Tübingen: Niemeyer.

Bublitz, W. (1992) Transferred negation and modality. *Journal of Pragmatics*, 18, 551–77.

Burrows, J. F. (1992) Computers and the study of literature. In C. S. Butler (ed.), *Computers and Written Texts*. Oxford: Blackwell, 167–204.

Cameron, D. (1990) Demythologizing sociolinguistics: why language does not reflect society. In J. E. Joseph and T. J. Taylor (eds), *Ideologies of Language*. London: Routledge, 79–93.

Cameron, D. (1992) *Feminism and Linguistic Theory*, 2nd edn. London: Macmillan.

Cameron, D. and Bourne, J. (1989) *Grammar, the Nation and Citizenship: Kingman in Linguistic and Historical Perspective*. University of London, Institute of Education.

Campanelli, P. and Channell, J. M. (1994) *Training: an Exploration of the Word and the Concept with an Analysis of the Implications for Survey Design*. London: Employment Department.

Canter, D. (1992) An evaluation of the 'cusum' stylistic analysis of confessions. *Expert Evidence*, 1(2), 93–9.

Carney, E. (1994) *A Survey of English Spelling*. London: Routledge.

Carter, R. (ed.) (1982) *Linguistics and the Teacher*. London: Routledge & Kegan Paul.

Chafe, W. (1986) Evidentiality in English conversation and academic writing. In W. Chafe and J. Nichols (eds), *Evidentiality: the Linguistic Encoding of Epistemology*. New Jersey: Ablex, 261–72.

Chafe, W. and Nichols, J. (eds) (1986) *Evidentiality: the Linguistic Encoding of Epistemology*. New Jersey: Ablex.

Channell, J. M. (1980) More on approximations. *Journal of Pragmatics*, 4, 461–76.

Channell, J. M. (1990) Precise and vague quantities in writing on economics. In W. Nash (ed.), *The Writing Scholar*. Newbury Park, CA: Sage.

Channell, J. M. (1993) The coding and extraction of pragmatic information in a dictionary data-base. Unpublished, Cobuild.

Channell, J. M. (1994) *Vague Language*. Oxford: Oxford University Press.

Chomsky, N. (1957) *Syntactic Structures*. The Hague: Mouton.

Chomsky, N. (1965) *Aspects of the Theory of Syntax.* Cambridge, MA: MIT Press.

Chomsky, N. (1970) Linguistic theory. In M. Lester (ed.), *Readings in Applied Transformational Grammar.* New York: Holt, Rinehart & Winston, 51–60.

Chomsky, N. (1992) On the nature, use and acquisition of language. In M. Pütz (ed.), *Thirty Years of Linguistic Evolution.* Amsterdam: Benjamins, 3–29.

Church, K., Gale, W., Hanks, P. and Hindle, D. (1991) Using statistics in lexical analysis. In U. Zernik (ed.), *Lexical Acquisition.* Englewood Cliffs, NJ: Erlbaum, 115–64.

Church, K. and Hanks, P. (1990) Word association norms, mutual information and lexicography. *Computational Linguistics*, 16, 22–9.

Church, K. and Liberman, M. (1991) A status report on ACL/DCI. *Using Corpora.* Proceedings of 7th Annual Conference of University of Waterloo Centre for the New OED and Text Research.

Clark, K. (1992) The linguistics of blame. In M. Toolan (ed.), *Language, Text and Context.* London: Routledge, 208–24.

Clark, R., Fairclough, N., Ivanic, R. et al. (eds) (1990) *Language and Power.* BAAL Annual Meeting. London: CILT.

Clarkson, C. M. V. (1987) *Understanding Criminal Law.* London: Fontana.

Clear, J. (1993) From Firth principles: computational tools for the study of collocation. In M. Baker et al. (eds), *Text and Technology.* Amsterdam: Benjamins, 271–92.

Coates, J. (1982) *The Semantics of the Modal Auxiliaries.* London: Croom Helm.

Cole, P. and Morgan, J. L. (eds) (1975) *Syntax and Semantics. Volume 3, Speech Acts.* New York: Academic Press.

Comrie, B. (1981) *Language Universals and Linguistic Typology.* Oxford: Blackwell.

Cook, G. (1992) *The Discourse of Advertising.* London: Routledge.

Corfield, P. J. (ed.) (1991) *Language, History and Class.* Oxford: Blackwell.

Coulthard, R. M. (1992a) Forensic discourse analysis. In R. M. Coulthard (ed.), *Advances in Spoken Discourse Analysis.* London: Routledge, 242–58.

Coulthard, R. M. (ed.) (1992b) *Advances in Spoken Discourse Analysis.* London: Routledge.

Croft, W. (1990) *Typology and Universals.* Cambridge: Cambridge University Press.

Crowley, T. (1989) *The Politics of Discourse. The Standard Language Question in British Cultural Debates.* London: Macmillan.

Crowley, T. (1991) *Proper English? Readings in Language, History and Cultural Identity.* London: Routledge.

Danet, B. (1980) 'Baby' or 'fetus': language and the construction of reality in a manslaughter trial. *Semiotica*, 32(1/2), 187–219.

Davison, A. (1975) Indirect speech acts and what to do with them. In P. Cole and J. L. Morgan (eds), *Syntax and Semantics. Volume 3, Speech Acts.* New York: Academic Press, 143–85.

De Beaugrande, R. (1991) *Linguistic Theory: the Discourse of Fundamental Works.* London: Longman.

Dixon, R. M. W. (1972) *The Dyirbal Language of North Queensland.* Cambridge: Cambridge University Press.

Eagleton, T. (1983) *Literary Theory.* Oxford: Blackwell.

Edmondson, W. (1981) *Spoken Discourse.* London: Longman.

Fairclough, N. (1989) *Language and Power.* London: Longman.

Fairclough, N. (1990) What might we mean by 'enterprise discourse'? In R. Keat and N. Abercrombie (eds), *Enterprise Culture.* London: Routledge, 38–57.

Fairclough, N. (1992) *Discourse and Social Change.* Cambridge: Polity.

Fasold, R. (1992) Linguistics and grammatics. In M. Pütz (ed.), *Thirty Years of Linguistic Evolution.* Amsterdam: Benjamins, 161–76.

Fillmore, C. J. (1969) Toward a modern theory of case. In D. A. Reibel and S. A. Shane (eds), *Modern Studies in English.* Englewood Cliffs, NJ: Prentice Hall, 361–75.

Fillmore, C. J. (1992) Corpus linguistics or computer-aided armchair linguistics. In J. Svartvik (ed.), *Directions in Corpus Linguistics.* Berlin: Mouton, 35–60.

Firth, J. R. (1935) The technique of semantics. *Transactions of the Philological Society,* 36–72.

Firth, J. R. (1957a) *Papers in Linguistics.* London: Oxford University Press.

Firth, J. R. (1957b) A synopsis of linguistic theory, 1930–1955. *Studies in Linguistic Analysis,* Special Volume, Philological Society, 1–32.

Firth, J. R. (1964) *Tongues of Men* and *Speech,* ed. P. Strevens (reprints from 1937, 1930). London: Oxford University Press.

Firth, J. R. (1968) *Selected Papers of J. R. Firth 1952–1959,* ed. F. R. Palmer. London: Longman.

Fish, S. (1980) *Is There a Text in This Class?* Cambridge, MA: Harvard University Press.

Flew, A. (1975) *Thinking about Thinking.* London: Fontana.

Fontenelle, T. (1990) Grammatical codes and definition patterns: a closer look at a computerized dictionary. Paper to International Conference on Computational Lexicography, Balatonfüred, Hungary, Sept 1990.

Fontenelle, T. and Vanandroye, J. (1989) Retrieving ergative verbs from a lexical data base. *Dictionaries. Journal of the Dictionary Society of America,* 11, 11–39.

Foucault, M. (1972) *The Archaeology of Knowledge.* London: Tavistock.

Foucault, M. (1980) *Power/Knowledge,* ed. C. Gordon. London: Harvester.

Fowler, R. (1991a) Critical linguistics. In K. Malmkjaer (ed.), *The Linguistics Encyclopedia.* London: Routledge, 89–93.

Fowler, R. (1991b) *Language in the News: Discourse and Ideology in the Press.* London: Routledge.

Francis, G. (1991) Nominal group heads and clause structure. *Word,* 42(2), 144–56.

Francis, G. (1993) A corpus-driven approach to grammar: principles, methods and examples. In M. Baker et al. (eds), *Text and Technology.* Amsterdam: Benjamins, 137–56.

Francis, W. N. (1979) Problems of assembling and computerizing large corpora. In H. Bergenholtz and B. Schaeder (eds), *Empirische Textwissenschaft.* Berlin: Scriptor, 110–23.

Frawley, W. (1987) Review article: T. A. van Dijk (ed.), *Handbook of Discourse Analysis. Language*, 63(2), 361–97.

Freebody, P. and Baker, C. (1985) Children's first schoolbooks. *Harvard Educational Review*, 55(4), 381–98.

Fries, C. C. (1952) *The Structure of English*. New York: Harcourt, Brace & Co.

Garfinkel, H. (1967) *Studies in Ethnomethodology*. Englewood Cliffs, NJ: Prentice Hall.

Garfinkel, H. and Sacks, H. (1970) On the formal structures of practical action. In J. McKinney and E. Tiryakian (eds), *Theoretical Sociology*. New York: Appleton-Century-Crofts, 337–66.

Garside, R., Leech, G. and Sampson, G. (eds) (1987) *The Computational Analysis of English*. London: Longman.

Gellner, E. (1959) *Words and Things*. London: Gollancz.

Gerbig, A. (1993) The representation of agency and control in texts on the environment. Paper to AILA Congress, Amsterdam, August 1993.

Gibbons, J. (ed.) (1994) *Language and the Law*. London: Longman.

Giddens, A. (1979) *Central Problems in Social Theory*. London: Macmillan.

Giddens, A. (1984) *The Constitution of Society*. Cambridge: Polity.

Giddens, A. (1987) Nine theses on the future of sociology. In *Social Theory and Modern Sociology*. Cambridge: Polity, 22–51.

Giddens, A. (1991) *Modernity and Self-identity*. Cambridge: Polity.

Goffman, E. (1981) *Forms of Talk*. Oxford: Blackwell.

Goldman, L. (1994) Accident and absolute liability in anthropology. In J. Gibbons (ed.), *Language and the Law*. London: Longman, 51–99.

Goody, E. N. (ed.) (1978) *Questions and Politeness*. London: Cambridge University Press.

Gowers, E. (1954) *The Complete Plain Words*. London: HMSO.

Graddol, D. and Swann, J. (1988) Trapping linguists. *Language and Education*, 2(2), 95–111.

Graddol, D., Thompson, L. and Byram, M. (eds) (1993) *Language and Culture*. BAAL Annual Meeting. Clevedon: Multilingual Matters.

Gradon, P. (1946) The teaching of grammar. In V. de Sola Pinto (ed.), *The Teaching of English in Schools*. London: Macmillan, 65–83.

Greenbaum, S. (1969) *Studies in English Adverbial Usage*. London: Longman.

Green, G. M. (1990) Linguistic analysis of conversation as evidence regarding the interpretation of speech events. In J. N. Levi and A. G. Walker (eds), *Language in the Judicial Process*. New York and London: Plenum, 247–77.

Gregory, G. T. (1984) Community-published working class writing in context. In M. Meek and J. Miller (eds), *Changing English*. London: Heinemann, 220–36.

Gregory, G. T. (1986) Working class writing, publishing and education. Unpublished PhD Thesis. University of London Institute of Education.

Grice, H. P. (1967/1975) Logic and conversation. Unpublished MS, Harvard University, 1967. In P. Cole and J. L. Morgan (eds), *Syntax and Semantics. Volume 3*. New York: Academic Press, 41–58.

Gumperz, J. J. (1982a) *Discourse Strategies.* London: Cambridge University Press.

Gumperz, J. J. (1982b) Fact and inference in courtroom testimony. In J. J. Gumperz (ed.), *Language and Social Identity.* London: Cambridge University Press, 163–95.

Gurevitch, M., Bennett, T., Curran, J. and Woollacott, J. (eds) (1982) *Culture, Society and the Media.* London: Methuen.

Haegeman, L. (1991) *Introduction to Government and Binding Theory.* Oxford: Blackwell.

Hall, S. (1974) The television discourse: encoding and decoding. *Education and Culture*, 25. UNESCO.

Hall, S. (1982) The rediscovery of 'ideology'. In M. Gurevitch et al. (eds), *Culture, Society and the Media.* London: Methuen, 56–90.

Hall, S. (1991) And not a shot fired. *Marxism Today*, December, 10–15.

Halliday, M. A. K. (1971) Linguistic function and literary style. In S. Chatman (ed.), *Literary Style.* London: Oxford University Press, 330–68.

Halliday, M. A. K. (1976) Types of process. In G. R. Kress (ed.), *Halliday: System and Function in Language.* London: Oxford University Press, 159–73.

Halliday, M. A. K. (1978) *Language as Social Semiotic.* London: Edward Arnold.

Halliday, M. A. K. (1982) Linguistics in teacher education. In R. Carter (ed.), *Linguistics and the Teacher.* London: Routledge & Kegan Paul, 10–15.

Halliday, M. A. K. (1985a) *An Introduction to Functional Grammar.* London: Edward Arnold.

Halliday, M. A. K. (1985b) *Spoken and Written Language.* Geelong: Deakin University Press.

Halliday, M. A. K. (1990) New ways of analysing meaning. *Journal of Applied Linguistics*, 6, 7–36. Also in Pütz (1992, pp. 59–96).

Halliday, M. A. K. (1991) Corpus studies and probabilistic grammar. In K. Aijmer and B. Altenberg (eds), *English Corpus Linguistics.* London: Longman, 30–43.

Halliday, M. A. K. (1992) Language as system and language as instance: the corpus as a theoretical construct. In J. Svartvik (ed.), *Directions in Corpus Linguistics.* Berlin: Mouton, 61–77.

Halliday, M. A. K. (1993) Quantitative studies and probabilities in grammar. In M. Hoey (ed.), *Data, Description, Discourse.* London: HarperCollins, 1–25.

Halliday, M. A. K. (1994) *An Introduction to Functional Grammar*, 2nd edn. London: Edward Arnold.

Halliday, M. A. K. and Martin, J. R. (1993) *Writing Science.* London: Falmer.

Halliday, M. A. K., McIntosh, A. and Strevens, P. (1964) *The Linguistic Sciences and Language Teaching.* London: Longman.

Harris, S. (1984a) Questions as a mode of control in magistrates courts. *International Journal of the Sociology of Language*, 49, 5–27.

Harris, S. (1984b) The form and function of threats in court. *Language and Communication*, 4(4), 247–71.

Hartston, W. (1995) Words. *The Independent*, 6 January.

Hill, T. (1958) Institutional linguistics. *Orbis*, 7, 441–55.

Hodge, R. and Kress, G. (1988) *Social Semiotics.* Cambridge: Polity.

Hodge, R. and Kress, G. (1993) *Language as Ideology*, 2nd edn. London: Routledge.

Hoey, M. (ed.) (1993) *Data, Description, Discourse.* London: HarperCollins.

Hoggart, R. (1957) *The Uses of Literacy.* London: Chatto & Windus.

Holmes, J. (1983) Speaking English with the appropriate degree of conviction. In C. J. Brumfit (ed.), *Learning and Teaching of Languages for Communication.* London: CILT, 100–13.

Hopper, P. J. and Traugott, E. C. (1993) *Grammaticalization.* Cambridge: Cambridge University Press.

Hudson, R. (1994) About 37% of word-tokens are nouns. *Language*, 70(2), 331–9.

Hunston, S. (1993a) Projecting a sub-culture: the construction of shared worlds by projecting clauses in two registers. In D. Graddol et al. (eds), *Language and Culture.* Clevedon: Multilingual Matters, 98–112.

Hunston, S. (1993b) Professional conflict: disagreement in academic discourse. In M. Baker et al. (eds), *Text and Technology.* Amsterdam: Benjamins, 115–34.

Hymes, D. (1971) *On Communicative Competence.* Philadelphia: University of Pennsylvania Press.

Iser, W. (1974) *The Implied Reader.* Baltimore and London: Johns Hopkins University Press.

Jenkins, R. (1989) On the world triumph of Oxford English. *The Independent Magazine*, 8 April, 14.

Johnson, M. G. (1990) Language and cognition in products liability. In J. N. Levi and A. G. Walker (eds), *Language in the Judicial Process.* New York and London: Plenum, 291–308.

Johnson-Laird, P. N. (1983) *Mental Models.* Cambridge: Cambridge University Press.

Jones, A. (1983) *Jury Service.* London: Robert Hale.

Joseph, J. E. (1990) Ideologizing Saussure. In J. E. Joseph and T. J. Taylor (eds), *Ideologies of Language.* London: Routledge, 51–78.

Joseph, J. E. and Taylor, T. J. (eds) (1990) *Ideologies of Language.* London: Routledge.

Jucker, A. H. (1992) *Social Stylistics. Syntactic Variation in British Newspapers.* Berlin and New York: Mouton de Gruyter.

Jucker, A. H. (1994) New dimensions in vocabulary studies. *Literary and Linguistic Computing*, 9(2), 149–54.

Kavanagh, P. J. (1988) Speaking up for Kingman and country. *The Daily Telegraph*, 30 April.

Kingman, J. (1988) *Report of the Committee of Inquiry into the Teaching of English Language.* London: HMSO.

Kniffka, H. (1981) Der Linguist als Gutachter bei Gericht. In G. Peuser and S. Winter (eds), *Angewandte Sprachwissenschaft: Grundfragen, Bereiche, Methoden.* Bonn: Bouvier, 584–634.

Kramarae, C. and Treichler, P. (1985) *A Feminist Dictionary.* London: Pandora.

Kress, G. (1989) *Linguistic Processes in Sociocultural Practice.* Oxford: Oxford University Press.

Kress, G. (1993) Cultural considerations in linguistic description. In D. Graddol et al. (eds), *Language and Culture*. Clevedon: Multilingual Matters, 1–22.

Kress, G. (1994) Text and grammar as explanation. In U. Meinhof and K. Richardson (eds), *Text, Discourse and Context*. London: Longman, 24–46.

Labov, W. (1970) The study of language in its social context. (in Labov, 1972, pp. 183–259).

Labov, W. (1972) *Sociolinguistic Patterns*. Philadelphia: University of Pennsylvania Press.

Labov, W. (1975) *What Is a Linguistic Fact?* Lisse: Peter de Ridder.

Labov, W. and Fanshel, D. (1977) *Therapeutic Discourse*. New York: Academic Press.

Lakoff, G. (1970) *Irregularity in Syntax*. New York: Holt, Rinehart & Winston.

Lakoff, G. (1972) Hedges: a study in meaning criteria and the logic of fuzzy concepts. *Papers of the Chicago Linguistic Society*, 8, 183–228.

Lakoff, G. (1987) *Women, Fire and Dangerous Things*. Chicago: University Press.

Lakoff, G. (1992) Metaphor and war. In M. Pütz (ed.), *Thirty Years of Linguistic Evolution*. Amsterdam: Benjamins, 463–81.

Lakoff, G. and Johnson, M. (1980) *Metaphors We Live By*. Chicago: University of Chicago Press.

Lakoff, R. (1969) Some reasons why there can't be any 'some-any' rule. *Language*, 45, 608–15.

Lawlor, S. (1988) *Correct Core: Simple Curricula for English, Maths and Science*. London: Centre for Policy Studies.

Lee, D. (1992) *Competing Discourses: Perspective and Ideology in Language*. London: Longman.

Leech, G. N. (1966) *English in Advertising*. London: Longman.

Leech, G. N. (1971) *Meaning and the English Verb*. London: Longman.

Leech, G. N. (1983) *Principles of Pragmatics*. London: Longman.

Leech, G. N. and Svartvik, J. (1975) *A Communicative Grammar of English*. London: Longman.

Leith, D. (1983) *A Social History of English*. London: Routledge.

Lemke, J. L. (1989) Semantics and social values. *Word*, 40(1/2), 37–50.

Letwin, O. (1988) *Aims of Schooling. The Importance of Grounding*. London: Centre for Policy Studies.

Levi, J. N. (1992) On the adequacy of Illinois jury instructions for capital sentencing. Paper to 1992 Law and Society Association Meeting, Philadelphia.

Levi, J. N. and Walker, A. G. (eds) (1990) *Language in the Judicial Process*. New York and London: Plenum.

Levinson, S. C. (1983) *Pragmatics*. Cambridge: Cambridge University Press.

Ljung, M. (1980) Reflections on the English Progressive. *Acta Universitatis Gothoburgensis*. Goteborg.

Loftus, E. F. and Palmer, J. C. (1974) Reconstruction of automobile destruction: an example of the interaction between language and memory. *Journal of Verbal Learning and Verbal Behavior*, 13, 585–9.

Louw, B. (1993) Irony in the text or insincerity in the writer? The diagnostic potential of semantic prosodies. In M. Baker et al. (eds), *Text and Technology*. Amsterdam: Benjamins, 157–76.

Lyons, J. (1968) *Introduction to Theoretical Linguistics*. Cambridge: Cambridge University Press.

Lyons, J. (1977) *Semantics*. Two volumes. London: Cambridge University Press.

Lyons, J. (1981) *Language, Meaning and Context*. London: Fontana.

McAdam, E. L. and Milne, G. (1963) *Johnson's Dictionary: a Modern Selection*. London: Gollancz.

McTear, M. F. (1980) The pragmatics of *because*. Mimeo, Ulster Polytechnic.

Marenbon, J. (1987) *English, Our English*. London: Centre for Policy Studies.

Martin, J. R. (1985) *Factual Writing: Exploring and Challenging Social Reality*. Geelong: Deakin University Press (2nd edn, Oxford: Oxford University Press, 1989).

Marx, K. (1852) Der 18te Brumaire des Louis Napoleon. *Die Revolution*. In K. Marx and F. Engels, *Werke, Volume 8*. Berlin: Dietz, 1960.

Meinhof, U. and Richardson, K. (eds) (1994) *Text, Discourse and Context*. London: Longman.

Merquior, J. G. (1985) *Foucault*. London: Fontana.

Mey, J. and Talbot, M. (1988) Computation and the soul. *Journal of Pragmatics*, 12, 743–89.

Miller, J. (1993) Spoken and written language. In R. J. Scholes (ed.), *Literacy and Language Analysis*. Hillsdale, NJ: Erlbaum, 99–141.

Milroy, J. (1984) Sociolinguistic methodology and the identification of speakers' voices in legal proceedings. In P. Trudgill (ed.), *Applied Sociolinguistics*. London: Academic Press, 51–72.

Milroy, J. and Milroy, L. (1985) *Authority in Language*. London: Routledge & Kegan Paul.

Moon, R. (1994) The analysis of fixed expressions in text. In M. Coulthard (ed.), *Advances in Written Text Analysis*. London: Routledge, 117–35.

Morais, E. (ed.) (1980–1) *Skills for Learning*. Four volumes. Walton-on-Thames: Nelson/University of Malaya Press.

Morreal, J. (1979) The evidential use of *because*. *Papers in Linguistics*, 12(1/2), 231–8.

Myers, G. (1992) Textbooks and the sociology of scientific knowledge. *English for Specific Purposes*, 11, 3–17.

Myers, G. (1994) *Words in Ads*. London: Edward Arnold.

Nair, R. B. (1992) Gender, genre and generative grammar. In M. Toolan (ed.), *Language, Text and Context*. London: Routledge, 227–54.

Nash, W. (1982) *Kettle of Roses*. London: Hutchinson.

O'Barr, W. M. (1981) The language of the law. In C. A. Ferguson and S. Brice Heath (eds), *Language in the USA*. Cambridge: Cambridge University Press, 386–406.

O'Barr, W. M. (1982) *Linguistic Evidence: Language, Power and Strategy in the Courtroom*. London: Academic Press.

Palmer, F. R. (1974) *The English Verb*, 2nd edn. London: Longman.

Palmer, F. R. (1986) *Mood and Modality.* Cambridge: Cambridge University Press.

Phillips, M. (1989) *Lexical Structure of Text.* Discourse Analysis Monograph 12. Birmingham: English Language Research.

Phillipson, R. (1992) *Linguistic Imperialism.* Cambridge: Cambridge University Press.

Phillipson, R. and Skutnabb-Kangas, T. (1989) Wanted! Linguistic Human Rights. *Rolig-Papir,* 44, University of Roskilde.

Popper, K. R. (1972) *Objective Knowledge.* Oxford: Clarendon.

Popper, K. R. (1994) *Knowledge and the Body–Mind Problem.* London: Routledge.

Posner, R. (1963) The use and abuse of stylistic statistics. *Archivum Linguisticum,* 15, 111–39.

Prince, E. F. (1982) Language and the law: a case for linguistic pragmatics. *Sociolinguistic Working Paper* 94, SW Educational Development Laboratory, Austin, Texas.

Pullum, G. K. (1991a) *The Great Eskimo Vocabulary Hoax and Other Irreverent Essays on the Study of Language.* Chicago: University of Chicago Press.

Pullum, G. K. (1991b) Citation etiquette beyond Thunderdome. In G. K. Pullum, *The Great Eskimo Vocabulary Hoax and Other Irreverent Essays on the Study of Language.* Chicago: University of Chicago Press, 147–58.

Püschel, U. (1991a) Journalistische Textsorten im 19. Jahrhundert. In R. Wimmer (ed.), *Das 19. Jahrhundert: Sprachgeschichtliche Wurzeln des heutigen Deutsch.* Berlin: De Gruyter. 428–47.

Püschel, U. (1991b) Ein Privatschreiben aus Gent vom 19. Juni berichtet folgendes. In *Akten des VIII. Internationalen Germanisten-Kongresses,* Tokyo 1990, 30–8.

Pütz, M. (ed.) (1992) *Thirty Years of Linguistic Evolution.* Amsterdam: Benjamins.

Quirk, R. and Greenbaum, S. (1973) *A University Grammar of English.* London: Longman.

Quirk, R., Greenbaum, S., Leech, G. and Svartvik, J. (1972) *A Grammar of Contemporary English.* London: Longman.

Quirk, R., Greenbaum, S., Leech, G. and Svartvik, J. (1985) *A Comprehensive Grammar of the English Language.* London: Longman.

Raban, J. (1989) *God, Man and Mrs Thatcher.* London: Chatto & Windus.

Renouf, A. (1987) Corpus development. In J. McH. Sinclair (ed.), *Looking Up: an Account of the COBUILD Project in Lexical Computing.* London: Collins, 1–40.

Renouf, A. and Sinclair, J. McH. (1991) Collocational frameworks in English. In K. Aijmer and B. Altenberg (eds), *English Corpus Linguistics.* London: Longman, 128–44.

Richards, I. A. (1929) *Practical Criticism.* New York: Harcourt Brace.

Robins, R. H. (1961) John Rupert Firth. *Language,* 37(2), 191–200.

Rosch, E. H. (1975) Cognitive reference points. *Cognitive Psychology,* 7, 532–47.

Sacks, H. (1992) *Lectures on Conversation, Volume 1,* ed. G. Jefferson. Oxford: Blackwell.

Said, E. (1978) *Orientalism.* London: Routledge & Kegan Paul.

Sampson, A. (1992) *The Essential Anatomy of Britain.* London: Hodder & Stoughton.

Sampson, G. (1980) *Schools of Linguistics*. London: Hutchinson.

Sampson, G. (1987a) Probabilistic models of analysis. In R. Garside et al. (eds), *The Computational Analysis of English*. London: Longman, 16–29.

Sampson, G. (1987b) The grammatical database and parsing scheme. In R. Garside et al. (eds), *The Computational Analysis of English*. London: Longman, 82–96.

Saussure, F. de (1916) *Cours de Linguistique Générale*, ed. C. Bally et al. Lausanne: Payot.

Scannell, P. (1986) The stuff of radio. In J. Corner (ed.), *Documentary and the Mass Media*. London: Edward Arnold, 1–26.

Schegloff, E. A. (1972) Notes on a conversational practice: formulating place. In D. Sudnow (ed.), *Studies in Social Interaction*. New York: Free Press, 75–119.

Searle, J. R. (1969) *Speech Acts*. London: Cambridge University Press.

Searle, J. R. (ed.) (1971) *The Philosophy of Language*. London: Oxford University Press.

Searle, J. R. (1975) Indirect speech acts. In P. Cole and J. L. Morgan (eds), *Syntax and Semantics. Volume 3*. New York: Academic Press, 59–82.

Searle, J. R. (1976) A classification of illocutionary acts. *Language in Society*, 5, 1–23.

Searle, J. R. (1979) *Expression and Meaning*. London: Cambridge University Press.

Shuy, R. W. (1993) *Language Crimes*. Oxford: Blackwell.

Simpson, P. (1993) *Language, Ideology and Point of View*. London: Routledge.

Sinclair, J. McH. (1965) When is a poem like a sunset? *A Review of English Literature*, 6(2): 76–91.

Sinclair, J. McH. (1966a) Taking a poem to pieces. In R. Fowler (ed.), *Essays on Style and Language*. London: Routledge & Kegan Paul, 68–81.

Sinclair, J. McH. (1966b) Beginning the study of lexis. In C. E. Bazell et al. (eds), *In Memory of J. R. Firth*. London: Longman, 410–30.

Sinclair, J. McH. (1968) A technique of stylistic description. *Language and Style*, 1, 215–42.

Sinclair, J. McH. (1971) The integration of language and literature in the curriculum. *Educational Review*, 23(2), 220–34.

Sinclair, J. McH. (1972) *A Course in Spoken English: Grammar*. London: Oxford University Press.

Sinclair, J. McH. (1973) English for effect. *Commonwealth Education Liaison Committee Newsletter*, 3(11), 5–7.

Sinclair, J. McH. (1980) Discourse in relation to language structure and semiotics. In S. Greenbaum, G. Leech and J. Svartvik (eds), *Studies in English Linguistics for Randolph Quirk*. London: Longman.

Sinclair, J. McH. (1982) Linguistics and the teacher. In R. Carter (ed.), *Linguistics and the Teacher*. London: Routledge & Kegan Paul, 16–30.

Sinclair, J. McH. (ed.) (1987a) *Collins Cobuild English Language Dictionary*. London: HarperCollins.

Sinclair, J. McH. (ed.) (1987b) *Looking Up: an Account of the COBUILD Project in Lexical Computing*. London: Collins.

Sinclair, J. McH. (ed.) (1988) *Collins Cobuild Essential English Dictionary*. London: HarperCollins.

Sinclair, J. McH. (ed.) (1990) *Collins Cobuild English Grammar*. London: HarperCollins.

Sinclair, J. McH. (1991a) *Corpus, Concordance, Collocation.* Oxford: Oxford University Press.

Sinclair, J. McH. (1991b) Shared knowledge. In *Georgetown University Round Table on Languages and Linguistics 1991.* Washington, DC: Georgetown University Press, 489–500.

Sinclair, J. McH. (1992a) Trust the text. In M. Davies and L. Ravelli (eds), *Advances in Systemic Linguistics.* London: Pinter, 5–19.

Sinclair, J. McH. (1992b) Priorities in discourse analysis. In R. M. Coulthard (ed.), *Advances in Spoken Discourse Analysis.* London: Routledge, 79–88.

Sinclair, J. McH. (1992c) The automatic analysis of corpora. In J. Svartvik (ed.), *Directions in Corpus Linguistics.* Berlin: Mouton, 379–97.

Sinclair, J. McH. (ed.) (1995) *Collins Cobuild English Dictionary*, 2nd edn. London: HarperCollins.

Sinclair, J. McH. and Brazil, D. (1982) *Teacher Talk.* Oxford: Oxford University Press.

Sinclair, J. McH. and Coulthard, R. M. (1975) *Towards an Analysis of Discourse.* London: Oxford University Press.

Sinclair, J. McH., Jones, S. and Daley, R. (1970) *English Lexical Studies.* University of Birmingham, for Office for Scientific and Technical Information.

Slembrouk, S. (1992) The parliamentary Hansard 'verbatim' report. *Language and Literature*, 1(2), 101–20.

Sperber, D. and Wilson, D. (1986) *Relevance: Communication and Cognition.* Oxford: Blackwell.

Strevens, P. and Weeks, F. (1985) The creation of a regularized subset of English for mandatory use in maritime communications: SEASPEAK. *Language Planning Newsletter*, 11, 2.

Stubbs, M. (1980) *Language and Literacy.* London: Routledge & Kegan Paul.

Stubbs, M. (1983a) *Discourse Analysis.* Oxford: Blackwell.

Stubbs, M. (1983b) Can I have that in writing, please? Some neglected topics in speech act theory. *Journal of Pragmatics*, 7, 479–94.

Stubbs, M. (1984) Review of Sinclair & Brazil 1982. *Applied Linguistics*, 5(1), 71–4.

Stubbs, M. (1986a) *Educational Linguistics.* Oxford: Blackwell.

Stubbs, M. (1986b) A matter of prolonged fieldwork: towards a modal grammar of English. *Applied Linguistics*, 7(1), 1–25.

Stubbs, M. (1989) The state of English in the English state: reflections on the Cox Report. *Language and Education*, 3(4), 235–50.

Stubbs, M. (1990) Knowledge about language: grammar, ignorance and society. Special Professorial Lecture. Institute of Education, University of London.

Stubbs, M. (1995a) Collocations and semantic profiles: on the cause of the trouble with quantitative methods. *Functions of Language*, 2(1), 1–33.

Stubbs, M. (1995b) Corpus evidence for norms of lexical collocation. In G. Cook and B. Seidlhofer (eds), *Principle and Practice in Applied Linguistics.* London: Oxford University Press, 245–56.

Stubbs, M. (1996) Language and the mediation of experience: linguistic representation and cognitive orientation. In F. Coulmas (ed.), *The Handbook of Sociolinguistics*. Oxford: Blackwell.

Stubbs, M. and Delamont, S. (eds) (1976) *Explorations in Classroom Observation*. London: Wiley.

Stubbs, M. and Gerbig, A. (1993) Human and inhuman geography: on the computer-assisted analysis of long texts. In M. Hoey (ed.), *Data, Description, Discourse*. London: HarperCollins, 64–85.

Summers, D. (1993) Longman/Lancaster English language corpus: criteria and design. *International Journal of Lexicography*, 6(3), 181–95.

Svartvik, J. (1966) *On Voice in the English Verb*. The Hague: Mouton.

Svartvik, J. (ed.) (1992) *Directions in Corpus Linguistics*. Berlin: Mouton.

Svartvik, J., Eeg-Olofsson, M., Forsheden, O., Oreström, B. and Thavenius, C. (1982) *Survey of Spoken English*. Lund: Lund University Press.

Svartvik, J. and Quirk, R. (eds) (1980) *A Corpus of English Conversation*. Lund: Gleerup.

Swales, J. M. (1990) *Genre Analysis*. Cambridge: Cambridge University Press.

Sweet, H. (1891) *A New English Grammar: Logical and Historical*. Oxford: Clarendon.

Thomas, G. (1991) *Linguistic Purism*. London: Longman.

Thomson, A. J. and Martinet, A. V. (1969) *A Practical English Grammar*, 2nd edn. London: Oxford University Press.

Thomson, N. (1989) How to read articles which depend on statistics. *Literary and Linguistic Computing*, 4(1), 6–11.

Tiersma, P. M. (1993) Linguistic issues in the law. *Language*, 69(1), 113–37.

Toolan, M. (ed.) (1992) *Language, Text and Context*. London: Routledge.

Torode, B. (1976) Teachers talk and classroom discipline. In M. Stubbs and S. Delamont (eds), *Explorations in Classroom Observation*. London: Wiley, 173–92.

Trask, R. L. (1993) *A Dictionary of Grammatical Terms*. London: Routledge.

Trudgill, P. (ed.) (1984) *Applied Sociolinguistics*. London: Academic Press.

Ure, J. (1971) Lexical density and register differentiation. In G. Perren and J. L. M. Trim (eds), *Applications of Linguistics*. London: Cambridge University Press. 443–52.

van Dijk, T. A. (1979) Pragmatic connectives. *Journal of Pragmatics*, 3/5, 447–57.

van Dijk, T. A. (1981) Discourse studies and education. *Applied Linguistics*, 2(1), 1–26.

van Dijk, T. A. (1993) Principles of critical discourse analysis. *Discourse and Society*, 4(2), 249–83.

von Polenz, P. (1988) *Deutsche Satzsemantik*. Berlin: De Gruyter.

Walker, A. G. (1990) Language at work in the law. In J. N. Levi and A. G. Walker (eds), *Language in the Judicial Process*. New York and London: Plenum, 203–44.

Walter, B. (1988) *The Jury Summation as Speech Genre*. Amsterdam/Philadelphia: Benjamins.

Warnock, M. (1989) *Universities: Knowing our Minds*. London: Chatto & Windus.

Whorf, B. L. (1956) *Language, Thought and Reality*, ed. J. B. Carroll. Cambridge, MA: MIT Press.

Wight, J. and Norris, R. (1970) *Teaching English to West Indian Children*. Schools Council Working Paper 29. London: Methuen.

Williams, R. (1961) *The Long Revolution*. London: Chatto & Windus.

Williams, R. (1973) *The Country and the City*. London: Chatto & Windus.

Williams, R. (1976) *Keywords*. London: Fontana, 2nd edn 1983.

Williams, R. (1977) *Marxism and Literature*. Oxford: Oxford University Press.

Williams, R. (1985) Mining the meaning: key words in the miners' strike. *New Socialist*, March.

Willis, D. (1990) *The Lexical Syllabus*. London: Collins.

Woods, A., Fletcher, P. and Hughes, A. (1986) *Statistics in Language Studies*. Cambridge: Cambridge University Press.

Subject Index

Name Index